Ancestry. Jesus Hidden Secrets of Jesus' Ancestors (the series)

~ Behind the Scenes with David and Bathsheba~

Jana Jones McDowell

Table of Contents

Dedication

This book is respectfully dedicated to all who want to deepen their understanding of the Scripture due to a quest for knowledge that is never quite satisfied. Being a "forever-student" of the Bible with a continual thirst for knowledge is most likely part of the Lord's plan. In our searching for answers, we arrive at a better understanding of what He tells us through his Word.

May there always be one more question......

Foreword: Author's Notes ~ The Story of David and Bathsheba

*P***earl:** *David's Hebrew name: Dawid, from the Hebrew root Dod, meaning 'beloved'.*

◆◆◆◆◆◆◆◆◆◆◆

By exploring the ancestry of Jesus, in the series ***Ancestry.Jesus,*** we will expand our knowledge of our Christian-Jewish roots through exploration of the ancient characters of the Hebrew Bible that make up Jesus' family tree.

In this installment of the ***Ancestry.Jesus*** series, we will go 'behind the scenes' with David and Bathsheba and look at their lives from a Jewish perspective, putting everything into the context of the day. Furthermore, we will view their lives as was seen through their eyes as well as their descendant, Mary, the mother of the Messiah, Jesus Christ.

By viewing David's epic story in the context of the ancient Jewish culture, we will more fully understand how Mary, the mother of Jesus, would have viewed her famous ancestors and how David and Bathsheba's life story impacted her own.

Interestingly, we will also see how many parallels can be drawn from David's and Bathsheba's life experiences to our own lives as well, even though we live nearly three-thousands years later. Through looking at David and Bathsheba in the context of the day, we will see how their lives served God's glorious purpose, fitting into His Divine Masterplan which points forward to our eternal Savior, Jesus Christ.

It is the intent of this book to help us comprehend David's story as would have been understood by Mary, a devout Jewish young woman who had been schooled in the Torah, the Tanakh, and Mosaic culture and law. Descending from the line of Judah and on through David, the renowned King of Israel, Mary would have been keenly aware of her ancestors, due to the keeping of accurate records which had existed for centuries. She also would have put their stories into context and understood them in a different light than the reader of today.

Through a greater comprehension of David's story from a Jewish perspective, we in turn will discover more about our own Jewish-Christian roots, and gain greater insight about what God is trying to tell us through His Word.

Knowing our ancestry has always been a subject of interest to us as humans, and somewhat of an enigma. In the world in which we live in today, it is difficult to find connections to our past, which in some cases has been seemingly lost forever. To help us connect to our past in today's complex world, many people invest in DNA analysis kits to determine their ancestral roots, searching for long-lost relatives that make up the family tree.

The need for knowing where we came from, and who are ancestors were, seems to be *hard-wired* in us as humans. As a result of DNA analysis, we may go to great lengths to contact a person who is said to be a relative based on a simple test that is a result of the technology of today.

The ancient Jewish people obviously did not have DNA kits to determine their ancestry. However, they were proud of their heritage, and kept extremely accurate records concerning their ancestors and the tribes of Israel from which they descended. Often referring to their grandfathers and great-great grandfathers as their 'fathers', the Jewish people were well-versed in the extensive history of their ancestors, as the records were legitimized in the Torah, and well-validated in Jewish legal documents.

In this installment in the series of Jesus' ancestors, we will go behind the scenes and discover many hidden secrets about one of the most famous of all the ancient Jews in the Hebrew Bible, being David, the shepherd-boy who became king.

Of course, we will also delve deep and discover hidden secrets about his wife, Bathsheba, as she is the woman who produced the offspring that were ancestors of Jesus.

How will we discover their *hidden* secrets?

Of course, they aren't really secrets, as God wants us to deeply explore His Word.

Through a deep look at the Bible, as well as conflating information from ancient sources, including the Old Testament and commentaries from Biblical scholars (ESV Study Bible), the Masoretic text of the Hebrew Bible, and the ancient Rabbinical commentaries from Jewish literature as is compiled in the Midrash, we will come to understand the inner-most soul of David and his wife, Bathsheba.

We will uncover the meanings behind their feelings and actions, which were molded by the culture and religious practices of the day.

In examining the life of David from shepherd-boy through his reign as King of Israel, we will go behind the scenes of what is typically presented about his life. We will go to the depths of his very being understanding his life in the context of ancient day Judaism, as if we were right there experiencing life with him nearly three thousand years ago.

Through seeing David's life through his eyes and his perspective, we will relive his failures and accomplishments and first-hand experience his range of emotions from anguish to pure joy.

Through looking deep into the scripture and examining David's life, we will see how he truly was a man of God's heart.

Perhaps you as the reader grew up with Biblical stories concerning David.

What stories do you recall?

The most famous story by far is how David slew the mighty giant and noted warrior, Goliath, with just a sling and a single stone. After defeating Goliath the young-David cruised right in to become the famous king of Israel, right?

No, not exactly. It actually would be over a decade before David ascended to the throne.

Going behind the scenes of David's epic story we will journey back to antiquity, nearly three thousand years ago when God first chose David, the youngest and most-ignored son of Jesse to establish His dynasty. From there, we will experience his many trials as he slowly and determinedly ascended to become the King of Israel.

The covenant God made with David, being the Davidic Covenant, was of unsurmountable importance, as this covenant was an integral part of God's eternal plan of salvation of humanity.

The Davidic Covenant is why David's offspring play such an important role in God's promise of a coming Messiah. As was promised by God, from the lineage of David would come the ultimate Messiah, our savior, Jesus Christ.

Through examination of the life of David, we will see that God did not choose David to be front- and-center in the plan of salvation because he was the perfect, ideal person.

Far from it!

However, the Lord was always with David, as David was truly a man of faith.

Although David was a man of great faith in God, we will see how his life's journey was not an easy, walk-in-the-park to become the King of Israel.

Nor was David the 'perfect' man.

Brimming with drama and suspense, David's life was a rollercoaster of trials and obstacles to be overcome. Experiencing David's life allows one to soar to the heights of reliving his triumphs and feats, as well as plummet to the depths of his abysmal, sinful endeavors.

Nothing goes untouched in David's story, as he runs the gamut from being a pure, young, Divinely-anointed king-to-be, to orchestrating a murder for his own selfish needs.

Throughout David's life we will also see his faith in God swing to-and-fro, similar to a pendulum. But David's faith will always move back towards God as he repents and seeks forgiveness and direction.

By putting ourselves in the front-seat to travel with David down the rocky paths of his life, we will acquire insight as to how the most unlikely people are chosen by God to accomplish His Holy purposes.

Of significance is with the story of David becoming the newly anointed king-to-be of Israel, so begins a new era for Israel. Eventually, under David's leadership, Israel will transition to become a powerful monarchy, with expanded borders and success as a nation never before realized.

David however, was not Israel's first king, and his story as he rose to be the second king of Israel is packed with trials and tests. The drama around his rise to power encompasses experiences that will unravel and expose many hidden things about David and the people in his life that most Bible readers have never realized.

Close attention to David's story unveils an in-depth analysis of qualities of character that makes for a great leader. Determination, courage, extreme faith, and a 'shepherding' attitude towards his 'flock' are qualities that David possessed, making him unique among the kings of antiquity.

Interestingly, David's choices he made during his life to obey God's will, or to go against it, are applicable to all individuals.

We all face tests and trials in our life, and we, like David, must make the intentional choice to follow God's direction in order to fully realize the ultimate purpose He has for us.

Deep analysis of David's life will once again prove how God uses the most unlikely, and at times, the most unworthy people for His glory. Fitting into the grand scheme of the Lord's Masterplan, we will see how the trials David faced made him into the person that God ultimately created him to be.

David, because of God's promise through the Davidic Covenant, became the center of the genealogical ancestry of Jesus Christ, and was therefore pivotal in the Divine Masterplan of salvation for humanity.

Psalm 89:2-4
"For I said, Steadfast love will be built up forever, in the heavens you will establish your faithfulness.
You have said, I have made a covenant with my chosen one; I have sworn to David my servant;
I will establish your offspring forever, and build your throne for all generations."

A Little History - Putting David's Story into the Political and Spiritual Context of the Day

Pearl: *A question that may surface is 'how did Israel transition to become a monarchy, that being ruled by a single leader with absolute power'? We have read previously in the Bible that Israel was a theocracy, with God at the center of rule. How did Israel come to be governed by a human king?*

♦♦♦♦♦♦♦♦♦♦♦

After Joshua's conquest of the Promised Land of Canaan it was substantially under the control of the Israelites. The Israelites moved into their Promised Land, settling-in and raising families in their land that was their promised gift from Yahweh, the God of Israel.

David's ancestors, such as his great-great-grandparents Rahab and Salmon, lived during the notable time of Joshua's armies obtaining control of the land of Canaan. Both Rahab and Salmon were instrumental in the conquest of Jericho, leading to Joshua's successful take-over from the indigenous groups of Canaanites that occupied the land.

Even though Rahab was a Canaanite prostitute, she holds honor with the Israelite people, as she was instrumental in Joshua's army's success. Working with the love of the Lord in her heart, Rahab protected the spies that came to scout out the 'impenetrable' city of Jericho. Because of Rahab's courage to stand with the Israelites, Joshua and his men were able to conquer the city of Jericho and then move forward with future successes in Canaan.

Eventually some years later after Joshua's conquest of Canaan, rule over the land evolved into a period of time known as the 'Judges'. This era received its name due to the rule by as a series of judges who were chosen by God to govern His people. David's great-grandparents, Ruth and Boaz lived in Bethlehem during this period of time, and were known for their extreme faith and dedication to the Lord.

During the time of settling the Promised Land, Israel did not have friendly neighbors around its borders and was surrounded by many pagan nations. Even within the Promised Land, pockets of indigenous pagan Canaanites still existed in and among the Israelites who had settled after Joshua's conquest. With this 'incomplete conquering' of Canaan and its inhabitants, the Israelites were exposed to many cultures, all who worshipped pagan entities.

Many Israelites intermarried with the native pagan Canaanites, even though this was against God's commandments. As a result of this intermarriage, many Israelites adopted the Canaanite pagan culture and religion. This eventually led to many of the Israelites to turn away from God and to become idolatrous, pagan worshippers in order to 'fit in' with the people among them.

The pagan cultures surrounding the Israelites were wealthy and powerful. This especially seemed intriguing to the Israelites who had recently served as slaves in Egypt, prior to their exodus to the Promised Land under the leadership of Moses and Joshua.

The Israelites therefore tended to admire the other nations and cultures around them as these pagan cultures flourished with decadence and power. Seeing that these surrounding nations were governed by kings who exuded prestige and opulence, the Israelites came to envy their way of life.

The period of Judges was characterized by the Israelites' disobedience to God. The era described in the book of Judges had the typical, cyclical pattern of the Israelite people's disobedience in their turning away from God, which resulted in God delivering them into the hands of their enemies who surrounded them.

The oppression that resulted then caused people to repent and temporarily turn back to God, but only for a while, as soon they would again become disobedient.

These cycles of turning away from the Lord, then back to Him again when oppression overcame them, is referred to as *Deuteronomic cycles.* This cyclic pattern was predicted and warned about in the Book of Deuteronomy.

During this period of time, God's chosen judges attempted to govern and lead His people in order to avoid the havoc that resulted from the peoples' disobedience.

However, as soon as a Judge would die, the people would again become disobedient and as a result turned further away from the Lord.

Being governed by Judges was not an ideal situation as far as the Israelites were concerned, and the people longed for a different kind of leader. Rebellious and envying other nations, the Israelite people turned from the Lord and longed for a monarchy. The Israelite people desperately wanted a king to rule over them.

Samuel was the last in a long line of the Judges, and also served as God's prophet to listen to His people. As Samuel became older, the people of Israel asked Samuel to give them a king to replace him to rule over them so that they could be similar to the other nations encompassing their borders.

Even though God knew that this would eventually be destructive to the nation of Israel, He complied with the people's wish to be governed by a human king.

♦♦♦♦♦♦♦♦♦♦♦

*P**earl:** This request by the people was actually disrespectful of the Lord, as it showed their lack of trust in the Almighty. The Lord was their king and He had consistently demonstrated how He had waged war for them and protected them throughout the centuries.*

♦♦♦♦♦♦♦♦♦♦♦

God actually anticipated His people's desires to have a human king, as he saw how they desired to be like other nations and the pagan cultures around them. Even though it was against the Lord's plan, he would allow them to choose their first king who would govern them.

How did the people choose a king?

The period of the Judges came to a close with Samuel as the last of Israel's Judges, as well as one of the last of the many prophets in that era.

Even though Samuel would give up his role as a ruling judge, he still had a very important job to do for the Lord.

Samuel was chosen by God to be instrumental in bringing about the transition of Israel becoming a Monarchy through being the one who anointed Israel's first-ever king.

However, Samuel was hesitant to follow the people's request of granting them a human king, and asked the Lord for direction.

Samuel prayed and God answered him by saying,

"Obey the voice of the people in all that they say to you, for they have not rejected you, but they have rejected me from being king over them. According to all the deeds that they have done, from the day I brought them up out of Egypt even to this day, forsaking me and serving other gods, so they are also doing to you.

Now then obey their voice, only you shall solemnly warn them and show them the ways of the king who shall reign over them."
(1 Samuel 8:7-9)

From these verses it is apparent that the Lord was obviously displeased and saddened with the people's request for a king, as He himself was their king.

God was also displeased because His people aspired to be like other nations, as God's people were designed by the Almighty to be unique!

Since Creation, God had governed His people through giving His Word through priests, judges and prophets. Most importantly, Israel was His 'chosen nation.'

Now, God's people were turning away from Him once again.

Importantly, Israel was not to be like other nations and through the Laws given to Moses, God's treasured people were to be different. Other nations were fraught with immoral practices, including the worship of pagan idols. Other nations' people did not have belief and faith in the one, true God of Israel.

God protected and loved His people, whereas the pagan gods of other nations were false and useless. The Israelites now wanted to exchange their uniqueness of worshipping the one true God for the things of world, such as a king who would condone the practice of idolatry and not uphold Mosaic Law.

All because the Israelite people had envied the Canaanites who had remained after the conquest of the Promise Land. They had succumbed to the materialistic temptations of this world and now they wanted to be just like the pagan Canaanites.

The Israelites thought that having a king would make them powerful, and would give them 'status' among other nations that surrounded their borders.

✦✦✦✦✦✦✦✦✦✦✦

*P**earl:** God's answer to the people's request for a human king was to have Samuel give them a king, in the person of Saul.*

Saul would become Israel's first king.

*Saul from the tribe of Benjamin was actually slated only to be a temporary ruler. The permanent ruler of Israel was destined to come from the tribe of Judah, as was stated in Jacob's blessing **(Genesis 49:10).** The choice of Saul being of the tribe of Benjamin is hinted at in Jacob's prophecy to his son, Benjamin, **"and kings will come out of your loins"**, referring to Saul who was a descendent of Benjamin **(Genesis 35:11**).*

However, due to the conditions under which this king was requested, the Lord only would appoint His temporary ruler for His people until the proper time came for a king of God's own choosing.

✦✦✦✦✦✦✦✦✦✦✦

In reference to Saul, the first king of Israel, the prophet Hosea said of the word of God,

> **"He destroys you, O Israel, for you are against me, against your helper.**
> **Where now is your king, to save you in all your cities?**
>
> **Where are all your rulers – those of whom you said, Give me a king and princes?**
>
> **I gave them a king in My anger, and I took him away in My wrath."**
> **(Hosea 13:11)**

Israel had asked for the wrong king of king **(1 Samuel 8:4-9)** when they asked for a king to rule them. They wanted to exchange their unique glory as people of the Almighty God, for status in the world.

But for now, against God's warnings, Saul was appointed the first king of Israel.

The Israelites were pleased with their new king and looked forward to being a monarchy. After all, Saul was impressive and looked-the-part, as he was handsome and tall. He was the epitome of a leader in appearance, but we shall see this was in appearance only.

As for Saul,

"There was a Benjamite, a man of standing, whose name was Kish son of Abiel, the son of Zeror, the son of Bekorath, the son of Aphiah of Benjamin.

Kish had a son named Saul, as handsome a young man as could be found anywhere in Israel, and he was a head taller than anyone else."
(1 Samuel 9:1-5)

God will however eventually reject Saul from being king of Israel.

Saul demonstrated many character-flaws not fitting of a king, including lack of leadership and true caring for his people. His main flaw however, being his disobedience and rebelliousness of the will of the Lord, lead to his ultimate demise.

In time, God directed Samuel, the prophet, to anoint the King of Israel of *God's choosing, rather than man's choosing.*

David the shepherd-boy, son of Jesse, grandson of Obed and the great-grandson of Ruth, the Moabitess and Boaz of the tribe of Judah, will be God's future choice for the King of Israel.

Through the lineage of David, God will work to further His ultimate promise of the coming Messiah.

Jesus Christ, a descendant of David will fulfill God's promise of salvation for humanity, and will be the Messiah of Israel and of the world.

Isaiah 11:1-16, entitled *The Righteous Reign of the Branch, " The Messiah will transform the world,"* describes the Messiah's triumph over evil,

"There shall come forth a shoot from the stump of Jesse, and a branch from his roots shall bear fruit.

And the spirit of the LORD shall rest upon him, the spirit of wisdom and understanding, the spirit of counsel and might, the spirit of knowledge and the fear of the LORD.

And his delight shall be in the fear of the LORD.

He shall not judge by what his eyes see, or decide disputes by what his ears hear, but with righteousness he shall judge the poor, and decide with equity for the meek of the earth; and he shall strike the earth with the rod of his mouth, and with the breath of his lips he shall kill the wicked.

Righteousness shall be the belt of his waist, and faithfulness the belt of his loins."
(Isaiah 11:1-5)

The reference to Jesse, David's father who is of the lineage of Judah, indicates that the Messiah will come from the heir of David. This verse continues the theme found in *Isaiah 7:10-14, and Isaiah 9:1-7.*

Isaiah, in *11:1-5,* portrays the Messiah as a shoot growing from a stump remaining after God's judgement against the Israelites' first choice of their king. The Messiah, descending from Jesse, unlike humanity before him, will bear the fruit of a new world.

The apostle Paul makes reference to this verse in Isaiah when he talks about the "armor of God" in *Ephesians 6*. The parallel Paul makes is to 'put on' the armor, meaning to put on or 'wear' the Messiah, Jesus Christ, as spiritual warfare against evil.

(Ephesians 6:11, 13-14)

"Put on the whole armor of God, that you may be able to stand against the schemes of the devil. "

"Therefore take up the whole armor of God, that you may be able to withstand in the evil day, and having done all to stand firm.

Stand therefore having fastened on the belt of truth and having put on the breastplate of righteousness and as hoes for your feet, having put on the readiness given by the gospel of peace."

Pearl: *As God's choice for the King of Israel, what would turn out to be David's legacy?*

We will see that he was a great leader and protector of his people, an esteemed warrior and even a great politician.

However, of paramount importance in regards to David's legacy, was that he had a heart for the Lord.

> **"For the LORD sees not as man sees; man looks on the outward appearance,**
> **but the LORD looks on the heart."**
> **(1 Samuel 16:7)**

Ultimately, as part of God's Masterplan, through David's offspring will come God's promised savior for humanity, Jesus Christ.

The step-by-step unfolding of God's plan, first realized in King David, and later fulfilled in the promised son of David, the Savior Jesus Christ, is summed up by the Apostle Paul in **Acts 13:17-23,**

> **"The God of this people Israel chose our fathers and made the people great during their stay in the land of Egypt, and with uplifted arm he led them out of it. And for about forty years he put up with them in the wilderness.**
> **And after destroying seven nations in the land of Canaan, he gave them their land as an inheritance.**
> **All this took about 450 years. And after that he gave them judges until Samuel the prophet.**
>
> **Then they asked for a king, and God gave them Saul, the son of Kish, a man of the tribe of Benjamin for forty years.**
>
> **And when he had removed him, he raised up David to be their king of whom he testified and said, I have found in David the son of Jesse a man after my heart, who will do all my will.**
>
> **Of this man's offspring, God has brought to Israel a Savior, Jesus as he promised."**

God fulfilled many promises to the leaders of Israel, especially to David and his Messianic heir.

As God stated in His Covenant with David, He promised the Eternal Throne through the Davidic Dynasty,

> **"I will raise up your offspring after you, who shall come from your body, and I will establish his kingdom. He shall build a house for my name, and I will establish the throne of his kingdom forever.**

I will be to him a father, and he shall be to me a son. When he commits iniquity, I will discipline him with the rod of men, with the stripes of the sons of men, but my steadfast love will not depart from him, as I took it from Saul, whom I put away from before you.

And your house and your kingdom shall be made sure forever before me. Your throne shall be established forever."
(2 Samuel 7:12-16 ~ The Davidic Covenant)

The arrival in history of the son of David, the one who will rule on the Eternal Throne forever, is stated in the genealogy of Jesus Christ, the Messiah.

As Matthew writes in his Gospel, the making of the Messiah, Jesus Christ, stems from David.

Matthew demonstrates Jesus' legal Jewish claim to the throne, emphasizing Jesus' legal descent from David and Abraham.

"The book of the genealogy of Jesus Christ, the son of David, the son of Abraham."
(Matthew 1:1)

✦✦✦✦✦✦✦✦✦✦✦

P*earl: Throughout Biblical history Jews kept extensive genealogical records in order to establish a person's heritage, rights and inheritance. Due to his background as a tax collector before becoming a disciple of Jesus, Matthew had extensive scribal and record-keeping skills. As a Galilean Jewish-Christian, he was also well versed in the Hebrew Bible and in Messianic prophecy.*
✦✦✦✦✦✦✦✦✦✦✦

Therefore Matthew's writing of Jesus' descent from David draws from Hebrew Messianic expectations, and emphasizes Jesus' legal claim to the throne of Israel and eternity through David.

Matthew's opening words in his Gospel carried special significance to the Jewish people, as their ancestry was importantly intertwined with the Abrahamic and Davidic Covenants.

The name Jesus (Greek: Iesous) was most likely not used by Matthew, as this was the everyday name for Jesus' Hebrew name of Yeshua or Yehoshua (Joshua), meaning "Yahweh saves" **(Nehemiah 7:7, Matthew 1:21).**

As stated in Matthew 1:1, Jesus is known as Jesus Christ, where Christ (Greek: Christos) is derived from the Hebrew word mashiakh, (mashiach/messiah), meaning 'anointed' leader by God. This is especially significant as the word anointed points back to David as the anointed King of Israel. The designation of Messiah harkens back to Hebrew Bible prophecy in the promise of an anointed one who would righteously rule God's people as stated in the Davidic Covenant **(2 Samuel 7:11-16)**.

Through Matthew stating that Jesus is a son of David, the Jewish people would have had images of a Messiah with the royal lineage from David, who would rule in eternity.

Jesus Himself mentions He is from the lineage of David in the Revelation to John, stating that He is both David's son and his Lord, the source of his royalty,

> **"I, Jesus, have sent my angel to testify to you about these things for the churches. I am the root and descendent of David, the bright morning star."**
> **(Revelation 22:16)**

In mentioning that Jesus was also a son of Abraham, Matthew reaffirmed to the Jewish people the Abrahamic Covenant where God's calling and Covenant with Abraham established Israel as a 'chosen people'. What was also implied and is exegeted Matthew's rendition of Jesus' genealogy in his authored Gospel, is the Lord's promise that the whole world (all nations) would be blessed through Abraham's line as was written in **Genesis 12:1-3; 22:18.**

> **"I will make of you a great nation, and I will bless you and make your name great, so that you will be a blessing."**
> **(Genesis 12:2)**

> **"and in your offspring shall all the nations of the earth be blessed because you have obeyed my voice."**
> **(Genesis 22:18)**

Luke, in his Gospel also claims Jesus' descent from David. In contradistinction to Matthew's account, Luke emphasizes Jesus' biological descent from David and Adam.

✦✦✦✦✦✦✦✦✦✦✦

Pearl: The promise of God to Abraham (the Abrahamic Covenant) saying that his descendants will be a blessing to all nations is fulfilled in the Davidic Covenant and ultimately with the coming of Jesus Christ with the New Covenant.

✦✦✦✦✦✦✦✦✦✦✦

God made a covenant with Abraham saying,

> **"Look toward heaven, and number the stars, if you are able to number them. So shall your offspring be."**
> **(Genesis 15:5)**

"Behold, my covenant is with you, and you shall be the father of a multitude of nations.
No longer shall your name be called Abram, but your name shall be Abraham, for I have made you the father of a multitude of nations.
I will make you exceedingly fruitful, and I will make you into nations, and kings shall come from you.
And I will establish my covenant between me and you and your offspring after you throughout their generations for an everlasting covenant."
(Genesis 17:4-7)

With the above background and context, we now will delve deep into the life of David. By first- hand experiencing his joys, trials, sins, and ultimately his repentance, we will come to see his complete surrender to Almighty God.

Importantly, we will also take a behind-the-scenes approach to the life of Bathsheba, as she is wife of David who produced the offspring who is in the ancestral line of Jesus.

Through Scripture, we will begin to understand the Lord's intentions as to why David was His chosen son to be a prominent figure in the enduring dynasty from which the ultimate Messiah, Jesus Christ, the savior of humanity will spring forth, bringing blessings to all nations.

As an integral part of God's divine Masterplan is that through David and Bathsheba, He is preparing the way for the ultimate salvation of humanity through His Son, Jesus Christ.

Prologue

Ca. 5 B.C., Nazareth, province of Galilee during the final years of the reign of Herod the Great.

Pre-Reading: Matthew 2, Luke 1

Virgin Mary, the future mother of Jesus, has found out that she will become pregnant

Playlist: "Let your Heart Beat Again" by Danny Gokey, "Yahweh, We Love to Shout Your Name" by Phil Wickham

Her heart was pounding in her chest as she ran through the hills, sometimes tripping over shrubs and rocks due to her haste.

Picking herself up each time, she determinedly continued on her journey. With her soul on fire for Yahweh *(YHWH : Hebrew)*, she pressed on, making her way through the hill country towards her cousin's house.

In one instant, her life had been changed forever.

Never again to be the young, innocent girl she had once been, she is now a woman with utmost responsibilities.

Stopping to catch her breath for a minute, she asked herself, could the baby inside of her really be the long-awaited Messiah? The savior sent from the Lord?

On one hand she was the scared to death, while on the other hand she was filled with excitement and anticipation concerning the plan for her future. With The Holy Spirit burning within her, what was once a tiny spark had now been kindled into a full-blown flame.

She was a peasant, teen-aged girl from Nazareth.

Her name was Mary.

The trek through the hill country of Judah was no easy hike, but Mary pressed on, filled with energy as she reflected about the events that had happened over the last few weeks.

This trip to visit her wise, older cousin, Elizabeth was definitely in order. Right now Mary really needed the comfort of a close family member who would understand her unusual predicament.
Besides, she had just heard the wonderful news that Elizabeth was pregnant!

This was an amazing miracle of the Lord, as Elizabeth and her husband Zechariah had prayed for a child for many years. In Elizabeth's old age, God has given them the gift of a child that they had so desired.

The journey from Nazareth to Elizabeth's home through the hills of Judea took several days, which had given Mary plenty of time to pray and ponder her situation.

Now Mary's thoughts turned to her recent, very unusual encounter with the angel, Gabriel.

Gabriel was overwhelming and powerful, to say the least! The supreme being had tried to comfort her when he first appeared, but Mary had still been scared out of her wits. He had appeared out of nowhere as she had been at the well drawing water for the evening meal.

Taken aback by Gabriel's power and magnificence, Mary had trembled in fear, paralyzed at first do or say much of anything.

Gabriel then formidably broke the news to her that soon she would become pregnant.

What? How can this be? Mary's mind began to churn, and her anxiety level rose.

Taken aback with disbelief, Mary collected her wits and pointedly asked Gabriel how she could possibly become pregnant while she was still a virgin? Thinking back on the encounter, she thought that she may have come across a little too bold with her question, but was glad she had stood up for herself.

After all, she was a virgin, and furthermore, she was not promiscuous!

What a predicament she was in!

She sure needed a friend right now. Knowing that Elizabeth was older and wiser gave Mary hope, as perhaps she could help explain these unusual circumstances. Being well educated in Mosaic Jewish law, and hearing excerpts from the Torah from readings was one thing, but at Mary's young age she knew she still had a lot to learn.

Mary thought back on the events of her recent life. Soon after reaching childbearing age a few months earlier, she had been promised in marriage to Joseph.

Joseph was a righteous man, and she was honored to soon become his wife.

Mary looked back fondly on the celebration of the announcement by their families of the couple's betrothment. She remembered the village-wide party honoring them as the young couple who would soon be married. The wedding and their subsequent co-habitation would be happening in the next year or so, but until then they were considered formally engaged.

The village party given in Mary and Joseph's honor last week had been a wonderful celebration of their marriage-to-be, complete with gift giving! She thought back at how pleased her father had been, his smiling face etched in her memory. Mary knew he was hoping for many grandsons in the future.

But then, just three days ago there was the mysterious, frightening encounter with the angel sent by God, named Gabriel.

Gabriel had appeared out of nowhere, and announced to Mary the absolute impossible!

Luke 1:29
"The angel Gabriel, sent by God said to Mary, Behold, you will conceive in your womb and bear a son, and you shall call his name Jesus."

Gabriel had proclaimed that not only would she become pregnant, but the baby she would bear is the "Son of God."

Luke 1:35
"The Holy Spirit will come upon you, and the power of the Most High will overshadow you, therefore the child to be born will be called holy – the Son of God."

Pearl: *God had broken the silence of four hundred years with humanity, as He sent the angel Gabriel to communicate the Good News of the coming of His Son to Mary.*

♦♦♦♦♦♦♦♦♦♦♦

Thinking back on the encounter, Mary remembered how Gabriel had greeted her and had first informed her that she had found favor with God. Difficult to believe, but at least that had been encouraging.

But the next bit of news was even more unbelievable.

Gabriel told her that she would conceive a baby from the Holy Spirit, and that she would bear a son! She was told to name this baby, Jesus, meaning *"God Saves"*.

Gabriel went on to tell her that her son, the *Son of the Most High*, would be given the throne of his father David, and would reign over the house of Jacob forever. Gabriel finished by saying that His kingdom would never end *(Luke 1:26-38).*

Now that it had time to sink in, she was pondering her future and wondering why this all happening to her?

Mary's once-simple world was no more. Now she definitely needed to think about things that were a bit loftier than just her future wedding.

Mary had been called by God to do the impossible!

How was she going to accomplish all of this?

Mary doubted that she, an ordinary girl of fourteen, could ever amount to much of anything besides possibly a wife and hopefully a mother of many sons.

Now, Mary had been chosen to be the mother of the "Son of God".

Mary was worried about what her family would think? And the neighbors? How will they react to her pregnancy prior to marriage?

And to top it all off, how will they react when she claims that the father of this child is Almighty God Himself?

Everyone will think that she was not only promiscuous, but crazy as well. Wow, now there's a combination!

Mary shuddered at what the consequences for her for being pregnant from someone other her husband will be. Coming from an honorable, law-abiding family, she knew the consequences and the law concerning infidelity.

◆◆◆◆◆◆◆◆◆◆◆

Pearl: *Jewish law was very specific about this and can be found in* Deuteronomy *22:13-21.*

The law said that a women who committed adultery, if she was betrothed and not yet married, would be stoned to death by her family and friends in order to restore honor to their town.

◆◆◆◆◆◆◆◆◆◆◆

Again, her angst rose and Mary suddenly felt sick to her stomach. Sitting down for a moment under the shade of a tree, Mary's thoughts turned to what could be a horrific nightmare, not only for her but her family as well.

Mary tried to push back the thoughts of her being drug from her house and stoned by her own family. Her last visions on this earth would be of her once-happy home and beloved relatives, who were the very people who would end her life.

Why me? Mary asked herself again, and began to weep.

And even if the worst didn't happen, and she wasn't stoned to death, her life would be ruined. Joseph, being an honorable man might choose to quietly divorce her. If this would happen, what would her future hold? Mary knew the answer.

◆◆◆◆◆◆◆◆◆◆◆

*P**earl:** By cultural standards, Mary would then be expected to live in her father's house for the rest of her life as a single, divorced woman. She would not be allowed to marry, and would be forced to live in quiet isolation away from the rest of the village. Of course, she would not be allowed to have children, which meant that she would not have any means of survival in her old age. Mary would be forced to live out her life in poverty, and die a miserable, lonely death. In other words she would be forced to live the lie that she was promiscuous and crazy. Alone and criticized by her family and the townspeople, she would be an outcast of society.*

◆◆◆◆◆◆◆◆◆◆◆

Definitely, she thought, *her life was a mess.*

That's why Mary had decided to flee her town and visit Elizabeth.

Mary knew that Elizabeth and her husband, Zechariah, were wise and righteous in the sight of God. Elizabeth will certainly understand, and would be able to make sense of all of this!

Picking herself up, Mary continued the journey.

Finally, after several long days of traveling, Mary arrived at the home of Zechariah and Elizabeth.

All of Mary's anxiety disappeared as she received a heartfelt, loving greeting from her cousin, Elizabeth. After being ushered into Elizabeth's home with warm hospitality, the two settled in and began to talk.

From the outset, both expectant mothers knew something very extraordinary and divine was happening.

Upon Mary's arrival, the baby in Elizabeth's womb leaped with joy, and Elizabeth herself was filled with the Holy Spirit.

Then it happened. All of Mary's pent up emotions came bursting forth!

The young, scared-to-death, teenaged mother-to-be, burst forth with a song of praise to God, as she prayed these words,

Luke 1:47-55; Mary's Song of Praise: The Magnificat

"My soul magnifies the Lord, and my spirit rejoices in God my Savior; for he has looked on the humble estate of his servant.
For behold, from now on all generations will call me blessed; for he who is mighty has done great things for me; and holy is his name.
And his mercy is for those who fear him from generation to generation. He has shown strength with his arm; he has scattered the proud in the thoughts of their hearts; he has brought down the mighty from their thrones and exalted those of humble estate; he has filled the hungry with good things, and the rich he has sent away empty.
He has helped his servant Israel, in remembrance of his mercy.
As he spoke to our fathers, to Abraham and to his offspring forever."

PEARL: *THIS SONG DREW FROM HEBREW SCRIPTURES, AND WAS TRULY A DIVINE-INSPIRED COMPOSITION. IT WAS AS IF ALL OF MARY'S PENT-UP EMOTIONS WERE CHANNELED INTO HER PRAISE OF GOD.*

IMPORTANTLY, MARY'S PRAYER SETS THE STAGE FOR US TO EXAMINE MARY'S DESCENDANTS, AS SHE TOOK PRIDE IN THE GENERATIONS BEFORE HER. IT IS ALSO VERY OBVIOUS FROM HER WORDS THAT SHE WAS KNOWLEDGEABLE OF THE TORAH AND HOW GOD HAD SPOKEN TO ABRAHAM AND HIS OFFSPRING, WHO SHE REFERRED TO AS 'OUR FATHERS.'

◆◆◆◆◆◆◆◆◆◆◆

Mary knew that what she needed, and now was the time to regroup and solidify her faith. She needed to gain the strength to face the trials ahead.

Mary knew she needed to study God's Word, as Scripture will help her to understand why she had been chosen by God to do 'the impossible'?

Elizabeth realized just what her younger cousin needed. Elizabeth knew that Mary would be inspired through understanding who she was, and why she had been chosen as the woman who would bear the child who would fulfill God's promise to humanity.

Elizabeth knew that young Mary needed to identify with her ancestors. Her ordinary, yet extraordinary ancestors.

She needed to know their stories, and that she was not alone in her calling by God to do "the impossible."

Knowing information about where Mary came from will help identify where she is going, and help her through the trials ahead of her.

And there certainly will be trials.

This knowledge of "why me?," and what had played out in their previous family histories would be essential in building and solidifying Mary's faith.

The young peasant girl stayed with her cousin for 3 months. She would then return home and face her family with the news of her pregnancy.

During this time, her wise, older cousin described to her important information from God's Holy Word about their family tree. The family tree that will soon lead to Jesus, the Messiah.

By studying scripture and reliving stories of their ancestry, the two women would discover that the baby Mary was carrying was indeed the prophesized Messiah, Son of God.

◆◆◆◆◆◆◆◆◆◆◆

P*EARL: IMAGINE BEING THE YOUNG PEASANT GIRL WHO IS PREGNANT THROUGH THE HOLY SPIRIT. IMAGINE BEING MARY, THE FUTURE MOTHER OF JESUS CHRIST, OUR MESSIAH. IMAGINE THE CONSEQUENCES OF BEING PREGNANT WITHOUT BEING MARRIED IN THE ANCIENT CULTURE OF A JEWISH WOMAN.*

✦✦✦✦✦✦✦✦✦✦✦

Mary had to trust that God had a plan for her.

Mary had received God's calling, and now it was time for her to be obedient, and carry out the plan that God had for her.

***Pearl:** Keep in mind that Mary; being well taught in Jewish scripture had most likely heard the stories about the characters of the Hebrew Bible (Old Testament). She knew that the Messiah would come from the Davidic Dynasty to fulfill God's prophecy.*

*What is not clear is if she realized how important the Messiah would be to all of humanity. What she will find out after studying Scripture, is how important this baby she was carrying would be and how he would fulfill God's prophesy of **Genesis 3:15.***
After the fall of Adam and Eve from the Garden of Eden, God promised humanity that a savior would be born from a human woman who would ultimately defeat sin and death.

What Mary will discover is that she, the humble peasant teenager from Nazareth, was 'that' woman.

Mary was the woman carrying the baby who would defeat the Devil, and is the Savior of all humanity. The most important event in all of human history was about to happen.

We will see that Mary's baby will be God's promise of thousands of year's prior, which was given first to Adam and Eve, then on to Abraham continuing through his offspring. God's promise would take shape in the fulfillment of the prophecies, and culminate with the coming of the Messiah.

Most importantly, the coming of Jesus the Christ is the beginning of the New Covenant, a new enlightened relationship between God and all of mankind.

Mary and Elizabeth drew very close together over the next three months as they studied the Tanakh and discussed their ancestors. The stories they shared helped Mary understand how the people in her family tree were just ordinary people, some even considered by society to be unworthy, but who became extraordinary all because of the grace of God.

Understanding the stories in the Hebrew Bible about the people who were the ancestors of Jesus helped Mary gain the courage to do what she was meant to do, being to bear and raise the Son of God.

The Son of God, Jesus Christ, the Savior who changed the future of all those who believe.

Once and for all, Jesus took on the sins of all mankind so that we can never be separated from God, the Father.

We will now enter into the story of two of Mary's ancestors, as seen from her eyes.

The story about to unfold is concerning two of the most important and notable characters of the Hebrew bible, the story of David and Bathsheba.

First, let's put the story into the context of the day, as Mary and Elizabeth would have understood.

Act 1: Young David

Introduction:

Playlist: "God Only Knows" by King and Country, "God of All My Days" by Casting Crowns

Pre-reading: Psalm 69, and the Book of Ruth (David's great-grandmother)

The Jewish Rabbis hold that David, as a prayer, wrote Psalm 69 to the Lord concerning his turmoil during his very young life.

We are not given much information about David's childhood years, but assuming that in keeping with Jewish tradition, that David was describing his early life in **_Psalm 69,_** we can gain great insight into this time of his life.

We do know that David was born into the family of Jesse (_Hebrew: Yishai_), who was the son of Obed _(Hebrew: Oved)_, the grandson of Boaz and Ruth the Moabitess (of the Book of Ruth), and the great-grandson of Salmon and Rahab, the Canaanite prostitute. Of significance is that although David ancestry was predominately Jewish in origin, but through his father, Jesse, David was also of both Moabite and Canaanite extraction.

David's esteemed ancestors carried with them the legacy of righteous conduct and prestigious positions in the community. They were all God-fearing people who were dedicated to follow the Law of the Lord. Both Ruth and Rahab who were of non-Jewish origin (Ruth was of Moabite and Rahab was of Canaanite origin), fully converted to Judaism and are revered by the Jewish people for their righteous deeds.

David's father, Jesse, according to the Talmud and Midrash, served as the head of the Sanhedrin (supreme court of Torah law), and was a leading Torah authority in his day.

Jesse and his family lived in Bethlehem (_Hebrew: Beit Lechem_), as did his father and grandfather before him. David was the youngest son of Jesse in a family, which included seven older brothers and two sisters.

David and his siblings were raised in Bethlehem during the time that Israel first became a monarchy under the rule of King Saul. Emerging from the period of time of nearly three hundred years where the Israelite people were ruled by a series of Judges selected by the Lord, rule by a single king was a new experience. Undoubtedly, the transition from a theocracy to a monarchy took some getting used to by the Jewish people.

There is not a lot divulged in the Bible about how the Israelites viewed their newly appointed King Saul, but it is clear that God did not approve of their choice. Throughout the years of his reign Saul demonstrated many characteristics unfitting of a righteous king that was capable of leading God's people. Eventually, this led to God removing Saul from being the king and replacing him with his choice, who would be David.

Of interest is that David as he was growing up would have only experienced King Saul as the leader of Israel, even though his father and grandparents grew up during the rule of God's chosen judges. David's immediate ancestors would therefore have had a very different political background than he would have known, as David would have only experienced the political and spiritual climate that surrounded that of a monarchy.

It is also clear from rabbinical commentary that under the auspices of their father, Jesse, who served on the Sanhedrin, David and his siblings were raised in a God-fearing, Jewish environment. As Jesse was considered to be an authority on the Torah, his children were undoubtedly schooled in the Word of God.

Unfortunately, even though David was raised in a devout Jewish family we can deduce that David's early life was not a happy one according to David's own words in his prayer written in *Psalm 69*. Here, David describes a very difficult life as he was growing up.

Describing in *Psalm 69* how he was shunned not only by his brothers, but also by the Torah sages who sat in judgment at the town gates, David pours out his feelings of anguish. Apparently the disdainful attitude against David was carried over to even include the drunkards on the street corners.

To make matters worse, it was as if no one would provide young David with love, comfort and friendship.

No human that is, as David, even at a very early age, turned to Almighty God with demonstrable faithfulness and trust.

Pearl: What had David done to arouse such contempt from people in his family and his hometown of Bethlehem? His angst is palpable in his prayer to the Lord, as recorded in Psalm 69. Some excerpts are included to illustrate David's feelings.

David's prayer ~ Excerpts from Psalm 69: (1-3, 4, 8, 11-12, 19-21, 30, 33)

"Save me O God! For the waters have come up to my neck.

I sink in deep mire, where there is no foothold.
I have come into deep waters and the flood sweeps over me.

I am weary with my eyes crying out, my throat is parched. My eyes grow dim with waiting for my God."

"More in number than the hairs of my head are those who hate me without cause, mighty are those who would destroy me, those who attack me with lies.

What I did not steal must I now restore?"

"I have become a stranger to my brothers, an alien to my mother's sons."

"I am the talk of those who sit in the gate, and the drunkards make songs about me."

"You know my reproach and my shame and my dishonor, my foes are all known to you. Reproaches have broken my heart so that I am in despair.

I looked for pity, but there was none and for comforters, but I found none. They gave me poison for food and for my thirst they gave me sour wine to drink."

"I will praise the name of God with a song, I will magnify him with thanksgiving."

"For the LORD hears the needy and does not despise his own people who are prisoners."

✦✦✦✦✦✦✦✦✦✦

From these verses, one can feel the outpouring of passion from a burdened, tormented soul.

Through it all however, David continued to draw upon the strength of the Lord, praising and magnifying Him with thanksgiving.

✦✦✦✦✦✦✦✦✦✦

Pearl: What is the mystery behind David's tormented childhood?

Of interest is to look into the **Hebrew meaning** of the verse *"I have become a stranger to my brothers."* The Hebrew word for 'stranger' is **muzar**, which is from the same root as **mamzer,** meaning 'bastard' or 'illegitimate offspring'.

With this Hebrew meaning in mind, could David possibly be saying that he was treated as an illegitimate son by his family and by the people of his hometown of Bethlehem during his years of growing up?

Why was David treated as a 'bastard-son'?

♦♦♦♦♦♦♦♦♦♦♦

Let the mystery unfold, as David's story continues.

In reading David's story, keep in mind that this lowly, shepherd-boy who people shunned is the one who God will choose to be the ruler of the Israelite people.

Of utmost importance, from David's ancestry will spring the one true ruler of all eternity, the Messiah, Jesus Christ.

Scene 1: Young David ~ 'The Ultimate Worship Director'

Playlist: "Giants" by Sanctus Real, "Yes I Will" by Vertical Worship

Pre-Reading: 1 Samuel 16, Psalm 144

Timeframe: Ca. 1000 B.C. David is now seventeen-years old and is the shepherd of his father's flocks in an area just outside of the city of Bethlehem. Saul has been the King of Israel for several years now, but has fallen into disfavor with the Lord.

Standing with his back to the sun rising above the vast plains surrounding Bethlehem, David diligently watched over his flock of sheep.

34

His eyes scanning the flock continuously, David carefully observed each herd-member's every movement as the sheep happily grazed the dew-laden grass in the early morning hours.

The dazzling morning illumination served as a backdrop for the young man, setting his crown of titian-colored hair aglow, forming a halo around the chiseled features of his face.

Ruggedly handsome, but far from being boulevardier, David exuded an unexplainable vibrancy and charismatic appeal. His naturally fair skin, tanned from hours of working in the grasslands tending his flocks, had taken on a ruddy hue.

Considering David's fit, muscular build and athletic prowess, it was apparent that he was no stranger to many hours of physical work in the fields.

David's prominent physical feature, however, were his beautiful eyes.

Gazing into David's eyes were like looking at a multifaceted tsavorite garnet, sparkling jasper green with golden-aurulent hues. His eyes were stunningly captivating and intense, but most of all, they were kind.

Looking into David's eyes served to glean information into the very nature of his inner soul. Through his eyes one could tell that his strong, warlike appearance and exceptional courage was balanced harmoniously with the *chesed* of his heart.

David also had an exceptional work ethic, as he took pride in his job as a shepherd who tended to his father's flocks. Being that he was the youngest of seven older brothers, David had been the one who was delegated to do the hard, long, tedious hours of shepherding the sheep.

Always thinking of the best plan to care for his flocks, David had creatively instrumented an optimal protocol for his herds to graze according to each individual's strength and maturity.

David's plan allowed the young lambs to graze the tender grass first, as they were incapable of chewing and digesting the tougher, older grass in the fields. He then allowed the older sheep access to the medium-aged grass, which they could efficiently harvest. Finally, David allowed the strong, youthful sheep to eat the tougher, older-aged grass, as they could effectively harvest and digest the aged growth.

David was extremely protective of his flock, and even had risked his own life on several occasions when predators had attacked. Being endowed with unusual strength and courage, he had been known to fight off bears and lions to save his sheep from the disaster of being killed by these vicious predators.

God had blessed David with an uncanny, keen sense of thought processes and physical adeptness that led to him having the superb capabilities of a warrior.

As a young man tending his sheep in the fields alone, David learned to hone his skills to protect his flock from vicious wildlife that lived in the area surrounding the vast grasslands. Using simple tools such as a sling and rocks gathered from the land, he could expertly kill even the most stealth, viscous predator who stalked the young lambs of his flock.

David had also trained his sheep to come to the sound of his voice, as they learned that he provided protection for them and their young, as well as sustenance.

However, shepherding could also be tedious work, so David was subjected to hours of potential boredom in the fields. Even though these hours could be long, he occupied himself in a positive way to serve the Lord so that he would not lose his concentration and neglect his shepherding duties.

Putting these long, lonely hours to good use, David learned to play the lyre and compose beautiful music and hymns of praise to Yahweh. David found his joy and passion, singing praises to the Lord through the hymns and music he created.

David had composed many hymns while shepherding, setting poetic words of praise to Yahweh to complement his musical tunes. He found that he felt close to the Lord when he could worship Him through music.

*P**earl:** David had a heart for the Lord, even from a very young age. The worship hymns David created would later be sung by the Jewish people in praise of Yahweh and incorporated into the Hebrew Bible Book of Psalms. Writing the majority of the Psalms, David came to be known as 'Israel's sweet psalmist'.*

◆◆◆◆◆◆◆◆◆◆◆

David spent many long, lonely hours in the pasturelands, but was rewarded by the joy he felt through worshipping God through his created music. He directed all of his God-given musical and poetic talents to praise the Lord.

While tending to his sheep, and composing hymns on his lyre, David would sing with fervor to the Lord in the pastures where his sheep grazed. There were no people present, but the sheep were an appreciative audience.

The sheep never complained, as David would often work, and re-work his tunes to perfection, sometimes hitting an off-note or two.

All for God's Glory!

David, a young man with a sincere heart for the Lord, was the epitome of God's beautiful creation of humanity.

David had a heart for God, and for all of His Creation. This was seen and remembered by the Almighty.

✦✦✦✦✦✦✦✦✦✦✦

Pearl: As David was a young man and a 'warrior-in-training' he wrote Psalm 144, requesting God equip him to fight for the sake of his people. At a very young age David realized that the plan for his life was to further God's purpose for his people. He will later learn that as king of Israel, he would not be allowed to pursue selfish ends with the power that God has graciously bestowed upon him.

✦✦✦✦✦✦✦✦✦✦✦

Psalm 144 of David: (1-2, 9-10)
"Blessed be the LORD, my rock, who trains my hands for war, and my fingers for battle;
He is my steadfast love and my fortress, my stronghold and my deliverer, my shield and he in whom I take refuge, who subdues peoples under me.

I will sing a new song to you, O God; upon a ten-stringed harp I will pay to you, who rescues David his servant from the cruel sword."

Scene 2: Within Minutes

Ca. 1000 BC
Setting: Bethlehem

Playlist: "Show Me Your Glory" by Third Day, "Nobody" by Casting Crowns and Matthew West

Pre-reading: 1 Samuel 15, and 16, Psalms 8, 19, 20, 21, 39, 143, and 144

Everyone in Bethlehem and the surrounding towns had heard about the proposed visit of the acclaimed prophet and judge, Samuel.

Bethlehem was abuzz with gossip concerning the reason behind Samuel's visit. The townspeople anxiously anticipated the honored prophet's arrival, as Samuel did not regularly travel to cities in the land, especially a small town such as Bethlehem.

When Samuel first arrived in Bethlehem the town-elders were brimming with trepidation. They were soon put at ease when they were told the occasion for Samuel's visit was for a special sacrificial offering to the Lord.

In the background however, lurked more information.

"And the LORD regretted that he had made Saul king over Israel."
(1 Samuel 15:35)

Samuel was told by the Lord to go to Bethlehem to find a king of God's choosing. This new king would be a son of Jesse, who was the son of Obed.

The LORD said to Samuel, "how long will you grieve over Saul, since I have rejected him from being king over Israel?
Fill your horn with oil, and go.
I will send you to Jesse the Bethlehemite, for I have provided for myself a king among his sons."
(1 Samuel 16:1)

However, Samuel was fearful to make the trip to Bethlehem. Afraid that Saul would find out that Samuel was going to Bethlehem to find a new king to replace him, Samuel questioned the Lord. Samuel was aware of Saul's violent temper, and was reluctant to make the trip to Bethlehem as the Lord intended.

Filled with worry about how King Saul would retaliate against him, Samuel asked the Lord,

"How can I go? If Saul hears it, he will kill me."
(1 Samuel 16:2)

In order to defuse Saul's potential anger and an adversarial encounter, the Lord instructed Samuel to take a heifer and provide a sacrificial feast for the townspeople to worship Yahweh.

One more important thing - at the Lord's direction, Samuel was to be sure to invite Jesse to the sacrificial feast.

God instructed Samuel to be sure to,

"Invite Jesse to the sacrifice, and I will show you what you shall do.
And you shall anoint for me him whom I declare to you."
(1 Samuel 16:3).

Samuel did as the Lord instructed and headed to Bethlehem. He sent word ahead of his visit that he was going to provide a sacrificial feast for the townspeople. In his preemptive message, Samuel was very clear that Jesse and his sons should be on the guest list for the feast!

In response to this gracious invitation by Samuel, David's father Jesse gathered up his sons and headed into town that morning for the big event. Not all of Jesse's sons made the trip, however.

One son had been told by Jesse to stay home. The one son that didn't make Jesse's guest list to attend the festivities was David.

Obedient to his father, David stayed home and tended to his father's sheep, just like any other day.

Just like any other day. Or so David thought.

Later on this same day, David was routinely attending the sheep in the field. Seeing motion out on the horizon, he shielded his eyes against the late afternoon to view a man who was hurriedly approaching him.

From a distance David noticed that the stranger appeared to be summoning him, as he was wildly waving his arms and seemed distressed. There could be no mistake the man was intent on getting his attention.

David stood quietly in the field and continued to shield his eyes against the sunlight to look at this mystery man striding across the pasture towards him.

The stranger, obviously unaccustomed to hiking through the grassland, was having a great bit of trouble navigating the unpredictably rough terrain. Tripping several times, he haltingly approached David and his herd of sheep.

Closing the distance between them, David walked towards the man and politely greeted him.

With hasty acknowledgement and a brief introduction of who he was, the stranger unexpectedly requested that David immediately accompany him to Bethlehem. The man hurriedly explained that the prophet Samuel refused to continue on with the sacrificial festivities without first meeting David.

Surprised by the stranger's odd request, David politely obliged, but insisted that he must first herd the flocks to the safety of their sheepfold.

The man grudgingly agreed and followed along as David took the time to herd the flocks to their safe-haven for the evening.

After the flocks of sheep were settled in, David and the mysterious man who was sent by Samuel to retrieve him, headed together into the town of Bethlehem.

Before David knew what had happened he was at the gathering in the city in the presence of the elders and the prophet Samuel. Totally out of his element, David became apprehensive due to the large crowds of townspeople and the cacophony of the festivities.

Noticing that his father and his brothers were already present and standing away from the crowd of people who had gathered, David started to head towards his family.

Huddled together away from the crowds, Jesse and David's brothers were talking among themselves in inaudible whispers. David noticed that his brothers seemed to be disappointed and somewhat angry, making him wonder what had previously taken place that led to their disgruntled moods.

As David approached, his brothers eyed him with contempt and began to chide him. The young men quieted their voices as their father gave them a harsh, sidelong glance.

David felt hurt and disgraced by his brothers' words and actions, so he solemnly moved forward to join the gathering of townspeople, instead of staying with his family.

Samuel looked up from talking with some people in the crowd and seeing David approach, hurriedly went to greet him.

Looking straight into David's beautiful eyes, Samuel knew that David was a man of God's heart.

"Now he was ruddy and had beautiful eyes and was handsome."
(1 Samuel 16:12)

Gently taking David by his arm, Samuel guided him a safe distance away from the discordant sounds and activities of the festivities, stopping just short of his father, brothers, and a group of townspeople who seemed to be very interested in the whole ordeal.

Holding a ram's horn filled to the brim with oil, Samuel began praying earnestly to the Lord. Embracing David close to his side as he prayed, Samuel lifted his face to the Heavens above.

As Samuel continued to pray, the oil in the ram's horn he was holding began to bubble-over the brim, unable to be contained within its confines.

And the LORD said to Samuel,

"Arise, anoint him, for this is he."
(1 Samuel 16:12)

Samuel then poured the oil from the ram's horn onto David's head.

"Then Samuel took the horn of oil and anointed him in the midst of his brothers."
(1 Samuel 16:13)

40

Pearl: *The Rabbis in the Midrash exegeted from these verses in **1 Samuel 16** the following concerning the event about David's anointment:*

*David was anointed with oil referred to as **'shemen ha-mishcha'**, the anointing oil prepared by Moses, which had been preserved throughout the years. The significance of the oil mixed by Moses was the reminder that the monarch's success was fully dependent on his ability to follow in the footsteps of Moses, who the Jews considered to be their nation's first and greatest leader.*

*From David forward, a king of Davidic stock would be anointed with the oil referred to as **'shemen ha-mishcha'**.*

◆◆◆◆◆◆◆◆◆◆◆

Hardening as it dripped down over David's hair, the shemen ha-mishcha took on the appearance and shape of pearls and precious stones. It was if a crown had been mysteriously formed from the anointing oil. The horn then refilled itself, and as Samuel continued pouring it over David's head, it began flowing down onto the collar of his garment.

As David was anointed with the shemen ha-mishcha which formed into a crown of royalty, Jesse and David's brothers stood looking on with disbelief, which soon turned to fear. Shaking uncontrollably, David's brothers backed away from the holy event and hurriedly headed for home.

After Samuel anointed David with oil,

> **"The spirit of the LORD rushed upon David from that day forward."**
> **(1 Samuel 16:13)**

David had been endowed with the Divine Spirit and was enveloped by the supernatural power of God.

The flame for God in David's heart would continue to be fanned into a fire that could not be extinguished by any obstacle that he would face in his future.

Pearl: *After David was anointed, the celebration did not last long – most likely less than an hour or less.*

Within minutes, history had been forever changed.

Soon after David's anointment, Samuel departed to Ramah *(1 Samuel 16:13).*

David then subsequently headed back home to tend to his father's flock of sheep. Proceeding as just another day, David went out the next morning to protect and tend to the flocks.

Summary Pearl of Scene 2: What does the Bible say about the events surrounding David's anointment?

Let's start with what we know from God's Word:

- *Samuel went to Bethlehem on the direction from the Lord to anoint the next king of Israel*
  - o *Samuel was afraid that the current king, Saul, would have him killed if Saul knew of his intentions*
  - o *Samuel therefore was instructed to go to Bethlehem under the premise of having a sacrificial feast for the townspeople*
    - ▪ *Samuel was told by the Lord to invite Jesse and his sons, as one of Jesse's sons would be God's choice of the next king of Israel*
- *Samuel paraded Jesse's sons before the Lord to see which one he was to anoint as the new king*
  - o *Each son was magnificent in appearance, and looked like "king-material"*
- *God did not choose any of Jesse's sons that shown to Him*
- *After God's disapproval of each son, Samuel ran out of options. Frustrated, Samuel asked Jesse if all of his sons were present?*
- *Jesse admitted that he had left his youngest son, (David) home to care for the sheep*
- *Samuel instructed Jesse that David should be fetched immediately to join the festivities, so that the Lord could see **all** of Jesse's sons*
- *Unexpectantly, David was God's choice to be the next King of Israel*
  - o *David, the most unlikely, youngest son that had been left at home by his father, turned out to be the anointed One – the son of Jesse, chosen by God, above all of his other sons*
  - o *Everyone was surprised at this choice including Jesse, David's brothers, the elders of Bethlehem, and all of the townspeople*
- *After his anointment, David went home to his life-as-usual as a shepherd, tending to his father's sheep*

With these facts from the Bible presented, one can try to imagine how David would have felt upon his anointment as the next king of Israel.

Elated, yet confused, are some emotions that come to mind. Everything happened very quickly, and David was not aware of all of the circumstances surrounding his anointment.

The celebration held by Samuel most likely ended soon after David's anointment, as Samuel had already delayed the festivities for quite a while waiting for David to arrive.

42

After David was anointed, the party most likely ended with the sacrificial offering, and the final eating of the meal. The people of the town then went home and Samuel departed for home as well.

Essentially, David had very little time to celebrate, if there even was any celebration.

We don't really know if there was celebration, or just confusion after David's surprise anointment.

We also are unaware of how David was received by his brothers once all were back at their home.

There are many unanswered questions. For instance:

What did David's brothers have to say about all of this after they were shunned and their 'unworthy', younger brother was chosen instead of them?

What did the people of Bethlehem have to say?

Did the townspeople question the whole anointment process of David the shepherd, and wonder what was to become of King Saul?

❖❖❖❖❖❖❖❖❖❖❖

Pearl: If the townspeople were similar to people of today, which we must assume they were, there was much talk about what had just happened! The townspeople must have had a lot of questions about the events of the day.

Questions must have surfaced among the people of Bethlehem after David's anointment, such as "who is this David – he's just a shepherd boy?"

Perhaps the people questioned why was David chosen, and not the other magnificent sons of Jesse to be the next king?

And of course, another important issue must have been...

Does King Saul even know of this????

❖❖❖❖❖❖❖❖❖❖❖

Pearl: An interesting fact that helps put things into context was that the procedure for a king's appointment in ancient Israel required two things. First, being that the future king is the choice of God, and second that he be the choice of the citizens of Israel.

❖❖❖❖❖❖❖❖❖❖❖

43

Therefore, in order for a king to obtain his position, it was necessary to have **dual consent**, first of God, and also the people of Israel **(Deuteronomy 17)**.

To fulfil both of these requirements, the king must be first anointed by a prophet, designating that he will rule with God's consent. To then fulfil the requirements that he will rule as the choice of the citizens, the consent of the Sanhedrin, the seventy-one members High Court of Israel, must be obtained.

Of significance is that the Sanhedrin was not consulted – God made His choice known that David was to be the next King of Israel. There is no mention about the Sanhedrin being consulted.

Did David not meet with the Sanhedrin's approval, or were they even in the picture?

Interestingly, God did not leave it up to them. God had made His choice, and that was that!

News traveled fast about David's anointment by the prophet Samuel!

The elders and townspeople at the festivities had witnessed the anointment of David. Being a small town, those that were not present most likely heard very quickly about the news of the happenings that momentous day in Bethlehem.

Undoubtedly, the news of David's anointment spread like wildfire.

Pearl: Within minutes the town was abuzz with talk about the controversial anointment that had just taken place. The townspeople asked each other, "Why David?"

After the conclusion of the festivities, the elders of the town were undoubtedly skeptical of the event of David being anointed as the next king. Not knowing of Saul's rejection by the Lord as king, the elders must have felt it their responsibility to take matters into their own hands and inform Saul's tribunal about this controversial event.

Within a matter of minutes, a messenger departed from Bethlehem to spread the word to Saul's Tribunal about the anointment of some unknown young man who would serve as his replacement as king.

In a matter of minutes history would be changed forever.

How did this all happen? What was not disclosed to David?

Let's go behind the scenes to establish what David did **not** know at the time he was anointed the next king of Israel by the Lord.

1 Samuel 16,
Pre-reading: Psalms 8, 19, 20, 21 and 143

Playlist: "We Were Meant To Be Courageous" by Casting Crowns

David's soul thirsted for knowledge of how to proceed with his new charge.

As the newly anointed one of the Lord, David knew that he was the one who would be God's servant to lead the people of Israel, and that God would always be with him.

◆◆◆◆◆◆◆◆◆◆◆

P*earl: Psalm 143 epitomizes David's feelings of how his soul thirsts for the Lord,*

"Let me hear in the morning of your steadfast love, for in you I trust. Make me know the way I should go, for to you I lift up my soul."

"Teach me to do your will, for you are my God!
Let your good Spirit lead me on level ground!"
(Psalm 143: 8,10)

◆◆◆◆◆◆◆◆◆◆◆

How did events unfold to result in David becoming the newly anointed King of Israel?

David had been unaware of what had happened in the moments before his arrival to the city, and was also not privy to the events preceding Samuel's visit.

Days before, after God had rejected Saul as the King of Israel, the Lord had sent Samuel to find Jesse in Bethlehem.

◆◆◆◆◆◆◆◆◆◆◆

P*earl: Why Jesse of Bethlehem? God was working behind the scenes, and had provided for Himself a king among Jesse's sons.*

◆◆◆◆◆◆◆◆◆◆◆

Samuel however, was reluctant to go to Bethlehem, even though the Lord had instructed him to do so. Samuel feared that Saul would kill him if he found out he was going to anoint another king.

Samuel knew King Saul well and was well aware that Saul had a temper. Samuel knew that Saul's temper was short, and that he could become very aggressive when he was angry.

The Lord therefore instructed Samuel to tell Saul and the people that he was going to Bethlehem to perform a sacrificial feast of praise.

God also was clear in His instructions that Samuel was to invite Jesse and his sons to the festivities. God told Samuel that He would show him what he should do to find the next king.

Once Samuel arrived and the festivities began, he set out on his mission from the Lord to meet Jesse and his sons. The young men were presented before Samuel one-by-one, starting with the oldest son, Eliab.

Eliab was indeed magnificent!

Samuel looked upon Eliab, who was tall and handsome in appearance. Thinking that Eliab certainly fit the bill for being king-material, Samuel thought that he would surely be the one!

Eliab, like Saul was taller than most men, very charismatic and endowed with the physical stature befitting of a monarch.

But the Lord had different plans.

The Lord clearly told Samuel,

> *"Do not look on his appearance or on the height of his stature, because I have rejected him.*
> *For the LORD sees not as man sees; a man looks on the outward appearance.*
> *But the LORD looks on the heart."*
> *(1 Samuel 16:6-7)*

♦♦♦♦♦♦♦♦♦♦♦

Pearl: *As noted in the ESV, the heart in scripture refers to a person's inward moral and spiritual life. From a person's heart will flow his actions, which will be demonstrated by his obedience to the Lord.*

♦♦♦♦♦♦♦♦♦♦♦

Rejected and deflated, Eliab walked with his down back to his father and brothers. Bewildered, Jesse then summoned his second oldest son Abinadab, and made him pass before Samuel. Again, the Lord made it clear that he was not the one.

One-by-one, each of Jesse's remaining seven sons were brought forth and presented to Samuel, but rejected by the Lord to become the next king of Israel.

Finally, in frustration Samuel asked Jesse if the young men who were present were _all_ of his sons?

"Are all your sons here?"
(1 Samuel 16:11)

Jesse replied,

"There remains yet the youngest, but behold he is keeping the sheep."
(1 Samuel 16:11)

Jesse had left David home, as apparently he did not consider his youngest son worthy enough to meet with the great prophet, Samuel.

Samuel requested that Jesse send for his youngest son immediately!

Halting the festivities, Samuel insisted that they shall not proceed with sacrificial offering until he had the opportunity to meet with Jesse's youngest son.

Upon David's arrival, God then indicated to Samuel that of all of Jesse's sons, the one whom people thought was the least likely of all, was indeed the Almighty's choice.

David was anointed to become the future King of Israel, and the Spirit of God empowered him for service.

David rejoiced in the Lords strength and wrote **Psalms 20 and 21,** prayers to the Lord in request for success of the Davidic king and thanksgiving for answering the request.

"May the LORD answer you in the day of trouble. May the name of God of Jacob protect you."
(Psalm 20:1 A Psalm of David)

"His glory is great through your salvation; Splendor and majesty you bestow on him. For you make him most blessed forever, you make him glad with the joy of your presence.

For the king trusts in the LORD;
and through the steadfast love of the Most High he shall not be moved."
(Psalm 21:5-7 A Psalm of David)

God then began training David to lead His people and serve as the next great King of Israel.

As the Divine Spirit entered the newly anointed David, it departed from Saul, for David had replaced him as God's servant as the anointed one *(1 Samuel 16:14).*

◆◆◆◆◆◆◆◆◆◆◆

Pearl: *So begins the long story of the strife and struggles between Saul and David.*

Saul, of course was not keen on the idea of being replaced, as he felt that he deserved to retain the right-to-reign as King of Israel.

Even though the Lord had anointed David, He didn't tell David to pack his suitcases and move into the royal palace quite yet. Things weren't quite so simple as David ascending to the throne, and Saul quietly exiting stage left.

Almighty God proclaimed that Saul would continue to stay in power as the legal ruler of Israel. While Saul was still serving as King, the Lord began working behind-the-scenes to train David to be His king.

As David was His choice, the Lord intended for David to not just be a good king, but to be a great king.

The Lord wanted David to lead the people back towards Him, and make the nation of Israel a nation under God, as it was originally meant to be.

Being disqualified as king of Israel, Saul was actually unaware at the time of David's anointment that his successor was David. He was also unaware of when his reign would end.

Saul only knew that his kingdom had been given to a man after the Lord's heart.

In contrast to Saul, David trusted in the Lord and had a heart for God.

"Now I know that the LORD saves his anointed; he will answer him from his holy heaven with the saving might of his right hand.

Some trust in chariots and some in horses, but we trust in the name of the LORD our God.
They collapse and fall, but we rise and stand upright.

O LORD, save the king!
May he answer us when we call."
(Psalm 20: 6-9, A Psalm of David)

Saul did however know that he had been usurped as King.
Immediately after David had been anointed, the Holy Spirit was removed from Saul, and a harmful spirit from the Lord began to torment him.

"Now the Spirit of the LORD departed from Saul,
and a harmful spirit from the LORD tormented him."
(1 Samuel 16:14)

♦♦♦♦♦♦♦♦♦♦

After David's anointment, Saul was like a king-without-a-crown, in that his rule and spirit were weakened. Without the spirit of the Lord within him, Saul was without purpose, living in fear and consumed with angst and fear *(1 Samuel 16:14).*

♦♦♦♦♦♦♦♦♦♦

P*earl: The Lord working undercover is a common theme throughout the Bible. In these circumstances, God instruments Saul's fear as an opportunity for David to enter into Saul's service.*

♦♦♦♦♦♦♦♦♦♦

Saul is still serving as the king, but becomes melancholy and moody. Saul knows that he has been rejected by the Lord as the leader of Israel and most likely heard rumors of his replacement.

Saul continued to live in his palace in Gibeah, just north of Jerusalem. Noticing Saul's severe depression and moodiness, his servants said to him,

"Behold now, a harmful spirit from god is tormenting you.
Let our lord now command your servants who ae before you to seek out a man who is skillful in playing the lyre, and when the harmful spirit from God is upon you, he will play it, and you will be well."
(1 Samuel 16:16)

Saul agreed, and told his servants to provide him with such a man.

One young servant, knowing David to be a skillful musician, suggested to Saul that David should play beautiful music and sing to help his depression.

♦♦♦♦♦♦♦♦♦♦

P*earl: Of interest is that the servants identified that Saul had a harmful spirit that was tormenting him. What we don't know is if the servant who suggested that David was specifically the one who should be chosen to be of service to Saul knew that David had been anointed by the Lord as the next King. The servant also expounded on David's other qualities, specifically that that the Lord was with David.*

"Behold, I have seen a son of Jesse the Bethlehemite, who is skillful in playing, a man of valor, a man of war, prudent in speech, and a man of good presence, and the LORD is with him."

49

Saul himself told his messengers to travel to Bethlehem to find Jesse and say,

"Send me David your son, who is with the sheep."
(1 Samuel 16:19)

After receiving the message from Saul, Jesse was honored and sent his son David to Saul in Gibeah.

Saul soon became very fond of David, as his music was very soothing and helped ease his anxiety.

Saul even appointed David as his armor-bearer, and asked Jesse to let David remain in his service.

Pearl: *An armor-bearer in the day served as a personal attendant to the king, and also had a close personal relationship with their master.*

But as we shall see, Saul's favor towards David will soon morph into extreme jealousy and anger.

✦✦✦✦✦✦✦✦✦✦✦

For now, David entered Saul's service at the palace and found favor in his sight.

"Whenever David played his music of worship to the Lord in Saul's presence, the harmful spirit departed from Saul."
(1 Samuel 16:23, 2 Chronicles 5:13-14)

Whenever David was summoned to Saul's palace he composed and sang music of worship that was intended to calm Saul. David's music was not only beautiful, but being music of worship to the Lord, caused the harmful spirit to flee from Saul.

Pearl: Because of his many songs of praise to the Lord that David wrote, he became known as the "sweet psalmist of Israel" (2 Samuel 23:1).

A Psalm of David that he may have played for Saul is **Psalm 8,** a hymn of praise. **Psalm 8** speaks of the Almighty Creator who enabled His children a privileged place in His creation

~Excerpts from Psalm 8~
"O LORD, our Lord, how majestic is your name in all the earth! You have set your glory above the heavens.
Out of the mouth of babies and infants, you have established strength because of your foes, to still the enemy and the avenger."
(Psalm 8:1-2)

"When I look at your heavens, the work of your fingers, the moon and the stars, which you have set in place, what is man that you are mindful of him, and the son of man that you care for him?"
(Psalm 8:3-4)

Interlude: Mysteries Surrounding David

~The story of David will continue, but for now there are some mysteries surrounding David that the reader may be contemplating. ~

- Before heading further into the life story of David in *1 & 2 Samuel,* you may wonder and question where in the story is David's mom?

As this is a book that looks deep into the life story and character of David as an ancestor of Jesus, one may wonder why there is no mention in the Bible of David's mother. There is only mention of David's father, Jesse.

Throughout the Bible, although it is arguably primarily patriarchal in nature, there has been mention of many influential matriarchal figures, either as wives or mothers.

For example, the book of *1 Samuel* begins with the story about Samuel's mother Hannah, and her prayer asking the Lord for a child in her barrenness.

- Secondly, a question may arise as to why David had been excluded from such an important event as the festivities with Samuel, when all of his brothers attended along with his father Jesse *(1 Samuel 16).*

  - There is no explanation of why this partiality existed on Jesse's behalf, which serves to pique the reader's curiosity as to why David is treated differently by his father as compared to all of his brothers.

- Third, why did Samuel need to write the scroll of Ruth to justify David's lineage after he had been anointed by God to be King? Why was David's lineage ever in question?
  - The *Talmud (B.B. 14b)* holds that the prophet Samuel is the author of the Book of Ruth. This is a commonly-held-thought in Rabbinic Judaism, as is stated in the Talmud and is reiterated by well-known Jewish

51

scholars, such in the Introduction of the *Judaica Books of The Hagiographa, the Book of Ruth.*

Of importance and significance is the question as to why was explaining David's lineage so important? Was David's true ancestry in question?

Delving a little deeper into the Midrash containing commentaries from Rabbis on the Hebrew Bible, the author found some interesting discussion concerning these questions that were raised above.

To begin with, much of the controversy seems to originate from David's great-grandmother Ruth, especially concerning her Moabite heritage.

And of course, it always also seems to circle-back to the sins of mankind. In this case, it is centered on Jesse and his divorce of his wife and his attraction to her maidservant.

And now, for the mystery of David's hidden story.

~Pearls from the Midrash: "David's Hidden Story"
Pre-reading: Psalm 40

O nce Saul figured out that it was David that was going to replace him, the proverbial 'wheels' started turning in Saul's head. Fearful of failure and defeat, Saul began to instrument a plan to keep David from succeeding him.

It is not clear when exactly Saul figured out that David was his successor, but the word must have spread soon after the happenings at the festival with Samuel in Bethlehem.

The town of Bethlehem was small, and it is a good possibility that the majority of the townspeople, along with the elders, were present for the festivities.

Undoubtedly, the anointment of young David with a horn full of bubbling oil that miraculously turned into a crown must have raised a few eyebrows.

Word would eventually travel through the land about David's anointment, and questions would be raised to as whether this lowly shepherd-boy was fit to be King of Israel.

Saul's council, their jobs also on the line if Saul were to be replaced as king, soon stepped-in to prevent Saul's dismissal.

After all, Saul was rejected by God, and soon to be ousted from his very powerful and influential job as King of Israel. Along with Saul, his tribunal would also be out of a job.

Undoubtedly, Saul and his loyal band of followers began to search for some 'dirt' on David in order to keep him from ascending to the throne.

Anything and everything was fair game for Saul and his tribunal of influential men, even if it wasn't the truth.

Saul and his council of men decided to first start with questioning David's ancestry.

Why did David's ancestry matter?

In ancient times, proof of heritage was very important for a king-to-be. Most of the time the kingship was handed down from father to the eldest son. Saul knew that the Law of Moses stating this in Deuteronomy had to be enforced.

How could Saul prove that David was not justified because of his ancestry to become king?

Saul jumped on the fact that David's heritage was tainted by Moabite ancestry.

Knowing that David's great-grandmother was a Moabitess before converting to Judaism, brought up extreme controversy concerning David's 'worthiness' to take the throne as King of Israel.

David's Moabite heritage apparently created quite a stir among Saul and his tribunal, to the point that they tried to keep David from taking the throne to which he had been anointed by the Lord.

The Talmud **(Yev. 76b, 77a)** relates that Doeg the Edomite, who was head of Saul's tribunal, contested David's eligibility for the throne. The tribunal even questioned David's eligibility to 'enter the assembly of God,' meaning that David was technically not permitted to marry Jewish women since he was of Moabite extraction (**Deuteronomy 22:4).**

The controversy surrounding Moabite lineage also relates to David's father, Jesse, as he was the grandson of Ruth, the Moabite. Jesse's wife was of pure Jewish extraction, so her ancestry was never questioned.

Eventually we will circle-back to David's mother and speculation about David's lineage from the line of Judah through Jesse, as we uncover some interesting information.

Trying to make sense of the controversy surrounding David, we will delve deep into ancient literature written by Jewish Rabbis in the Talmud and the Midrash.

Some background taken from the ancient Rabbi's commentaries provides context concerning David's heritage and his 'unusual' treatment by his brothers.

The following summary concerning the controversy surrounding David is provided:

✦ In the Midrash, scholars such as Shoresh Yishai, writes that after David was anointed that Samuel wrote the Book (Scroll) of Ruth to trace David's lineage as the son of Jesse as proof of his heritage.

   o **The Scroll of Ruth was written to legitimatize David to enter the assembly of the Lord and to occupy the throne.**

   o In **Psalm 40** David actually tells of how the Scroll (Book) of Ruth was prescribed for him.

> **"Then I said, Behold, I have come;**
> **In the scroll of the book it is written of me;**
> **I delight to do your will, O my God;**
> **Your law is written my heart."**
>
> **(Psalm 40:7-8, A Psalm of David)**

✦ The Rabbis discuss at length in the Midrash that Samuel wrote the Book of Ruth after David was anointed King of Israel to legitimatize David to enter the assembly of God and to occupy the throne of Israel.

✦ The Talmud **(Yev. 76 b, 77 a)** discusses that Doeg the Edomite, who was the head of Saul's tribunal, contested David's eligibility for the throne.

✦ Doeg the Edomite also contested David's eligibility to enter the assembly of God, meaning that he should not be permitted to marry Jewish women due to his Moabite heritage **(Deuteronomy 22:4).**

✦ The Talmud relates that this question was previously asked and was answered years before when it came up about Ruth, the Moabitess, who married Boaz of the tribe of Judah. The Torah scholars replied after much deliberation that the Torah clearly indicated that a Moabite (male of Moab origin), **but not a Moabitess** (female of Moab origin) was prevented entry into the assembly of God.

   o This ruling was reflected in the Jewish Halachah, and clearly states that a Moabite, but not a Moabitess, is forbidden to enter the assembly of God.

✦ Samuel therefore composed the Book of Ruth to trace the root of Jesse, which will stand as a banner to the nations to tell everyone that David is descended from the family of Ram and of Boaz of the tribe of Judah.

   o The decision of Boaz to marry Ruth (a Moabitess) would no longer be contested and the Torah and the Halachah (Jewish religious laws from the oral Torah) would support this.

✦ Ultimately, this cleared David's heritage, as he was descended from a Moabitess (not a Moabite), who converted fully to Judaism prior to her marrying a Jewish man.

To readers of today, this all sounds very confusing and it is helpful to go back to what the Law of Moses said in Deuteronomy.

Under the laws set forth in Deuteronomy, Moabites were banned from the assembly of God and worship of the Lord forever.

Deuteronomy 23:2-4
"No one born of a forbidden union may enter the assembly of the LORD. Even to the tenth generation, none of his descendants may enter the assembly of the LORD. No Ammonite or Moabite may enter the assembly of the LORD. Even to the tenth generation, none of them may enter the assembly of the LORD forever because they did not meet you with bread and with water when you came out of Egypt and because they hired against you Balaam the son of Beor from Pethor of Mesopotamia to curse you."

The Israelites were also instructed to not seek their peace or their prosperity all of your days forever **(Deuteronomy 23:6)**.

At the time of Judges, the **Halachah** (the collective body of Jewish laws derived from the written and oral Torah) was unclear about permitting a <u>Moabite woman</u> to marry an Israelite man. If Moabites were banned from the assembly of God forever, it certainly was not generally accepted, even if it was within the realm of the law.

However, if the Moabite woman embraced Judaism **prior** to her marriage according to halachic requirements (which stated that it had to occur in the presence of a beth-din, a Rabbinic tribunal) and were sincere converts, their conversion would be accepted, and she would be allowed to enter the assembly of God

What does this have to do with David?

As mentioned, David is the great-grandson of Ruth the Moabite. Ruth had been married to Mahlon, son of Elimelech and Naomi from the tribe of Judah. Upon Mahlon's death, Ruth eventually remarried Boaz, also from the tribe of Judah, and they had a son named Obed. Obed fathered Jesse, and Jesse fathered David.

Assuming simple, Mendelian genetics apply, and that Ruth was 100% Moabite, Obed would have been half Moabite, Jesse one-quarter Moabite, and David would therefore be one-eighth (12.5%) Moabite.

Was marrying a Moabite legal according to the Torah in ancient Judaism?

Many ancient Jewish Rabbi commentators state that Naomi and Elimelech's sons (Mahlon and Chilion) married women who were actually forbidden to them by the Torah. The question then arises if the two women (Ruth and Orpah) embraced and converted to Judaism prior to their marriage to Mahlon and Chilion?

Some Jewish rabbis commented that they doubt if conversion prior to marriage occurred. They point out that even if they were proselytes, they may have converted to Judaism out of fear of their husbands, or for insincere reasons for the purpose of marriage.

It's complicated; to say the least, and many scholarly exegetes have debated over divergent theories relating to conversion of a gentile woman to Judaism, and the timing of her conversion if she is marrying a Jewish man.

The Talmud has laws of conversion to Judaism and there was considerable debate over the timing and legality of Ruth's conversion to Judaism.

The Torah does not exactly forbid a Moabite to convert, only to enter the Assembly of God.

In the Talmud however, this is understood to mean that a Moabite convert may not marry a pedigreed Jew (Yevamot 77b), but may marry another convert.

Interestingly, the Talmud relates the question of does the Halachah apply to a Moabi**tess (female from Moab)** as well as to a Moabite (male from Moab)?

Samuel the prophet addressed this issue, and ancient scholars agreed that the Torah was precise in writing the word **Moabite**, meaning that Moabite males (referred to as a Moabite) are forbidden to marry a Jew, but Moabite females (referred to as a Moabitess) are allowed.

Samuel apparently later composed the Book of Ruth to substantiate this Halachah so it would no longer be disputed.

This legality was of utmost importance as the question was not if Ruth converted, but how she could have legally married Boaz.

Of significance is without a legal marriage of Ruth to Boaz there would be profound implications as far as their descendants, especially impacting David's legality of becoming King of Israel.

The Book of Ruth is a book that substantiated the Halachah of the Jewish people, and legitimized Ruth's legacy of her royal ancestry in the Davidic dynasty.

Nonetheless, this legal decision was also included in the canon of the Talmud due to the profound implications it has on legitimizing the Davidic dynasty, from which the Messiah will be descended.

◆◆◆◆◆◆◆◆◆◆◆

Pearl: The Book of Ruth essentially put the rumor that David could not legitimately be chosen as king to rest, once-and-for-all!

◆◆◆◆◆◆◆◆◆◆◆

Hidden Midrashic Pearl: *Of interest is that the issue of the 'Moabite heritage' didn't start with David being anointed as the new King of Israel. It actually started before David was ever born. It also stems from humanity's sinful* nature. How is that?

✦ Jesse had his doubts concerning the Halachah years before, relating to the stigma of his Moabite extraction.

✦ An ancient Midrash commentary states that Jesse separated from his wife Nitzevet, after she gave birth to, and raised all of Jesse's sons prior to David.

✦ After Nitzevet birthed seven sons, Jesse 'suddenly' felt that he was 'forbidden' to be married to a Jewess, as he had a grandmother who was a Moabite.

✦ The Rabbi's discussed in the Midrash that most likely Jesse's own feelings of his Moabite heritage that suddenly surfaced after all of these years actually involved 'another woman' (Yalkut Machiri).

  o The Rabbi's in the Midrash comment that Jesse had taken notice of his wife's attractive servant. He intended on taking her as his wife and desired to have children with her.
  o According to Jesse's line of thought, these children would not carry the stigma of Moabite extraction as the servant was a convert to Judaism, but was not a Jewess. It was therefore perfectly legal for Jesse to marry the servant within the Talmud as Jesse, being of Moabite extraction but a Jewish convert, could legally marry another Jewish convert who was not of Jewish descent.
  o According to Jesse, because of his Moabite descent through Ruth, he was illegally married to Nitzevet, who was of Jewish lineage.

✦ In the meantime, Nitzevet was very upset and did not want the separation from Jesse. She desired to have more children with Jesse, as she was a devout Jewish wife.

✦ Jesse's wife's attractive servant actually cared very much for Nitzevet and told her of Jesse's plan to marry her.

  o The servant felt bad for Nitzevet and confided in her, telling her when the wedding was going to happen.

✦ Nitzevet and her handmaid then devised a plan to deceive Jesse.

  o On the wedding night of Jesse and the handmaid, the handmaid switched places with Nitzevet after the candles were extinguished for the evening.
  o Jesse, unaware of the switch, had sexual relations with Nitzevet instead of the servant whom he thought he had taken as his wife that night. (Apparently Jesse was drunk, or very tired, as he did not notice that the two women had switched places in the night).

- Nitzevet conceived David on that very occasion.

- When it became known that Nitzevet was pregnant, Jesse and his sons suspected her of having an affair and that the baby she carried was fathered by some other man besides Jesse.

- Nine months later when David was born, Jesse's sons wanted to stone their mother and the child to death for her crime.

- Jesse persuaded them not to kill them, but to keep David as their 'slave' and tend to their flocks.

  - Of interest is that the job of shepherd was considered to be very lowly by the Jewish people, and it is even stated that shepherds are not considered reputable in the Talmud.

- David continued to live with Jesse and his other sons, but served as a slave for the family as he was not considered worthy due to his speculative lineage of being an illegitimate son not fathered by Jesse.

- Importantly, David served as a shepherd for Jesse's sheep.

  - This was considered to be a sign that David would be the shepherd of the Jewish people.

- Commentaries point out that many great leaders were tested by the Almighty in the capacity of shepherds, such as David, Amos, Moses and Jacob.

- Throughout his childhood years, David grew up as a slave to his brothers who treated him with disdain and contempt.

- Years later, when David was anointed as king David's mother, Nitzevet wept with joy.

  - She had kept her secret that David was Jesse's son as to not disgrace Jesse. She absorbed the humility and shame of her pregnancy with David out of respect for Jesse.

- Jesse was a distinguished leader in Bethlehem and served as head of the Sanhedrin (supreme court of Torah law).

- David wrote **Psalm 69** to describe his feelings of his untold humiliation and disgrace during his youth. It describes how he was shunned by his brothers and by the townspeople.

◆◆◆◆◆◆◆◆◆◆◆

After many years of silence when David was anointed as the future King of Israel, Nitzevet finally knew that David's humiliation would come to an end.

It was obvious now that David was from the lineage of Judah, as he was anointed the king of Israel, and was indeed Jesse's son.

*David addressed his being anointed as King when he wrote **Psalm 118:22-23.***

The Psalm is actually part of the thanksgiving Psalms of the Egyptian Hallel (Hebrew: Praise) sung by the Jewish people on Passover in celebration of their freedom from exile in Egypt.

Psalms 118:22-24
"The stone that the builders rejected has become the cornerstone.
This is the LORD's doing;
it is marvelous in our eyes.
This is the day that the Lord has made;
let us rejoice and be glad in it. "

Summary Pearl:

As far as the idea that the Jewish people did not respect Ruth, being Moabite, this is definitely not the case. It is apparent after reading the commentaries of Rabbis in the Midrash that the Jewish people hold Ruth in the highest regard.

Ancient rabbinical scholars do not dispute David's lineage from Ruth and Boaz through Jesse.

We, as Christians, also acknowledge David's lineage through Jesse as it is stated in the Gospels of Matthew, Luke, and the Book of Ruth.

Importantly, we read in the Book of Isaiah that it is prophesized that the Messiah would come from the line of Jesse.

Pearl: David ~ King-to-be of Israel~ Let the Trials Begin!

David had been anointed as King of Israel, but the Lord knew that he needed further direction and guidance before actually taking the throne.

David is at this time a 'King-in-Training'.

David was a very young man when anointed King of Israel by the Lord, probably only in his late teens. Now as he becomes an adult, it is time for him to learn the life-skills that will lead to him not only becoming a great king, but also the foreshadow of the Messiah.

David was meant to be a great king, one who will restore the faith of the Israelite people and their worship of the one, true God Almighty.

With the charge to make Israel a great nation under God, David had a huge responsibility to the Lord and to his people.

With the mind-set that David was to be the anointed-one in His Masterplan, God has already endowed David with many attributes of a great king.

For instance, David was not only an imaginative, skilled, creative musician but also a brave warrior. A warrior that not only could fight in battle but also well versed in the science and strategy of war. In both the Bible *(1 Samuel 16:18)* and in the Midrash, David was described as having a keen intellect, capable of good judgement and giving sound advice.

Last but certainly not least, the Lord was with David *(1 Samuel 16:18, 17:37, 18:12, 20:13, 2 Sam 5:10, 7:3,9)*.

David was a God-fearing man. Of interest is as the Rabbis of the Midrash discuss, a man with all of these talents usually pursues his own desires, but David followed the Lord's will, casting his own interests and desires aside.

God would therefore always be at David's side to help and to protect him *(1 Samuel 16:14-29)*.

Much of the 'making of David' into a great leader and his training to become king had already taken place in the years of his being a shepherd. The Lord had purposely put David into the position of being a slave to his brothers, taking on the labors that they shunned. Through these life-experiences as a young man, David learned invaluable life-skills that would be put to use in the years to come.

For instance, a very important life-skill that David mastered was the use of the sling in battle.

While shepherding, David's expertise with the sling had served him well as he had to fight off many predators over the years while tending to the sheep. The sling was a simple tool that once mastered was a deadly instrument of warfare. Unlike a sword, it was small, portable and could be armed with rocks taken from the land.

Although it was hard on him, David also learned the important life-lessons of humility. While his brothers were pursuing their own desires, David learned perseverance and patience, as he had to deal with the mundane, yet important tasks that needed to be done.

In the time following David's anointing, God further honed and groomed David to be king. The years to come will at times be painful for David, as he continuously must learn to overcome the obstacles that God will place in his life.

God, the ultimate Gardener, set out in His "pruning" of David to become a great king and importantly, the foreshadow of the Messiah.

It seemed as though the Lord would often be coming after David with the sharpest of gardening shears, pruning and trimming away the branches that were merely dead wood and not needed.

But it was all part of His Master plan.

Immediately after God anointed David as the 'King-to-be' of Israel, life just seemed to go on as usual. In this usualness-of-life mentality, David undoubtedly became discouraged, thinking that he was not worthy to be king.

Feeling not worthy would have been expected, especially if David was aware of the political environment surrounding his anointment as future king. Before David could even take the throne, Saul's council attempted to find every reason for David not to become the person God designed him to be.

Perhaps Samuel spent some time with David as a mentor, encouraging and educating him by giving him knowledge of his ancestors. This seems plausible, as Samuel was a prophet and a judge during the time that David's great-grandparents, Ruth and Boaz were living in Bethlehem.

As David wondered how he, a lowly shepherd-boy could ever attain the skills needed to become a mighty warrior and king of Israel, a vivid picture comes to mind of Samuel relating the story of his great-grandmother, Ruth the Moabitess.

During the long hours David target-practiced with his sling and rocks, it is likely that Samuel told him of Ruth's love of the Lord and her perseverance to overcome obstacles placed in her life.

The parallels between Ruth and David are many, as both had to persevere and overcome many obstacles in their lives. It is striking to learn how Ruth and David were *similar in their faithfulness to the Lord, and persisted through unwanted circumstances in order to become who God had designed them to be.*

Both Ruth and David were considered unworthy but the Lord used their perceived brokenness in society's eyes to become elite figures that were paramount in the ancestry of the Messiah, Jesus Christ.

✦✦✦✦✦✦✦✦✦✦✦

Scene 4: The Proposed 'Impeachment' of David

Setting: *A meeting of Saul's Royal Council, the Tribunal, in the King's Palace in Gibeah just north of Jerusalem*

Time Frame: *Shortly after David's Anointment as the King of Israel*

Reference: *The Talmud **(Yev. 76 b, 77 a)** including commentaries by Rashi and others in the Judaica Books of the Prophets, the Books of Samuel 1 & 2.*

The room was filled with loud, pointedly angry conversation. Heated debates were ongoing as the group of men argued their sides about a very controversial topic.

With an authoritative command, Doeg the Edomite attempted to bring the group of men making up Saul's Royal Council known as his Tribunal, to order. Anxious to get the meeting on-track, Doeg was on a mission to fulfill his own self-serving agenda.

The members of Saul's Royal council continued to talk heatedly among themselves, but Doeg, who served as head of the Tribunal, finally quieted them with the resounding noise of his gavel, forcefully pounding it down upon the wooden table.

The conglomerate of men making up the king's Tribunal had agreed to hold the meeting emergently early in the morning, as the previous day had unfolded quite unexpectantly.

There was a very important reason the council had been brought together, and the air was filled with apprehension, and fueled with anger.

The council's paramount motive for the emergency meeting was for one intention. The council needed to quickly and succinctly find a legal reason to impeach the newly anointed future King of Israel.

✦✦✦✦✦✦✦✦✦✦✦

Pearl: *Why did the members of the council feel threatened by David, the newly anointed king-to-be?*

News had spread quickly about the shepherd-boy who had been anointed as the future king of Israel just hours before, in the small town of Bethlehem. This news took the Tribunal completely by surprise. To their dismay, the esteemed Tribunal had not even been consulted concerning the newly anointed king.

❖❖❖❖❖❖❖❖❖❖❖

None of the Tribunal members had even the slightest suspicion that David, the youngest son of Jesse, would be anointed as the future King. Feeling threatened, the Tribunal members were fully aware that soon the power and prestige they had enjoyed for the time during Saul's reign would soon come to an end.

Saul, the reigning King of Israel looked on in anticipation, waiting for this nightmare to end.

Saul knew that he had been disobedient to the Lord several times during the many years of his reign as king, but was shocked that he would soon be cast aside. How could he exist as a common man when he had once held the power and prestige of a king?

Saul's only hope for continuing on as king was in these men who served on his tribunal.

Saul knew that the powerful men of his Tribunal could restore and uphold his position as king, even though it was obvious that he had been rejected and removed by the Lord Himself.

After the meeting was called to order, Saul quietly exited the room, having confidence that Doeg the Edomite would make sure that the council would unanimously vote to impeach the new king-to-be.

Much deliberation ensued as the meeting progressed. Heated words were exchanged among the members of the royal council as emotions boiled to the surface.

The angry conversation centered on David, the young shepherd boy. The council members kept asking each other, "why had young David been anointed to be the future-king of Israel?"

This just can't be possible, the council members mused, as this definitely was not their idea.

Nor was it in their best interest. Saul's tribunal needed to impeach David before things escalated beyond their control.

The group of Tribunal members intentionally set out to find a reason to keep David from ascending to the throne. The Tribunal of men knew they had to find a legal reason to make David ineligible to be the new king-to-be.

Soon the discussion turned to David's ancestry. The men brought up the old news that David had a tainted lineage – he was of Moabite descent!

Talk turned to David's great-grandmother Ruth the Moabitess. The Tribunal re-visited the old lies of those who claimed Ruth did not convert to Judaism prior to her marriage to Boaz of Bethlehem, the judge and descendant of Jacob and his son, Judah.

Doeg, as head of the council, reiterated that Ruth, being a Moabite had no right to legally enter into the assembly of God, as there was no evidence that she had converted to Judaism prior to her marriage.

Lying about Ruth's faithfulness to the Lord, Doeg falsely accused Ruth of converting to Judaism to appease her future husband. He pointed out that this meant that Ruth could not legally marry a Jewish man, and have children and future descendants with rights to Jewish privileges.

The council then moved to vote that Ruth the Moabitess' marriage to Boaz was not legal and therefore her son, Obed was essentially illegitimate. As Obed was the father of Jesse, David's father, their decision would delegitimize David's lineage and his rights to the kingship of Israel.

Ruth's descendants, produced as a result of her union with Boaz, would not be considered to be Jews, and therefore not considered to be worthy of any claim to Israeli royalty. Nor would they even have claimed to enter the assembly of God.

After the discussion was brought forth about David's tainted Moabite heritage, the lies became even worse.

Saul's council continued on in their discussion to slander David's mother, saying she had an illegal affair outside of marriage with another man. Drawing erroneous conclusions that David was actually not fathered by Jesse, the council discussed that David was definitely unfit for being King of Israel, as he was not even a son of Jesse who was of the lineage of Judah.

The lies continued to be fabricated as the men of Saul's royal council brought the motion forth that David was not worthy, due to his tainted and even speculative heritage, to ascend to the throne as the King of Israel.

The claims against David's ancestry were not true, but the council moved forward to impeach David in a matter of minutes, even before he could celebrate his newly anointed position as King of Israel.

✦✦✦✦✦✦✦✦✦✦✦

Pearl: *David's mother had never come forth with the truth about the night of Jesse's wedding to her handmaid. She never revealed to anyone about the scheme she and her handmaiden devised to prevent Jesse from fathering children with anyone but her. David's lineage from Jesse had always been questioned, but upon his anointment to be King by God Himself, David's mother thought that the rumors had been put to rest.*

Even after Jesse married his wife's handmaid, and David's mother had given birth to Jesse's youngest son David, David's mother had protected the reputation of his father and not disclosed the truth that David was Jesse's son. After all, Jesse was a prominent figure in the Sanhedrin, and who was she to dispute his reputation.

Only David and his mother knew that he was indeed Jesse's son, and therefore descended of the lineage of Judah. David's mother often laughed at how people were so unobservant to not notice the resemblance of David to his true father, Jesse. Both men had the titian-colored hair, green eyes and ruddy complexion that had been passed on through Ruth, the Moabitess.

Of course, one other knew the truth about David – the Lord Almighty.

All in the Lord's plan!

♦♦♦♦♦♦♦♦♦♦♦

With the meeting drawing to a close, the council members agreed among themselves to make a ruling against David.

With David's lineage proving him to be of Moabite descent through Ruth the Moabitess, and his parentage furthermore in-question, the ruling was made to impeach David before he ever even set one foot near the throne.

The motion was voted on first by an oral vote, which passed unanimously. Next it needed to pass a written vote by all present to be considered legal.

It seemed as though David was defeated before his reign as king ever even had a chance.

But God had other plans for David. Sinful humans, with their self-serving agendas, would not thwart the Lord's Divine plans.

Suddenly the door swung open!

As a result of Divine-interference, Samuel suddenly appeared in the doorway with a scroll rolled up neatly in his hand.

Churning up the drama, Samuel strode deliberately towards the council waving the written document wildly in the air.

"Enough", Samuel proclaimed! "Read the truth"!

Presenting the scroll of the Book of Ruth, Samuel slammed it down on the table for the council to read. Spreading the pages clearly before them on the table, Samuel presented the evidence of truth behind David's ancestry.

Documenting Jewish Halachah describing Ruth the Moabitess' legal marriage to Boaz and her acceptance into the assembly of God, the question of David's heritage being tainted was finally cleared.

Samuel also clearly stated David's genealogy in the final words of the Book of Ruth, legitimizing that David was a son of Jesse.

Samuel stood before the council, reading the final sentences of the scroll of Ruth being the detailed genealogy of David,

"Now these are the generations of Perez: Perez fathered Hezron, Hezron fathered Ram, Ram fathered Amminadab, Amminadab fathered Nahshon, Nahshon fathered Salmon, Salmon fathered Boaz, Boaz fathered Obed, Obed fathered Jesse, and Jesse fathered David."
(Ruth 4:18-22)

The men knew not to doubt Samuel as he was a prominent figure in Israel - Samuel had served as a Judge for many years, and was a prophet of the Lord.

Finally, the rumors saying that David was not eligible to rule as the anointed King of Israel were set to rest with the truth in the Book of Ruth.

Samuel had set the truth free, and David would therefore rightfully ascend to the throne as King of Israel.

♦♦♦♦♦♦♦♦♦♦♦

*P**earl:** This genealogy is also documented in **1 Chronicles 2:5-15**. Of interest is that David has three foreign women in his ancestry, being Tamar, Rahab and Ruth which is documented in **Matthew 1:3, 5** and **Ruth 4:12, 21**.*

*Of future significance is that the Messiah, the Lion of the tribe of Judah, is the root of Jesse and the root and descendant of David **(Genesis 49:9, Isaiah 11:10, Romans 15:12, Revelation 5:5** and **22:16).***

♦♦♦♦♦♦♦♦♦♦♦

David, hearing of the drama from Samuel, composed a prayer of thanksgiving to the Lord as he attended to his duties as shepherd.

David composed **Psalm 20** to God in thanksgiving and praise.

Psalm 20: 6-9

"Now I know that the LORD saves his anointed; he will answer him from his holy heaven with the saving might of his right hand.

Some trust in chariots and some in horses; but we trust in the name of the LORD our God.
They collapse and fall, but we rise and stand upright.

O LORD, save the king!
May he answer us when we call."

David also composed **Psalm 40** in reference to the Book of Ruth being written on his behalf to trace his lineage, legitimatizing him to enter the assembly of the Lord and to occupy the throne as King of Israel.

Psalm 40:7-8

"Then I said, Behold, I have come; in the scroll of the book it is written of me:

I delight to do your will, O my God;

Your will is written my heart."

As we will see in the unfolding of David's story, since Saul and his council were unsuccessful in impeaching David from legally ascending to the throne, they would then proceed to take extreme measures.

Saul will become obsessed at keeping David from taking the throne.

As a result of his obsession, Saul would compromise the well-being and safety of the people and the nation of Israel. Over the next several years, Israel will become a nation and people without an effective leader and protector.

Before taking the throne, David will continue to gain the respect and approval of the people of Israel.

Importantly, David will continue to turn to God for direction and focus on bringing the Lord back into the heart of the nation of Israel, and the Jewish people.

In contradistinction, Saul will continue to plummet in a downward cycle of evil, neglecting his duties as standing-king, and focusing all of his energy to keep David from ascending to the throne.

Saul will become obsessed with one agenda.

That being to kill David.

Act 2: The Champion

1 Samuel 17

Playlist: "I Raise a Hallelujah" by Bethel Music, "Nobody" by Casting Crowns and Matthew West, "Confidence" by Sanctus Real, "Word of God" by Jeremy Camp

Pre-Reading: Psalm 9, 21, 144

<u>*Introduction and Background:*</u>

Psalm 144: (1-2, 9-10) My Rock and My Fortress
~A Psalm of David~

"Blessed be the Lord, my rock, who trains my hands for war and my fingers for battle, he is my steadfast love and my fortress, my stronghold and my deliverer, my shield and he in whom I take refuge, who subdues peoples under me.

I will sing a new song to you O God; upon a ten-stringed harp I will play to you, who gives victory to kings, who rescues David his servant from the cruel sword."

Shortly after David's anointment by God he was summoned to serve in Saul's court, to do of all things, play music.

Subject to periods of mood changes ranging from uncontrollable anger to melancholy and severe depression, Saul was in search of anything that could help since the Holy Spirit had departed from him.

Since David had been endowed with extraordinary talents of playing and composing worship music to the Lord, David was commissioned to help Saul, as the music David played in Saul's presence seemed to ease his severe mood swings.

Members of Saul's court were relieved to have David around to play his music, as king Saul would settle down from his awful tantrums.

As a result of the calming of Saul's anger, David's talent of calming Saul led to David becoming very liked among Saul's servants. With an uncanny ability to lift everyone's spirits, even Saul's, David quickly became the favored-one among Saul's court.

Even though David was anointed King of Israel, Saul was still acting as the legal-reigning king. With great humility, David continued to accept this and worked honorably around Saul's court.

After Saul's Tribunal had been unsuccessful in their attempt to impeach David from his anointed position of king-to-be, Saul reluctantly performed as a 'lame-duck', not knowing when David was to formally take the position as king. Saul seemed at this point to ignore the fact that the Lord had dismissed him and living life as usual, continued ruling from the palace. Suffering from severe depression, as the Lord was no longer with him in his quest to rule Israel, Saul became more and more pre-occupied and self-serving.

Even considering how awkward of a situation this was for David to serve Saul in his court, David always treated Saul with utmost respect. David remained humble and showed humility toward his superiors, even though he was the anointed-one who was destined to eventually serve as King of Israel.

David knew he was receiving continuous instruction and guidance by the Lord, and the time would be revealed to him when he was to step-up to be the rightful king.

At this point in his life David did not live in Saul's palace permanently. David's home continued to be in Bethlehem, which was 10 miles away from the palace, and easily traveled in less than a day. Maintaining his duties of tending to his father's sheep, David continued to serve as a shepherd out of love for his flock and respect for his father.

In the context of the day, the reigning king of Israel traditionally went to battle to fight along with his troops. Not being the exception to this tradition, Saul always accompanied his army of men into battle.

The time came when the Philistines were threatening Israelite territory, so Saul had gathered his army and departed from the palace to fight to retain their land.

David's three eldest brothers had previously joined the Israelite army and therefore followed Saul into battle. David, not being a member of Saul's army, returned home to Bethlehem to serve in his shepherding duties.

The Israelite army was currently stationed in the Valley of Elah, which was close to Bethlehem running westward from the hill country of Judah toward Gath. The Israelites were defending their land in Judah as the Philistine army was planning a takeover.

Besides shepherding, Jesse had assigned other duties to David while he was home. One of these duties was to take food to the Valley of Elah for his brothers while they served in Saul's army.

One day Jesse asked David to take roasted grain, bread and cheese to his brothers and the commander of their army unit while they were encamped in the Valley of Elah. Jesse also wanted a report back from David on how his three eldest sons were doing while they were away. The brothers had been away for quite some time, and Jesse was concerned about their welfare.

The Philistine army had assembled their forces at Socoh, about fourteen miles west of Bethlehem, which was in the land of Judah. They had set up camp between Socoh and Azekah, which was two miles to the northwest.

Saul and his Israelite army were camped in the Valley of Elah, drawing up a battle line to meet the Philistines. The Philistines wanted to gain control of the Valley of Elah as this would give them entry into the hill country of Judah.

While the camps of each of the armies were in the valley, the strategists from each rival army daily ascended the mountains on either side of the camps to keep track of the enemy.

The Philistines occupied one hill, and the Israelites the hill opposite. There had been some scrimmages between the two armies, but no clear winner had been determined. The armies had continued to face each other for several months.

◆◆◆◆◆◆◆◆◆◆◆

P*earl: 'The Champion' and Rules of Warfare*

*According to custom and rules of warfare in the context of the day, each army would choose a man referred to as a **champion** to represent them. The chosen champion would represent the entire army.*

This champion would challenge a designated man of the opposing army, being their designated champion, to a duel. This was done in lieu of a full-blown war between the two armies.

The two champions of each opposing side would battle until one of them died or surrendered.

The champion who won would be held in high regard, as his victory would ensure that the land they were fighting over would be taken into the hands of the champion's army and people.

Of importance was also that the winning army would enslave the losing army into their ranks.

Furthermore, the people of the losing army's country would also be assimilated and would become slaves of the winning country's people.

This custom decreased the amount of killing of people and led to the growth and power of the winning army and nation as a whole, as all the people of the losing nation were assimilated into the dominant nation.

Putting this into context, the assimilation of the losing side meant that the people of the nation who lost would be enslaved and be forced to adopt the culture and the laws of the dominant society.

The women of the losing nation would be forced to marry men from the dominant society, bear children and bring their offspring up in the culture of the society.

The losing country would essentially lose more than a battle; they would end up losing their freedom as well as their entire culture, background and religious beliefs.

A lot was therefore at stake for the nations when they chose the 'champion' to represent them.

Careful consideration of the champion to represent them was undertaken, as well as intensely sizing-up the enemy. Things to consider when probing the enemy's resources were the person chosen that was the enemy's champion, his experience and what sort of armor and weapons the champion wielded.

◆◆◆◆◆◆◆◆◆◆◆

The Philistines had carefully chosen their champion to represent them in a duel against the Israelites. The Philistine champion was an acclaimed officer of the army who would emerge twice daily from his battle camp and would verbally torment the Israelites. An accomplished warrior, the champion had never been overcome in battle.

The Israelites had not gained enough courage to send forth a champion of their own as the Philistine champion was a very intimidating and foreboding opponent. Known throughout the land for his large stature and loud voice, the Philistine champion carried the title of "Goliath from Gath."

For the last forty days, Goliath had come forward every morning and evening and had taken his stand. He had offered to fight on behalf of the Philistine army against any champion that Israel would put forward for a duel.

◆◆◆◆◆◆◆◆◆◆◆

Pearl ~ *Goliath's Intimidation Factor: Goliath was an enormous man to say the least. At the height of six cubits and a span, he stood about nine-feet-nine-inches tall. Along with his overwhelming stature, Goliath also had a very intimidating personality. He also had one more thing going for him - Goliath was considered to be impenetrable due to the technologically advanced armor that he wore. This armor was the best in all of the land and like nothing the Israelites had ever seen.*

◆◆◆◆◆◆◆◆◆◆◆

With his loud voice that carried for miles and his immense, foreboding stature Goliath was well aware that he could instill fear into the heart and soul of any man that dared to even consider fighting him.

By modern day standards, Goliath would be considered to be both a bully and a beast!

Adding to Goliath's intimidation factor of his immense size, his body armor was technologically advanced. Being the best in all the land, Goliath's *techno-armor* was nothing like the Israelites had ever seen or experienced before!

❖❖❖❖❖❖❖❖❖❖

Pearl: Goliath's 'Techno-Armor'

- Goliath's body armor was made of solid copper and bronze.
  - ○ His body was covered entirely by a coat of bronze, which was reinforced by shields of iron, resembling the scales of a fish.
  - ○ The coat of armor weighed about 125 pounds *(consisted of 5000 sheckels of bronze).*
  - ○ He also had bronze armor that completely shielded his legs and shoulders.

- His spear, made of copper and iron, had a head weighing 15 pounds.

- Goliath wore a helmet constructed of bronze. In addition to providing head protection, the helmet also had a copper javelin protruding from the back that covered his neck and extended down between his shoulders.

  - ○ The helmet was specifically designed to protect his neck from the sword of his enemies.

Wearing the advanced techno-armor Goliath was not only a very large man of considerable training and experience, but was also impenetrable.

In addition, he had a shield-bearer who went before him for even further protection against the enemy!

❖❖❖❖❖❖❖❖❖❖

Every day for the last forty days Goliath had come forth from the Philistine camp to taunt the Israelites wearing his *techno-armor.*

Calling out with an earth-shaking war cry, Goliath dared the Israelites to choose an individual to come and fight him in a duel. Knowing full well that he was undefeated and was wearing the best armor that money-could-buy, Goliath had the audacity to continually taunt the Israelites for the last forty days.

73

With ravings of his own self-worth flying from his mouth, Goliath also shouted profane utterances against the God of Israel.

Trying to goad the Israelites into fighting him, Goliath continually demeaned the one, true God.

The Philistine's wanted to invade the southern area of Israel-Judah and was encroaching on Israel to take the Valley of Elah as their own. If the Philistine's were successful, they would assimilate the Israelite army and all the people of Israel. Their intent was to grow in power and land, killing most of the nation's men and taking the women and children as slaves.

A lot was at stake for the Israelites, but under the leadership of Saul they were paralyzed with fear. No progress to protect the land and their people had been made, and time was running out.

Day after day, the ranks of the Israelite army would retreat back to the safety of their camp when Goliath came forth to challenge them. The spirit of the Israelites to fight for their country and their God was dwindling day by day. Becoming discouraged and fearful, the Israelites felt as if they had run out of viable options.

Goliath came each day and shouted out to the Israelites,

"Why have you come out to draw up for battle? Am I not a Philistine and are you not servants of Saul?
Choose a man for yourselves and let him come down to me.
If he is able to fight with me and kill me, then we will be your servants.
But if I prevail against him and kill him, then you shall be our servants and serve us.
I defy the ranks of Israel this day.
Give me a man, that we may fight together !"
(1 Samuel 17:8-10)

♦♦♦♦♦♦♦♦♦♦♦

Pearl: *With his words Goliath had just accused the Israelites of being 'servants of Saul'. Goliath, being a man of a pagan culture, did not understand the true relationship the people of Israel had with God and that they were the Lord's servants, not Saul's servants.*

Goliath's words were therefore a direct insult to the Israelites, and importantly a direct insult to God.

Goliath was well aware that his words and presence elicited fear among his opposition and therefore continually day-after-day taunted the Israelites with his threats and disdainful talk of their God.

♦♦♦♦♦♦♦♦♦♦♦

The Israelites led by Saul, were terrified and refused to send out a champion to duel with Goliath. Each day Goliath appeared and made threats against Saul and his Israelite army. Each day the Israelites were stricken with great fear and retreated to camp *(1 Samuel 17:11).*

Until the day David arrived.

Scene 1: Standing Up For God

Playlist: "Nobody" by Casting Crowns

David set out for Elah at his father's request to deliver food and check on the status of his brothers. Making the short journey in a matter of hours, he carried rations that would last his brothers and their commander for several few weeks.

As he traveled, David couldn't help but wonder why the battle was taking so long. He realized a lot was at stake for the Israelites as the Philistines were a formidable opponent. But why had the Israelites not yet taken a stand against the enemy?

Upon his arrival to the Israelite camp, David immediately heard off in the distance the ominous war cry of a man shouting disdainful words of defiance to the ranks of the Israelites.

Hearing the commotion emanating from the battle line, David quickly unloaded the food he had brought at the camp base and proceeded to the battlefield to search for his brothers.

David located his brothers and the rest of the troops some distance from the battle line. Talking with them, David noticed that the men seemed very fearful and apprehensive, especially when they heard the piercing voice coming from a distance. Turning to see where the loud battle cry stemmed from, David saw Goliath approach close to the ranks of the Israelite army for the second time that day.

David looked around at the ranks of the Israelite army, and to his amazement saw all of the men withdraw from the battle line with fear. Many began to prepare to flee back to camp as Goliath came closer.

With his ominous threats and booming voice uttering disdainful comments, the huge Philistine champion lumbered up to the battle line from his camp across the way. Armed in his *techo-armor*, Goliath was not able to travel at a fast pace, nor make any quick moves. However, his intimidating nature seemed to scare the Israelites, as many of the men retreated back to their camp in fear.

As Goliath trudged forward shouting at the Israelites, the rest of the men of the Israelite army who had remained at the battle line quaked in fear. David observed as they too gathered their weapons and hastily retreated, as they had done every day for the last forty days.

As they retreated towards camp, a few of the Israelite men spoke to David telling him that this huge man had come to defy Israel. They went on to say that King Saul was desperate to have the man killed, and therefore promised great riches and his daughter's hand in marriage to the man who could accomplish the feat!

The men told David,

"Have you seen this man who has come up?
Surely he has come up to defy Israel.
And the king will enrich the man who kills him with great riches and will give him his daughter and make his father's house free in Israel."
(1 Samuel 17:25)

❖❖❖❖❖❖❖❖❖❖

Pearl: *Saul had essentially said that he would award the Israelite champion who slayed Goliath with the gift of riches, his daughter in marriage, and the promise of him and his extended family being free from taxation and all obligations to the palace.*

❖❖❖❖❖❖❖❖❖❖

David couldn't believe what was happening! Not caring about Saul's promises, David was sickened by how this Philistine was demeaning his God and his nation of Israel. Someone needed to stand up to this disgusting Philistine!

Thinking to himself, David wondered why were these men of Israel retreating from this Philistine fool?

David had no interest in the riches Saul promised, but he knew that he was the one who had to stand up to this Philistine who defied the God of Israel, Yahweh!

David posed the question to his fellow Israelites,

"What shall be done for the man who kills this Philistine and takes away the reproach from Israel?
For who is this uncircumcised Philistine, that he should defy the armies of the living God?"
(1 Samuel 17: 26)

Immediately grasping the spiritual nature of the battle, David saw Goliath's challenge as defiance toward God Himself.

With his extreme faith, David knew that this pagan Philistine-creature was now as 'good-as-dead', since he had profaned the honor of God!

❖❖❖❖❖❖❖❖❖❖

Pearl: *Why did David point out that the Philistine was 'uncircumscribed'? What was the meaning behind his statement?*

77

David had essentially asked the question, who was this <u>uncircumcised</u> Philistine who has the audacity to taunt the ranks of the living God?

Being uncircumcised indicated that Goliath was a pagan, who did not believe in and worship the one, true God of Israel.

Harkening back to the Covenant of Circumcision God made with Abraham in the Torah, David's comments implied that he knew that Goliath was not a descendant of Abraham. He therefore did not have a Covenant with the Lord, nor was he a God-fearing man. Furthermore, this idolatrous man and his descendants did not have rights to God's Promised Land, which the Lord had promised to Abraham's descendants **(Genesis 17)**.

The 'sign' of the covenant God made with Abraham and his offspring in **Genesis 17** was circumcision.

Having this sign of circumcision as a seal of the Abrahamic Covenant was two-fold. First, it indicated that as the descendants of Abraham, those who were circumcised were entitled to the Promised Land of Canaan. Secondly, and of utmost importance, it focused on the importance of the royal line of Abraham (and David) from which God's blessings will come forth in the birth of the Messiah, Jesus Christ, the one true ruler of Israel and of all humanity.

As God said to Abraham,

"I will give to you and your offspring after you the land of your sojournings, all the land of the Canaan, for an everlasting possession, and I will be their God.

This is my covenant which you shall keep, between me and you and your offspring after you: Every male among you shall be circumcised.

You shall be circumcised in the flesh of your foreskins, and it shall be a sign of the covenant between me and you."
(Genesis 17:8-11)

✦✦✦✦✦✦✦✦✦✦✦

Pearl: So just who was 'Goliath' in Midrashic tradition?

According to tradition stated in the Midrash, Goliath was one of Orpah' four sons. When Orpah, the sister of Ruth and daughter-in-law of Naomi, turned her back on Ruth and Naomi on their journey to Bethlehem, Orpah returned home to the low-moral standards and evil ways of the Moabites.

On that day, Orpah cast off her supposed-conversion to Judaism, and then proceeded to sink to abysmal depths of promiscuity, which was a hallmark of the Moabite culture.

On that very night rabbinic tradition states she became intimate with one hundred Moabites and from this episode conceived Goliath.

The Rabbis say that Orpah's son, Goliath, was spared forty days when he defied Israel in reward for the forty steps Orpah took with Ruth and Naomi, before she turned back to her idolatrous culture.

After forty days, Orpah's son Goliath would be slain by David, Ruth's great-grandson.

Ruth had persisted to go with Naomi, fully converting to Judaism and became the great-grandmother of King David and a progenitor of the Messiah.

Ruth's actions stood in stark contrast to Orpah, who gave up Judaism and returned to her Moabite people, becoming the mother of the evil Goliath who taunted the people of the living God.

According to Rabbinical tradition, Orpah has been associated with the Philistine giants who are understood to be descendants of the Nephilim, also known as the Rephaim. These giants were the pre-Israelite inhabitants of Canaan. Goliath, believed to be one of four sons of Orpah, is thought by many rabbinic scholars to have been descended from the Nephilim (Rephaim), who became known as the giants from Gath.

This concept is also mentioned in **2 Samuel 21:16, 18, 20, 22,** and **1 Chronicles 20:4-8.**

David did not fear the Nephilim giants, or their foreboding heritage that haunted the Israelites ever since they had originally attempted to conquer the Promised Land of Canaan. David was undaunted by Goliath's stature, and certainly had faith on behalf of God to successfully defend the Almighty's honor.

♦♦♦♦♦♦♦♦♦♦♦

Eliab, David's older brother, upon hearing David's willingness to stand up to Goliath and for the Lord, became very angry with David.

Perhaps he thought that David was just 'showing-off' in front of Saul and his ranks, but he then went on to falsely accuse David of having evil in his heart.

♦♦♦♦♦♦♦♦♦♦♦

Pearl: In light of the fact that Eliab was witness to God's anointment of David, his reproof seemed to be unjustified.

Eliab said to David,

"Why have you come down?
And with whom have you left those few sheep in the wilderness?

I know your presumption and the evil of your heart, for you have come down to see the battle."
(1 Samuel 17:28)

❖❖❖❖❖❖❖❖❖❖❖

David wisely chose to not engage in defensive conversation with his brother. Instead he took charge of the situation and spoke directly with Saul, offering to fight with Goliath, the Philistine.

David said to Saul in regards to Goliath,

"Let no man's heart fail because of him.
Your servant will go and fight with this Philistine"
(1 Samuel 17:32)

Saul reminded David that he was but a youth, and that the man he was offering to fight was a mighty man of war who had been doing this for many years. Besides, he was impenetrable with his technologically advanced body armor.

David countered with examples of his skills learned from fighting off lions and bears while defending his father's sheep.

"Your servant used to keep sheep for his father.
And when there came a lion, or a bear, and took a lamb from the flock, I went after him and struck him and delivered it out of his mouth.
And if he arose against me, I caught him by his beard and struck him and killed him.
Your servant has struck down both lions and bears, and this uncircumcised Philistine shall be like one of them, for he has defied the armies of the living God."
(1 Samuel 17: 33-36)

David showed more willingness to do battle for the Lord and his people than any seasoned warrior of Saul's had shown!

Full of confidence instilled by his faith in the Lord, David went head-on with the mighty warrior who took the Lord's name in vain.

While the warriors in the Israelite army cowered in fear, David stepped-up to defend the nation and people of Israel and the living God.

David went on to say,

"The Lord who delivered me from the paw of the lion and from the paw of the bear will deliver me from the hand of this Philistine."
(1 Samuel 17:37)

Saul, finally convinced by David's determination to fight, agreed and told him to go into battle against Goliath. Saul added that may the Lord be with him.

♦♦♦♦♦♦♦♦♦♦♦

Pearl: David followed in the footsteps of his ancestors: *The parallels of David's determination to fight Goliath to Ruth's determination to stay with Naomi in this last passage are vividly apparent. With Ruth's declaration of faith to go with Naomi and comply with her beliefs concerning the living God of Israel, one can see how her great-grandson, David, emulated her determination.*

Both Ruth and David overcame obstacles of resistance set forth by mankind to stay obedient to God and live according to His plan.

Parallels can also be drawn which include Rahab, David's great-great grandmother.

Rahab, like David, chose to risk her life in honor of the one true living God of Israel.

Similar to Ruth, Rahab turned her back on her pagan culture to convert to Judaism out of obedience to God.

All three, David, Ruth and Rahab, showed determination to follow the Lord and to be obedient to His will.

♦♦♦♦♦♦♦♦♦♦♦

David now must move forward with his preparation for battle against Goliath.

Although Saul clothed him with his own coat of armor, helmet and sword, David cast them off preferring to wear only the *armor of God.*

Relevant New Testament verses

Romans 13:12
"So let us cast off the works of darkness and put on the armor of light."

Paul was calling Christians to put off evil works and live in the light of Jesus Christ.

Ephesians 6:10-11, 13-18
"Put on the whole armor of God"

"Be strong in the Lord and in his mighty power.
Therefore take up the whole armor of God, that you may be able to withstand in the evil day, and having done all, to stand firm.

Stand therefore having fastened on the belt of truth, and having put on the breastplate of righteousness, and as shoes for your feet, having put on the readiness given by the gospel of peace.
In all circumstances take up the shield of faith, with which you can extinguish all the flaming darts of the evil one, and take the helmet of salvation and the sword of the Spirit, which is the word of God, praying at all times in the Spirit."

✦✦✦✦✦✦✦✦✦✦

Pearl: *In order to reveal God's Divine nature and offset the Philistine's profanation of God, David must perform a true miracle. This could only be accomplished by not taking refuge behind man-made armor and weapons, but through wearing the whole armor of God.*

✦✦✦✦✦✦✦✦✦✦

David took only his shepherd's staff and his sling and set out to gather his unlikely weapon-of-choice.

Going to the brook, David chose five smooth stones from the river's edge and tucked them into his shepherd's pouch.

Armed with only his staff, sling and five smooth stones taken from the river, David put on the whole armor of God to fight evil.

✦✦✦✦✦✦✦✦✦✦

Pearl: *Why did David choose five stones? Was this just the number of stones, which would fit into his pouch, or is God trying to get us to think through this detail, which is clearly mentioned in all of the versions of the Old Testament?*

There are several Midrashic interpretations which all agree that there is definitely significance in why David chose five stones. However, the exact reason for the number five is disputed.

The reasons mentioned by the Rabbis vary.

One idea is that David chose one stone for God, whose name Goliath had blasphemed, while the other four stones avenged the honor of the Torah and the three patriarchs of Israel. Which three patriarchs who are honored are not mentioned.

Rabbis also exegete that perhaps David took five stones for backup, 'just-in-case' he missed the first few times.

No matter why David chose 5 stones to go into battle against Goliath, of significance is it only took one to slay him!

Personally, I think the one stone was in honor of God. It only took one stone, and God was the One behind it.

◆◆◆◆◆◆◆◆◆◆

Scene 2: David Brought a Rock to a Sword-Fight
Pre-Reading: *1 Samuel 17:48-58, Psalms 9, 20, and 28*

Playlist: *"I Raise a Hallelujah" by Bethel Music, "Until the Whole World Hears" by Casting Crowns*

As David approached Goliath and his shield-bearer in preparation for battle, Goliath noticed his opponent's staff, but did not see his true weapon of the shepherd's sling.

Confident with his prowess with his weapon-of-choice, David adeptly held his sling in the grip of his hand, out of Goliath's sight.

When he should have been trembling in fear, instead David had the confidence that the Lord had instilled within him.

Although David was not fearful, Saul's entire army was watching the whole ordeal with trepidation, as they knew the outcome was surely in the Philistine's favor and that their doom was imminent.

Expecting to face off with a seasoned warrior who would be wearing armor and carrying an imposing sword and a javelin, Goliath thought this was a ludicrous attempt at war by the Israelites.

Goliath couldn't believe his eyes, Instead of a sword, a young lad was coming after him carrying a stick!

After sizing up David, who was obviously inexperienced and ill prepared for a sword-fight, Goliath thought that he would slay this young man with ease. The bully that he was, Goliath then decided to taunt David to further add to the humiliation of the Israelites.

Disdainfully Goliath said to David,

"Am I a dog, that you come at me with sticks?"
(1 Samuel 17:43)

Goliath then cursed David, saying that he would kill him and give his flesh to the birds and the beasts.

David responded to Goliath with faith in the Lord saying,

83

"You come to me with a sword and with a spear and with a javelin, but I come to you in the name of the LORD of hosts, the God of the armies of Israel whom you have defied.

This day the LORD will deliver you into my hand, and I will strike you down and cut off your head.

And I will give the dead bodies of the host of the Philistines this day to the birds of the air and to the wild beasts of the earth, that all the earth may know that there is a God in Israel, and that all this assembly may know that the LORD saves not with sword and spear.

For the battle is the LORD's and he will give you into our hand."
(1 Samuel 18:45-47)

David, courageous and full of faith in God, ran toward the battle line to meet Goliath. Digging into his shepherd's bag, he palmed one stone and slung it in his sling.

David then drew back and swung the sling in circumferential movements gaining torque with his motions. He then released the rock at the exact endpoint needed for maximum velocity and accuracy.

The rock hurled with utmost speed through the air in a miraculous trajectory, striking the giant Philistine in his forehead.

Even though Goliath was wearing his techo-helmet for the utmost protection humanly possible, God orchestrated the miracle of the stone striking his head in just the right location.

The stone sank deep into Goliath's head and the lofty giant fell on his face to the ground.

"And David put his hand in his bag and took out a stone and slung it and struck the Philistine on his forehead.
The stone sank into his forehead, and he fell on his face to the ground."
(1 Samuel 17:49)

Goliath had been stopped dead-in-his-tracks.

Scripture clearly states that Goliath fell forward after being struck in his forehead by David's rock. The Rabbis exegete that Goliath fell forward burying his mouth in the dirt, which was well deserved, as this was the mouth that had blasphemed the Lord. They also comment that Goliath fell forward on his chest, crushing the name of Dagon, his pagan god, whose name was engraved in his evil heart.

Midrashic Rabbinic opinion of the killing of Goliath was that it was indeed a true miracle.

Discussing the event, the Rabbis came up with the following in-depth commentary.

First, Goliath was wearing a helmet. The rock that embedded in his forehead had to have had just the right position through the perfect trajectory to land in the exact place on his forehead which was not protected by the helmet.

Second, Goliath fell forward after being struck, rather than falling backwards. Falling forward signified that he fell on his heart, which was evil and had worshipped the pagan god, Dagan. Goliath also buried his blasphemous mouth in the dirt.

Goliath falling forward after being struck in the head was indeed a miracle as it defied the natural laws of physics. The Rabbis pointed out that a blow to the forehead severe enough to kill a man would have sent the victim backwards, rather than falling forward towards direction of the blow.

◆◆◆◆◆◆◆◆◆◆◆

David then took Goliath's own sword from its sheath and cut off Goliath's head.

"So David prevailed over the Philistine with a sling and with a stone, and struck the Philistine and killed him.
There was no sword in the hand of David.
Then David ran and stood over the Philistine and took his sword and drew it out of its sheath and killed him and cut off his head with it."
(1 Samuel 17:50-51a)

Seeing this horrific event and knowing that their champion was dead, the Philistine army fled in terror.

The battle of the Israelites against the Philistines was over! The Israelites were victorious!

"And the men of Israel and Judah rose with a shout and pursued the Philistines as far as Gath and the gates of Ekron, so that the wounded Philistines fell on the way from Shaaraim as far as Gath and Ekron."
(1 Samuel 17:52)

David had prevailed over the Philistine champion with just a sling and a single stone.

David, the shepherd boy had defeated a nine-foot-tall giant and esteemed warrior who was armed with the sharpest sword and was wearing the best technologically advanced armor of the day.

With just his shepherd's staff, sling and a single stone, David had defeated the enemy and became the Champion of all of Israel and Judah.

♦♦♦♦♦♦♦♦♦♦♦

Pearl: *God had orchestrated this miracle for one simple reason, being that David had a heart of faith and complete trust in the Lord.*

♦♦♦♦♦♦♦♦♦♦♦

The Israelite army chased the Philistines as far as Gath then returned and plundered their camp.

David took Goliath's head to a suburb near Jerusalem for exhibition, but kept Goliath's armor and sword in his tent.

David was a Champion for the people, but more than that he was a *Champion of the Faith!*

*Perhaps at this time, David wrote **Psalms 9, 20 and 28** to honor the Lord. Below are some excerpts from these relevant Psalms written by David.*

Psalm 9:1-2; 9-10

"I will give thanks to the LORD with all my whole heart; I will recount all of your wonderful deeds. I will be glad and exult in you; I will sing praise to your name, O Most High.

"The LORD is a stronghold for the oppressed, a stronghold in times of trouble. And those who know your name put their trust in you, for you, O LORD, have not forsaken those who seek you."

Psalm 28:7
"The LORD is my strength and my shield; in him my heart trusts, and I am helped; my heart exults, and with my song I give thanks to him."

Psalm 20: (7,8,9,10,13)
"For the king trusts in the LORD, and through the steadfast love of the Most High he shall not be moved.
Your hand will find out all your enemies; your right hand will find out those who hate you. You will make them as a blazing oven when you appear.
The LORD will swallow them up in his wrath, and fire will consume them.
You will destroy their descendants from the earth, and their offspring from among the children of man.
Be exalted, O LORD, in your strength!
We will sing and praise your power."

Things with David and Saul certainly did not end well with David's victory over Goliath.

In fact, the strife between them increased. Beginning with a curiosity about David, Saul began trying to find out who David really was.

Saul's curiosity of David resurfaced concerning his family tree.

Saul asked Abner, the commander of his army,
"Abner whose son is this youth?"
(1 Samuel 17:55)

✦✦✦✦✦✦✦✦✦✦

Pearl: *David's ancestry puzzled Saul at the time, and he tried to figure out who exactly this champion of the Israelites was. Saul immediately asked Abner, the general of his army about this valiant young man. Abner did not know who David was, or where he came from, as David was not a regular soldier. David seemed to be an enigma to everyone.*

What is odd is that Saul did not remember David from playing his lyre in the palace, or at least he did not let on that he did.

✦✦✦✦✦✦✦✦✦✦

When David returned to camp, Saul asked David who his father was.
David replied as he held the head of Goliath in his hands,
"I am the son of your servant Jesse, the Bethlehemite."
(1 Samuel 17:58)

Pearl: *Saul apparently wanted to know his background, as most commentaries have said that Saul was asking because he wanted David to stay in his palace permanently.*

The Midrash commentaries have other interpretations concerning Saul's inquiry into David's lineage.

The Rabbis point out that Saul was concerned that if David were from the line of Judah and Perez that he would be qualified for the throne. Saul at this point was on-guard against David, as he felt threatened by David's skills and by his royal lineage.

Saul already knew that the Lord had disqualified him as king, but some scholars say that he had become confused about who had been anointed to take his place, or did not know exactly whom God had chosen as His choice for the next king.

The Rabbis say that Saul then again consulted his legal counsel at this point, and they re-opened the questioning concerning David's Moabite heritage.

Saul's counsel was intent on legally disqualifying David from being eligible for becoming King of Israel, even though God had anointed him.

Knowing that he was a threat to Saul's kingship, Saul's counsel took this opportunity to again place stigma upon David's ancestry.

The head of the counsel, Doeg the Edomite chose to ignore the precedent set by Boaz's marriage to the Moabitess Ruth. He reopened the case and therefore cast a shadow of doubt on David's legitimacy for the throne. It is not clear if Samuel once again stepped-in to defend David, but apparently Doeg's efforts to disqualify David as the future king failed once again.

However, Saul did not give up so easily!

The episode of David slaying Goliath added fuel-the-fire of Saul's jealousy of David, which in turn will morph into an evil monster and ultimately destroy Saul's sanity.

✦✦✦✦✦✦✦✦✦✦✦

Scene 3: Jonathan

Even though Saul's jealousy and envy of David was taking root, Saul's first-born son, Jonathan, loved David as his own soul.

Jonathan was at the battle where David slew Goliath, as he was a member of his father's army.

As soon as Saul finished talking with David, Jonathan stepped-in to befriend David.

"the soul of Jonathan was knit to the soul of David, and Jonathan loved him as his own soul."
(1 Samuel 18:1)

Jonathan respected David and made a covenant with him. He even gifted him with his own robe, tunic, sword, belt and bow.

"Then Jonathan made a covenant with David, because he loved him as his own soul. And Jonathan stripped himself of the robe that was on him and gave it to David, and his armor, and even his sword and his bow and his belt."
(1 Samuel 18:3-4)

✦✦✦✦✦✦✦✦✦✦

*P**earl**: This action by Jonathan symbolized and foreshadowed the transfer of Saul's kingship to David. It is not clear at what point Jonathan realized that David was actually God's chosen one to become king. But Jonathan embraced David's ascension to the throne, even though his father did not.*

Of interest is that Jonathan should have legally been the heir to the throne as he was Saul's firstborn son, but unlike his father he was not envious or jealous of David.

Jonathan and David's friendship flourished from that day forward and lasted forever, with each sacrificing for one another in various ways.

✦✦✦✦✦✦✦✦✦✦

Saul took David into his service at this point in time and kept him permanently in his palace. David therefore moved from his home in Bethlehem to the palace to serve Saul full-time.

At this point in time, Saul seemed to love David as a son and treated him like family.

Was this just an act to deceive David?

We will never know. For now Saul acted as if he cared deeply for David.

But this loving-friendship would not last for long.

Unfortunately, Saul secretly harbored the detrimental emotions of envy and jealousy in his heart for David.

Pre-reading Ephesians 6:10-18

Pearl: *Putting on the Armor of God (Ephesians 6: 10-18)*

Before we go further, let's discuss how David 'suited up' for the fight of his life without using physical armor. David was strong in the Lord and essentially fought a spiritual, as well as a physical battle against the Devil when he confronted the enemy, Goliath.

Relating David's battle to ours of everyday life where we are in a constant battle against the Devil, it is relevant for us to exegete the words spoken by the Apostle Paul in *Ephesians 6: 10-18.*

Deconstructing *Ephesians 6: 10-18,* we can break down the spiritual armor that Paul spoke about into six pieces that must be worn to stand against the schemes of the Devil. With the seventh resource, being prayer, we will be fully equipped.

We first must recognize that these verses actually circle back around to *Genesis 3,* where the Devil and his demons made it their ultimate mission to usurp God's place in the lives of Adam and Eve and therefore of all humanity.

Throughout the rest of the Bible, we see humanity waging a continuous warfare against the Devil. Specifically, as we have studied, the Devil tries to upset God's Master plan through attempting to create chaos among the ancestors of Jesus so that the Messiah is never born on this earth. But as God prophesized in *Genesis 3:15*, a son born to woman will crush the head of the Devil.

How does this relate to us now?

First, we always need to be aware of the Devil's existence and of his schemes.

Second, we must realize we cannot defeat the Devil on our own, but need God's protection and His weapons.

This second point is an analogy that can be drawn to David as he put on the armor of God and therefore had supernatural ability to defeat the impenetrable, evil Goliath.

Back to the seven pieces of spiritual armor that Paul spoke of in Ephesians 6.

With this complete head-to-toe armor, we will have the Seven Spiritual resources given to us through Christ to defeat the Devil

- *The belt of Truth;* God is truth, the Devil is the Deceiver. We must arm ourselves with the 'belt' of truth of God's Word. We must delve into God's Word and know what God is trying to tell us so we won't be deceived by the voice of the Devil.
  - As Jesus said, *"If you abide in my word, you are truly my disciples and you will know the truth, and the truth will set you free." (John 8:31)*
- *The Breastplate of Righteousness:* The Biblical meaning of righteousness throughout the Bible is simply pursuing what is right. We find righteousness by becoming more Christ-like, as we are all sinners. When the Holy Spirit of Christ is within us we are able to be righteous. We must therefore put on the breastplate of righteousness and seek to become more Christ-like.
- *Shoes for your feet, having put on the readiness given by the gospel of peace:* The Gospel is the foundational truth that God has given us. Without the proper foundation or 'shoes', we are unable to be ready to fight the enemy. The Devil will do everything he can to cause us to doubt the Gospel and he will direct us away from God's Word. If we integrate and live out the Gospel as our foundation then the Devil cannot stand against us, because the Devil cannot stand against God.
- *Shield of Faith, with which you can extinguish all the flaming darts of the evil one:* Never lower your faith as it serves as a shield against the Devil. The opposite of fear is faith, so keep your faith strong through knowing God's Word, as this is the foundational tool He has given us.
- *Helmet of Salvation:* Because of our belief in Jesus, we know that our salvation is assured. Because of what Jesus did for us we are His adopted children and have been restored to have a relationship with God.
  - *Isaiah 59:17: "He put on righteousness as a breastplate, and a helmet of salvation on his head."* God opposes sin, but also forgives, as He has given us the armor of the Messiah, Jesus Christ.
- *Sword of the Spirit:* As Christians, we are equipped with the Holy Spirit living within us.
- *Prayer: Prayer is the main weapon of spiritual warfare.* Prayer demonstrates our submission to and dependence on God. By asking for direction and giving the Lord praise, we as Christians receive God's most powerful resource.

Act 3: Living With the Enemy

1 Samuel 18, Psalms 23 and 103

Playlist: "Bless the Lord, Oh My Soul," "Yahweh, We Love to Shout Your Name" by Phil Wickham, "Psalm 23" by Peter Furler

Introduction: While David was serving under Saul, he was successful on every mission he was sent on. This resulted in Saul giving David a very high rank in the Israelite army *(1 Samuel 18:6).*

The Israelite people loved David!

Blessed with a charismatic personality and a natural leadership ability, David earned the love and respect of the people. As he always treated people honestly and fairly, David quickly gained the respect of the men of the Israelite army, as well as all the people serving at the palace, including all of Saul's servants.

The people of Israel grew to respect David for his talents in warfare and his leadership abilities. Developing into a great leader, David's influence increased throughout all of the land. Gaining the trust of the people, David soared to heights of popularity.

In direct proportion to David's increasing success, Saul grew more and more jealous of David.

Jealousy, like the spread of a deadly cancer, began to infiltrate his very soul and soon Saul became obsessed with envy and anger towards David.

Saul's jealousy was initially fueled by David's popularity with the people and then grew exponentially over time.

In one particular incident that seemed to fuel Saul's hatred of David was when Saul and his army returned home with David from the battle with the Philistines. It had to do with a simple victory celebration.

The people of Israel realized the magnitude of the David's victory over the Philistine champion, Goliath. David had saved thousands of lives with his victory, and saved the people of Judah from being killed or enslaved by the Philistines.

As they traditionally did after a successful battle *(Exodus 15:20),* the women from all of the cities of Israel traveled to the king's palace to celebrate the army's victory over the Philistines.

The women congregated in the streets singing, dancing and playing tambourines in celebration of the Israelite victory. There was joy in the air as the people sang praises to the Lord, the King of Israel, and to the Israelite army *(1 Samuel 18:6-7).*

One of the verses from a song the women sang only served to deepen Saul's jealousy towards David.

The women of Israel sang out,

"Saul has struck down his thousands, and David his ten thousands."

(1 Samuel 18:7)

The women's praises of David fueled Saul's anger, which would soon turn to rage.

Saul was livid that David's name was mentioned in the same song as his. Furthermore, David was celebrated by the people as being more victorious than Saul, as the words of their song indicated that David struck down ten thousands of Israel's enemies versus Saul's thousands.

Becoming more suspicious and jealous of David, Saul now perceived David as being a definite threat to his kingship. Saul felt that he needed to get rid of David!

Feeling out of control and with depression overwhelming his senses, Saul began to plot David's demise.

The only way Saul could stop David from taking over as king, he reasoned, would be to take extreme measures against David.

Extreme measures - meaning Saul felt he had to kill David.

David was living with the enemy. Not knowing how much anger Saul harbored against him, David continued to serve Saul and live in the king's palace.

Scene 1: Every Day is an Adventure

The next day after the victory celebration, an evil spirit from the Lord engulfed Saul and he began to act like a madman *(1 Samuel 18:10).*

David was in the reading room of the palace composing music in praise to the Lord. Deep in concentration, he began strumming out a new tune on the lyre and thinking of lyrics that would complement the music.

Playing a tune to the words that had been placed upon his heart, David began to sing praise to the Lord,

"Bless the LORD, O my soul, and all that is within me, bless his holy name!

Bless the LORD, O my soul and forget not all his benefits,
Who forgives all your iniquity, who heals all your diseases,
Who redeems your life from the pit, who crowns you with steadfast love and mercy,
who satisfies you with good so that your youth is renewed like the eagle's.

For as high as he heavens are above the earth, so great is his steadfast love toward those who fear him;
As far as the east is from the west, so far does he remove our transgressions from us."

Bless the LORD, O My Soul ~ A Psalm Of David
(Psalm 103:1-5, 11-12)

As David bent down to reach for his Torah on the bench beside him, he heard the sound of a spear whistling through the air above his head.

With the deadly weapon narrowly missing him by less than an inch, David raised up to see what had just happened. Looking behind him, he saw that the trajectory of the spear had caused its sharp head to become embedded deep in the wall directly behind the chair in which he was sitting.

Saul then rushed into the room from his hiding place behind the door chanting senseless words at the top of his lungs, his eyes wild with rage!

Armed with another spear, Saul drew his arm back and hurled a second spear at David in another attempt to pin him to the wall.

Again, David ducked just in time to evade Saul's second attack on his life.

"And Saul hurled the spear, for he thought, I will pin David to the wall.
But David evaded him twice."

94

Saul could see that the Lord was with David, as no one should have been capable of moving that quickly to dodge both of his spears.

This frightened Saul even more, as he knew the Lord was with David, and was no longer with him.

"Saul was afraid of David because the LORD was with him, but had departed from Saul."
(1 Samuel 18:12)

To say the least, David needed to get away from Saul.

The Lord placed it upon Saul's heart to send David far away from the palace. Saul removed David from his presence by giving him command over a thousand men of the army. This new charge would take David far away from the palace, and out into the lands of Israel to command his army of men.

David with his extraordinary leadership abilities had tremendous success with his command. This served to threaten and frighten Saul even more. All of Israel and Judah loved David, making Saul even more jealous than before. *(1 Samuel 18: 13-16)*

◆◆◆◆◆◆◆◆◆◆◆

Pearl: *David in his despair but thankfulness for his life praised the Lord with confidence for His care with **Psalm 23: The LORD is My Shepherd.***

Relating to the duties of a shepherd from David's past life, he proclaims that the Lord is his shepherd, as He personally attends to David' care.

Psalm 23 ~ The LORD is My Shepherd
"The LORD is my shepherd, I shall not want. He makes me lie down in green pastures. He leads me beside still waters. He restores my soul. He leads me in paths of righteousness for his name's sake.
Even though I walk through the valley of the shadow of death, I will fear no evil, for you are with me;
Your rod and your staff, they comfort me.
You prepare a table before me in the presence of my enemies; you anoint my head with oil;
my cup overflows.
Surely goodness and mercy shall follow me all the days of my life;
and I shall dwell in the house of the LORD forever."

◆◆◆◆◆◆◆◆◆◆◆

Scene 2: David Becomes Saul's Son-in-Law
Psalm 12

Saul continued to plot to end David's life. Somehow, he thought, David has to die!

Saul decided to make ill-use of David's love for God, hoping that his faith in the Lord during warfare would lead to David being killed while fighting.

Saul thought,

"Let not my hand be against him, but let the hand of the Philistines be against him."
(1 Samuel 18:17)

To accomplish this Saul promised his eldest daughter, Merab, to David if he would be valiant for Saul and fight the Lord's battles.

In humble response David asked,

"Who am I, and who are my relatives, my father's clan in Israel, that I should be son-in-law to the king?"
(1 Samuel 18:17-19)

Saul then proceeded to not keep his promise to David, as he gave Merab to another man.

But then Saul tried again to plot against David. This time he thought he could use his second daughter, Michal, as a snare to destroy David.

Saul promised Michal's hand in marriage to David but as a *bride price* David needed to kill one hundred Philistines and provide their foreskins to Saul *(1 Samuel 18:25).*

Saul thought that the Philistines would surely kill David in his quest to kill one hundred of these foreboding, evil men!

Saul's plotting demonstrated his little faith in the Lord as he thought the Philistines could defeat David, even though the Lord was with him!

David, the over-achiever with the Lord's backing, countered Saul's request of one hundred Philistine foreskins by bringing two hundred instead. David proved to Saul that he had killed one hundred more than Saul had ever thought possible.

Michal and David went on to get married, but Saul continued to be David's enemy and plot his demise.

After David and Michal married, David moved back into Saul's immediate vicinity of the palace into a house nearby to live with his wife.

David, now Saul's son-in-law, had a very successful life by cultural standards. He had gone from a lowly shepherd-boy to holding an esteemed job in the palace. Now he was even in the king's family as the king's son-in-law with resultant guaranteed wealth, power and freedom from taxes.

David, so he thinks, is on top-of-the-world with a royal family and a prestigious job.

However, unbeknown to David, this is all about to change in a matter of minutes.

♦♦♦♦♦♦♦♦♦♦♦

Pearl: *So far, what have we learned about David and Saul's relationship?*

For starters, the Lord due to his disobedience has torn Saul's kingdom away from his rule. The Lord has promised it to David and anointed him as the King-to-be of Israel. When David was anointed to be the future king of Israel the Holy Spirit came upon him, endowing him with many gifts that have and will be used to further God's purpose.

When Saul was stripped of his rule, the Holy Spirit was removed from him and an evil spirit caused him to become insanely jealous of David. As a result, Saul has resorted to many treacherous actions and attempts on David's life.

In the meantime, Saul has remained in power as King of Israel as God is not ready for David to step into being the ruling king just quite yet. God is training David to become a great king through presenting him with numerous obstacles that David must conquer through having faith in the Lord.

During his training period with the Lord, David has remained a faithful and humble servant to Saul.

On the other hand, Saul, becoming a failed warrior for the Lord's purposes, has spiraled downward in his faith. Being consumed with murdering David, Saul has sunk to lowest-of-low.

In contradistinction to Saul, David has risen to become a mighty Holy warrior and an obedient servant of the Lord.

*David lamented how he was dominated by the unfaithful, and wrote **Psalm 12.***

Psalm 12: (1-5)
"Save, O LORD, for the godly one is gone; for the faithful have vanished from among the children of man.

Everyone utters lies to his neighbor; with flattering lips and a double hear they speak.

May the LORD cut off all flattering lips, the tongue that makes great boasts, those who say,

With our tongue we will prevail, our lips are with us; who is master over us?
Because the poor are plundered, because the needy groan, I will now arise, says the LORD;
I will place him in the safety for which he longs."

♦♦♦♦♦♦♦♦♦♦♦

Act 4: The Fugitive On-The-run

Pre-reading: 1 Samuel 19-20; Psalm 26, Psalm 22, Psalm 23, Psalm 5, Psalm 59, Psalm 11, Psalm 12

Playlist: "Love Moved First" by Casting Crowns

Introduction: The story carries on, and Saul's hatred of David continues to grow and develop into a mega-obsession. Putting the nation and people of Israel on the back burner, Saul continuously plots to destroy David.

Meanwhile, David continues to be successful against the Philistines in battle. In the light of his successes, David gains the trust and approval of the Israelites. David has served to make the nation of Israel great, and the people are thriving as never before.

Saul, becoming more and more jealous of David, and deranged by the day, has decided to step-up his attempts to kill David.

Saul moves from *trying* to use the Philistines to kill David, to *ordering* him killed.

Not wanting David's murder to appear, as it was his doing, Saul decided that it must appear as if it was done without his participation and any knowledge of the event.

Saul began to plot David's murder, but remained at arms-length so that he would not be implicated.

In order to implement his plan, Saul therefore chose to involve his son, Jonathan.

Scene 1: The Flight Begins

Taking his son aside along with a small group of his most loyal servants, Saul ordered them to kill David *(1 Samuel 19:1).*

Jonathan, being a true friend to David, warned David about his father's plot.

Jonathan also spoke well of David to his father, and brought about reconciliation between the two. Unfortunately, but expectantly, it was only temporary on Saul's part.

After David's continued success in war against the Philistines, Saul continued with his plotting once again to kill David.

"Then a harmful spirit from the Lord came upon Saul as he sat in his house with his spear in his hand."
(1 Samuel 19:9)

As David was playing his lyre in the palace, a fit of uncontrolled anger and rage gripped Saul and he approached David. Hurling his spear, Saul attempted to drive it into David, and pin him to the wall.

As if it was a macabre theatre effect, the spear quivered, as it lay buried deep into the wall behind where David had been sitting.

Fleeing quickly from the room, David narrowly evaded Saul as he strode angrily into the room to retrieve his spear.

As the Lord was with David, he was able to flee from Saul. David had once again come close to losing his life at the hands of crazy, deranged Saul.

David hurriedly escaped the palace and retreated to his home that he maintained with his wife, Michal. He sought her comfort and safety in the privacy of their home.

However, Michal told David that he really needed to leave, as she confided to him that she had heard of the plan of her father's to kill him.

Michal knew that Saul was going to send his men to David's house to hide and wait for just-the-right-time to murder David.

Michal told David,

"If you do not escape with your life tonight, tomorrow you will be killed."
(1 Samuel 19:11)

Michal, in effort to save David's life, let him down to safety through a window during the night. In the black of the night, the guards did not see David leave the premises.

Taking an image (*Hebrew: terapim*), which was of human size and shape, Michal put it in his bed with a pillow of goat's hair at its head to simulate David. Her attempt to outsmart the palace guards was successful.

When Saul's men came to David's house, Michal tricked them into thinking David was lying in his bead and was ill. The guards, not having the heart to murder David in his sleep, left the house and planned to return later.

Meanwhile, David was long-gone, as he had safely fled the area.

When Saul's men returned at Saul's orders to capture David, they found the terapim instead of David lying in David's bed.

Michal was not quite the devoted wife as first seemed however, as when Saul questioned his daughter about why she had allowed David to escape, she lied to her father.

Betraying David, Michal told Saul that David had threatened to kill her. This lie that Michal told Saul most likely fueled Saul's anger even more.

David ran from the palace, but unfortunately, he had nowhere to run.

◆◆◆◆◆◆◆◆◆◆

Pearl: *Does David turn to God in his time of need?*

Notice that at no point during this Scripture describing David's life is David turning to God.

At this point of his life, David leaned on people instead of God to try to help him with his problems with Saul. The people in David's life let him down, as they were unable to do anything to help David with his dilemma with Saul.

Eventually, David will turn back to God and ask for strength.

David then chose to turn to his trusted confidant and prophet, Samuel. After all, Samuel was the one who anointed him to be the future king. Surely Samuel will know what David should do!

◆◆◆◆◆◆◆◆◆◆

Fleeing from Saul's palace in Gibeah, David joined Samuel at Ramah. The two then moved on to Naioth, where David and Samuel stayed.

At this point David turned back to God. With great faith in the Lord, David prayed for strength.

Pearl: *According to the Midrash, David praised the Lord by reciting divinely inspired songs and praises to the Almighty. David is asking for strength and is praising the Lord, but it is not clear if he is asking for direction from God.*

◆◆◆◆◆◆◆◆◆◆

Psalm 59 was composed by David, and is fitting of his prayer for strength and protection at this time in his life. It was to the tune of *"Do not Destroy", a Miktam of David.*

Excerpts from Psalm 59: 1-4, 9-10

"Deliver me from my enemies, O God;

101

*be my fortress against those who are attacking me. Deliver me from evildoers and
save me from those who are after my blood.*

*See how they lie in wait for me!
Fierce men conspire against me for no offense or sin of mine, LORD. I have done no
wrong, yet they are ready to attack me.*

Awake, come to meet me and see!"

*"O my strength, I will watch for you, for you, O God, are my fortress.
My God in his steadfast love will meet me;
God will let me look in triumph on my enemies."*

Hunting David down, Saul soon found David with Samuel, causing David to once again flee and be on-the-run.

David has gone from one narrow escape from Saul's attempts on his life, to the next.

With nowhere else to turn, David then seeks out his friend, Jonathan.

David returned to Gibeah to confide in his friend Jonathan asking,

*"What is my sin before your father that he seeks my life?
(1 Samuel 20:1)*

Jonathan promised to try to help him, as he knew that his father would disclose his plans to him regarding David. Jonathan made a covenant with David, vowing to protect him, and David reciprocated.

But Jonathan also narrowly escaped danger from his father when Saul found out the two had talked. Jonathan now knew how serious things were, and that his father really was intent on killing David.

Even though his father was angry and humiliated him, Jonathan still protected David.

Jonathan and David parted ways when David fled from Saul's court a final time.

Jonathan said to David,

*"Go in peace, because we have sworn both of us in the name of the LORD, saying,
the LORD shall be between me and you, and between my offspring and your offspring
forever."
(1 Samuel 20:42)*

✦✦✦✦✦✦✦✦✦✦✦

Pearl: *This oath between Jonathan and David will turn out to have much significance later in David's life, when David as King of Israel will show Chesed to Jonathan's crippled son, Mephibosheth.*

◆◆◆◆◆◆◆◆◆◆◆

For now, David the anointed future-king of Israel is nothing but a lowly fugitive running for his life.

David, writing **Psalm 26,** continues to bless the Lord,

"Vindicate me, O LORD, for I have walked in my integrity and I have trusted in the LORD without wavering.

Prove me, O LORD, and try me;
Test my heart and my mind.

For your steadfast love is before my eyes, and I walk in your faithfulness.
I do not sit with men of falsehood, nor do I consort with hypocrites.

I hate the assembly of evildoers, and I will not sit with wicked;

I wash my hands in innocence and go around your altar, O LORD;
Proclaiming thanksgiving aloud, and telling all your wondrous deeds.
(Psalm 26 OF DAVID: 1-7)

David continues to flee from Saul's relentless attempts to kill him.

Saul, his army, and essential members of his court such as Doeg the Moabite, all worked around the clock to hunt down and kill David.

Doeg was well connected in the network and would find out information concerning David's whereabouts. Doeg would then report this information to Saul.

David was continuously on the run in fear of his life. A madman, as he knew it, had destroyed his life.

Unfortunately, unlike Saul, David was not in the *'royal power-party,'* nor did he have men to help him fight. In contrast, Saul the crazy, deranged individual being the acting-king of Israel had unlimited men and power at his fingertips.

David was left with no family or friends to turn to. In many ways, his identity had been destroyed, to the point that he was unrecognizable - *even to himself.*

David, with nowhere left to hide and nowhere to turn, took it upon himself to flee to Gath *(1 Samuel 21:10).*

Interlude ~ Pearls concerning Scene 1:

Why Gath?

*A*s the reader coming to this piece of information in ***1 Samuel 21:10,*** *you might possibly wonder why David fled from Saul straight into the hands of his enemies?*

Gath was a Philistine city and was where Goliath had lived prior to being killed by David. Since then, David had killed many Philistines in battle and had become famous for his conquests throughout all of Judah and Israel. Undoubtedly the Philistines harbored much hatred for David!

Could this possibly be a good decision for David to seek refuge in the city of the enemy?

Pondering David's decision, the following summarizes the possible reasons why David chose to seek refuge in the Philistine city of Gath.

- ✦ Perhaps David entered into enemy camp thinking that Saul would never follow him into such treacherous territory.
    - o Rabbinic commentators in the Midrash and many Biblical scholars think that David may have had the idea to serve the King of Gath, Achish, as an anonymous mercenary.

- ✦ Or maybe David made the decision to try to take refuge in Gath in a desperate attempt to try to turn his life around. He may have thought he could forge-out a new identity for himself.

    - o David may have been so overwhelmed with fear and exhaustion that he wasn't thinking clearly.
    - o David had exhausted all of his possibilities of people to lean on, and had been turned away or betrayed by everyone he had known.
    - o His past life no longer existed, and in many ways his identity had been erased, like the writing on a chalkboard.
    - o Did David think that the Philistines would not recognize him?

- ✦ David had been reduced to living the life of a wanted-fugitive, and ran to the most unlikely place anyone would think of finding him.

- ✦ Saul, being king of Israel had many men from Israel at his beck and call, and he had everyone hunting David down with orders to kill him on sight.

* Saul and his men would never enter Gath for fear-of-their lives. David, on the other hand took the chance that he would not be recognized and could hide from Saul.

Whatever the reason behind David's decision, he entered into the city of Gath.

Scene 2: Rising From Abysmal Depths

1 Samuel 21
Pre-reading: Psalm 34 and 56

Playlist: "Yes I Will" by Vertical Worship, "God Only Knows" by King and Country

D avid fled to the city of Gath.

With nowhere else to turn, and exhausted from running for his life from Saul, David had a moment of doubt and was deceived by the temptation to plummet into abysmal depths.

David decided to join forces with the enemy.

Upon entering the city of Gath, the servants of King Achish immediately caught on to the fact that this was the 'famous' David.

Asking themselves if this was the same man that slayed their Champion, Goliath, the servants were taken aback with amazement that David would be so bold as to enter their city.

They deduced that this was indeed the same David who had slayed Goliath, and the same David that the people of Israel had celebrated with singing and dancing.

"And David rose and fled that day from Saul and went to Achish the king of Gath.
And the servants of Achish said to him,
"Is not this David the king of the land?
Did they not sing to one another of him in dances."
(1 Samuel 21:10-11)

The people of Gath mocked David with the very words the Israelites had sung when they sang David's praise after he had slayed Goliath of Gath,

"Saul has struck down his thousands and David his ten thousands."
(1 Samuel 21:11)

The people of Gath were not hospitable when David arrived in Gath.

Needless to say, the welcoming committee for the city of Gath did not extend their invites to David with open arms, in fact their intention was to kill him!

◆◆◆◆◆◆◆◆◆◆◆

Pearl: Not quite grasping the reasoning behind David's coming to their city, Goliath's relatives and friends living among the people of Gath wanted to avenge Goliath's death by killing David.

Not only had David slain their 'champion' Goliath, but also he had gone on to kill many more Philistines while he was in Saul's command.

As a result, David had many angry Philistines who wanted to see him dead to reconcile the death of their family members and their nation's war-heroes.

◆◆◆◆◆◆◆◆◆◆◆

Pearl from the Midrash: The Rabbis comment in the Midrash that Goliath had several brothers. One of these brothers served as a bodyguard for Achish, the King of Gath. Upon David's arrival, Goliath's brothers recognized David, and came before the king to demand David's blood as revenge for slaying Goliath.

Respectful of David since he had been the head of Saul's army, King Achish came to David's defense. Achish pointed out that David had slain Goliath in battle, and this should not be revenged since he was doing his duty of defending his nation and people.

◆◆◆◆◆◆◆◆◆◆◆

Recognizing David, the men of Gath captured David and presented him as their prisoner to the King.

Standing alone in the midst of the enemy outside of the palace of the king of Gath, David needed to quickly come up with a plan to avoid being killed.

Progressing from bad to worse, this situation David is now faced with in Gath might very well be even more dangerous than his previous confrontations with Saul.

Once again, David seemingly had no way out alive.

Suddenly, as if acting the part of a deeply disturbed character in morbid play, David assumed the role of a madman!

Transitioning himself into living-out his dramatic acting role, David took himself into the depths of a stark, raving lunatic *(1 Samuel 21:13)*.

With his eyes wide and crazed, David began stumbling wildly around with no definite purpose. Spewing from his mouth came the utterances of nonsensible phrases.

Making himself even more distasteful and obnoxious, David moved around the room flailing his arms and with drool running down from the corners of his mouth.

Proceeding to wipe his hands in his spittle that collected on his beard, David wrote irrational statements with his wet fingers into the dust covering the doors of the palace walls.

The king and his army of Philistine men looked upon David with utter disbelief.

Looking at each other, the Philistines began to doubt that this was really *the* David that was once the mighty commander of Saul's army, and the one who had slain their champion, Goliath.

Certainly if he was once that man, the Philistines thought, he is not that man anymore.

The King of Gath, seeing David's foolish behavior, responded by saying to his servants to get David out of his presence.

King Achish told his servants,

> *"Behold, you see this man is mad.*
> *Why then have you brought him to me?"*
> *(1 Samuel 21:14)*

Then going on to say which may be one of the most difficult lines in the Bible to comprehend, King Achish said,

> *"Do I lack madmen, that you have brought this fellow to behave as a madman in my presence?"*
> *(1 Samuel 21:15)*

Apparently the King of Gath didn't think he needed another madman in his court, so he drove David away!

❖❖❖❖❖❖❖❖❖❖

P*earl: Why did King Achish imply that he did not lack madmen in his life, and that he certainly did not need any more madmen in his presence?*

Putting this statement into context, the Midrash states that Achish's wife and daughter were stricken with mental illness. Apparently the two women were prone to rave insensibly inside the palace. Upon seeing David's antics, King Achish did not want him anywhere near him, or in his city, as he did not want to deal with any more mentally-ill people and their ravings.

❖❖❖❖❖❖❖❖❖❖

Whatever the reason, David the mighty warrior and the anointed-one to be the next king of Israel, had sunk to abysmal depths in his life by pretending to be a madman.

Nonetheless, David had managed to escape the wrath of the king of Gath and his Philistine men. Even though David had killed Goliath and countless numbers of Philistines, David escaped death while in their grasps.

◆◆◆◆◆◆◆◆◆◆◆

Pearl: David has escaped death once again. In spite of a serious case of lack of judgement, which should have led to his death, David departed from Gath with life-and-limb.

Now David must rise from his abysmal depths and soar to new heights as he develops into the man the Lord intends for him to be. But first, he must ask the Lord for guidance.

*After the encounter at Gath, David composed **Psalms 34 and 56** in response to his fear and depression.*

*In **Psalm 34** David gave thanks for God's encouragement, and surrendered with complete humility to the Lord. In his cry for help, David received the Lord's direction and deliverance from his bad situation.*

David realized that he only had the Lord to depend on, and that was all he needed. He didn't need other people to help him out of his bad circumstances with Saul, the Lord was enough.

*David began **Psalm 34** with the words, **"I will bless the Lord at all times, his praise shall continually be I my mouth" (Psalm 34:1).***

Thinking about the encounter at Gath, David realized that even through the times when he didn't understand the Lord's plans, he should nevertheless praise the Lord for them.

Excerpts from Psalm 34: Of David when he changed his behavior before Abimelech so that he drove him out

"I sought the LORD, and he answered me and delivered me from all my fears."

"The angel of the LORD encamps around those who fear him, and delivers them."

"When the righteous cry for help, the LORD hears and delivers them out of all their troubles.

The LORD is near to the brokenhearted and saves the crushed in spirit.
Many are the afflictions of the righteous but the LORD delivers him out of them all. "
(Psalm 34: 4, 7, 17-19)

Scene 3: From Rock-Bottom to Rock-Star

1 Samuel 22-23, 1 Chronicles 12:6-18

Pre-Reading: 1 Samuel 22-23, 1 Chronicles 12, Psalms 142, 141, 64, 35 and 53

David departed from Gath and escaped to the cave of Adullam. Ten miles east of Gath, the cave in which David took refuge, was halfway between Gath and Bethlehem in the Forest of Hereth.

Here, deep in the depths of the cave, David prayed for refuge from his enemies. As David recorded his feelings in **Psalm 142,** it is apparent that he realizes that he has none to trust other than the Lord.

◆◆◆◆◆◆◆◆◆◆

Pearl: *Of note is that in this prayer David is praying for protection from persecutors but has no prayers for the enemies' downfall. It is similar to **Psalm 143,** in that David's troubles makes him aware of his own sin of not being as dependent on God as he knew he should be.*

Excerpts from Psalm 142: 4-7; A MASKIL OF DAVID when he was in the Cave of Adullam

"Look to the right and see there is none who takes notice of me; no refuge remains to me; no one cares for my soul.

I cry to you, O LORD, I say You are my refuge, my portion in the land of the living.

Attend to my cry, for I am brought very low!

Deliver me from my persecutors, for they are too strong for me. Bring me out of prison, that I may give thanks to your name!

The righteous will surround me, for you will deal bountifully with me."

◆◆◆◆◆◆◆◆◆◆

David then set up his headquarters at the cave of Adullam where he formed, and progressively increased the numbers in the ranks of his army. David had previously gained the support of many people of Israel while he had served under Saul.

The people remembered David, and upon hearing of his plight, gathered around him in support.

Word spread where David was hiding and soon his father, brothers and four hundred men assembled to support him. Bringing their families with them, these loyal followers of David gave up their homes in Israel to camp in the wilderness. All for David' cause.

Everyone who was distressed, in debt, or bitter as a result of Saul's rule gathered to David. He assembled the outcasts of Israel under his leadership, as they recognized that he was a man of the Lord, and that the Lord was with him *(1 Samuel 22:1-2).*

♦♦♦♦♦♦♦♦♦♦♦

Pearl: *Assembling the outcasts as a man of God brings to mind a parallel with how Jesus assembled his disciples. With the choosing of the disciples, twelve unexpected outsiders were chosen by God to change the world.*

Similarly, David assembled his ranks, being those who were outcasts under the leadership of Saul. They too, would change history.

♦♦♦♦♦♦♦♦♦♦♦

David organized his ranks into a massive, effective fighting force. He became their commander, as he was both a gifted leader and a warrior. The Lord had given David this gift of leadership and therefore the people were drawn to serve with him.

The group of men and their families would often assemble around the campfire during the nights in the wilderness. David consolidated his forces and chose the select few who would come to be known as his Mighty Men.

With the light of the fire illuminating his titian colored hair and handsome features, David talked of his battle plans. But importantly he led his men and their families to worship the Lord.

Writing his music and prayers to God, David, the ultimate worship director, would lead his people to sing in praise to the Lord.

Psalm 143: 8-10
"Let me hear in the morning of your steadfast love, for in you I trust.
Make me know the way I should go, for to you I lift up my soul.
Deliver me from my enemies, O LORD!
I have fled to you for refuge!
Teach me to do your will, for you are my God!
Let your good Spirit lead me on level ground!"

♦♦♦♦♦♦♦♦♦♦♦

Pearl: *David came out of his cave in Adullam transformed by the Lord, and then inspired people to further God's plan. This foreshadows and draws a parallel to Jesus, who was resurrected from death and came out of his burial cave to not only inspire people, but also redeem humanity in the eyes of God.*

The Lord not only transformed David's life, but He also restored broken relations with his family, as Scripture states that David's father and brothers also joined up with David in Adullam.

Recall that David's brothers treated him with disdain. Even his father, Jesse, had previously ignored his son, leaving him behind in the field with his sheep on the day that he was eventually anointed by the Lord as the next King of Israel.

♦ ♦ ♦ ♦ ♦ ♦ ♦ ♦ ♦ ♦

David however honored his parents and was concerned for their safety. Fearing that Saul might harm them in revenge against him, David took action to protect his mother and father from Saul's relentless aggression and anger towards him.

Knowing Saul's evil ways and brewing hatred, David sensed that this anger Saul harbored could very well be directed at the people who David cared about.

In order to protect his aging parents from harm that Saul may inflict, David took them to Mizpah in Moab to request that the king of Moab care for them,

"Please let my father and my mother stay with you, till I know what God will do for me."
(1 Samuel 22:3)

The journey to Moab would not have been easy for David's elderly parents, as it involved a considerable descent first to the Dead Sea, then a similar ascent up to the plateau of Moab.

David must have planned ahead of time and considered the hardships involved. The benefits of protection for his parents must have outweighed the disadvantages of the hardships involved in the travel.

Furthermore, David must have felt comfortable leaving his elderly parents in the care of the Moabite king.

♦ ♦ ♦ ♦ ♦ ♦ ♦ ♦ ♦ ♦

Pearl: *Why did David choose Moab as a place for his parents to escape Saul's anger? Remember that Ruth was a Moabite. After reading deeper in the Midrash concerning David's great-grandmother, Ruth, the Midrash states that Ruth was the daughter of the King of Moab. This sheds even more light on how much she obeyed God to follow her mother-in-law, Naomi, to Bethlehem. She truly shed off her old*

111

life, which must have been good as she was royalty, for a better life that God had is store for her as part of His Master Plan.

Now, years later David entrusted the care of his own parents with the King of Moab. The King that reigned in this day and time was most likely a descendent of the King that was Ruth's father. Interestingly, this lineage has come full circle, and David entrusted them with the care of his elderly mother and father.

David's Moabite heritage turned out to be significant in many ways.

For instance, no one would have suspected that a Moabite, who was an enemy of the Jewish people, would have served in such an important role as to be the protector of David's very own mother and father.

David entrusted his parents to the king's care knowing that they were safe from Saul as he would never be able to hide and seek out David's parents in the country of Moab. Saul would be considered an enemy to the Moabites, and would most likely be put to death if he showed his face in Moab.

◆◆◆◆◆◆◆◆◆◆◆

After securing safety for his parents, David then went to live in a stronghold in the wilderness across the Dead Sea.

◆◆◆◆◆◆◆◆◆◆◆

Pearl: *Scholars think that the stronghold was not in the land of Judah but may have been Masad, a mesa on the western shore of the Dead Sea.*

◆◆◆◆◆◆◆◆◆◆◆

While in the stronghold, David was joined by brave Gadite warriors, Benjaminites (from Saul's own tribe), and men from Judah. These men further strengthened and increased the ranks of David's army. David made them the leaders of his troops as they came to help him with his success.

Support for David continued to grow tremendously, as members from many tribes of Israel defected to join his ranks. Everyone knew God was with David *(1 Chronicles 12:8-18)!*

And a spirit enwrapped Amasai, the chief of the officers,
"To you, David, and with you, O son of Jesse: peace, peace to you and peace to your helper, for your God has helped you."
And David received them and placed them at the head of the troop."
(1 Chronicles 12:18, Hebrew Bible ~A New English Translation of the Hebrew Text)

◆◆◆◆◆◆◆◆◆◆◆

Pearl: *The Hebrew Rabbinic scholar, Rashi, comments in the Midrash that Amasai was indicating that David need not thank them for their help because it is from the Lord, and that is the meaning of 'for your God has helped you."*

The Rabbis also not that the word "peace" is repeated three times for emphasis, as is often done in the Hebrew language.

Also of note is that Amasai is David's sister's son. The Benjaminites had taken David's nephew with them to the stronghold to meet with David to make sure that David would trust them and not think that they were coming to capture him and deliver him into Saul's hands. By taking David's nephew with them, the sons of Benjamin, being of the same tribe as Saul, would be assured that David would see that they came in good faith, and not suspect them of any bad intentions.

◆◆◆◆◆◆◆◆◆◆◆

The prophet Gad then told David to depart from the stronghold and go into the land of Judah *(1 Samuel 22:5).*

David therefore went to the Forest of Hereth in Judah. With faith in the Lord, David went back to Judah, despite the danger lurking from Saul and his army.

In the meantime, back at the palace of Gibeah, Saul heard that David and his men had been discovered. With his officials by his side, Saul accused them and his son Jonathan of stirring David up, and that David was lying in wait for him.

Fearing that his servants and his son have conspired against him, Saul trusts no one, including the Lord.

Doeg the Edomite then betrayed David, telling Saul that he had visited Ahimelech, the priest in Nob. Doeg told Saul that Ahimelech had given David supplies and the sword of Goliath, which David had hidden there.

Infuriated, Saul summoned Ahimelech the priest, his son and all the priests who were at Nob to come to the palace. Accusing the priests of conspiring against him, Saul commanded his guards to kill the priests of the Lord, as their hand was with David. Disobeying Saul's command, the guards would not kill the priests.

Saul, turning to Doeg the Edomite, commanded him to kill the priests, which he did.

"Doeg the Edomite turned and struck down the priests, and he killed on that day eighty-five persons who wore the linen ephod. And Nob, the city of the priests, he put to the sword; both man and woman, child and infant, ox, donkey and sheep, he put to the sword. "
(1 Samuel 22:18)

One person escaped the massacre at Nob, being Abiathar, one of Ahimelech's sons. Narrowly escaping death, Abiathar immediately sought-out David.

✦✦✦✦✦✦✦✦✦✦

P*earl: David's Cover-up*

Several months ago just after speaking with Jonathan at the palace and fleeing Saul, David, being on the run with nowhere to turn, visited the priests at Nob. With good intentions to acquire food for sustenance and to pick up the sword he had used to decapitate Goliath, David arrived in Nob.

Speaking with the head priest, Ahimelech, David did not tell the whole truth behind his visit.

David covered up the fact that he was no longer in Saul's service and did not disclose to Ahimelech, or any of the priests at Nob, that Saul was actually searching for him with the intent to kill.

Unaware that Doeg the Edomite, head of Saul's Tribunal, was lurking around Nob in attempt to seek-out David's whereabouts, David accepted bread from the priests, picked up his sword and headed on his way. Doeg of course, communicated this to his boss, Saul. Of significance is that to Doeg the Edomite, these actions spelled conspiracy – it appeared as if the priests were supporting David, and conspiring against Saul and his supporters.

The ramification of David's lie to the priests of Nob is that he unintentionally put their lives in danger. Considering Saul's extreme jealousy and suspicion, Saul assumed that the priests were conspiring against him. In his altered mindset, Saul will take extreme measures against anyone who does not support him. Even priests!

✦✦✦✦✦✦✦✦✦✦

Confessing that he had visited Nob and obtained provisions from the priests in spite of the danger of Doeg the Edomite finding out and telling Saul, David admitted his sin to Abiathar.

David said to Abiathar,

> **"I knew on that day, when Doeg the Edomite was there, that he would surely tell Saul. I have occasioned the death of all the persons of your father's house. Stay with me, do not be afraid, for he who seeks my life seeks your life. With me you shall be in safekeeping."**
> **(1 Samuel 22:21-22)**

In his guilt and grief, David composed **Psalm 52, a maskil of David – when Doeg the Edomite had gone to Saul and told him: David has gone to the house of Ahimelek.**

*Excerpts from **Psalm 52***

"Why do you boast of evil, you mighty hero? Why do you boast all day long, you who are a disgrace in the eyes of God?
You love evil rather than good, falsehood rather than speaking the truth.
You love every harmful word, you deceitful tongue."
(Psalm 52: 1-4)

Pearl: Abiathar will stay as David's priest until David's death.
Abiathar forgave David and transitioning the priestly council from Saul to David, brought the ephod (the garment worn by the Jewish priests) with him as he came to be in David's service.

Abiathar will serve David for the rest of David's life. Solomon, David's son will eventually banish him after David's death.

Once David and his men left the stronghold and returned to Judah, David inquired of the Lord for direction.

David was told by the Lord to rescue the city of Keilah, three miles south of Adullam, which was being attacked by the Philistines *(1 Samuel 23:1-2)*.

♦♦♦♦♦♦♦♦♦♦♦

Pearl: Of note is that now David is now continually relying on the Lord for direction, and is carrying out His will. The Lord is with David and leading to his cause, as David's army has now greatly enlarged in number and power. At this point in time David's army of warriors has increased to six hundred men.

♦♦♦♦♦♦♦♦♦♦♦

Consulting the ephod that Abiathar had brought with him from Nob, David learned from the Lord that Saul was coming in pursuit of him to Keilah.

After saving the inhabitants of Keilah, David and his army therefore relocated to the wilderness of Ziph in the Judaean mountains, which is about five miles southeast of Hebron *(1 Samuel 23:13-14)*.

The wilderness of Ziph was essentially a desert - parched and dry.

Water was difficult to find, but David and his men persevered as they realized that Saul continued to search for them.

David wrote **Psalm 63** out of gratitude to God for not giving him into the hands of Saul.

Excerpts from **Psalm 63:1, 9-11**
"You, God, are my God, earnestly I seek you; I thirst for you, my whole being longs for you, in a dry and parched land where there is no water.

Those who want to kill me will be destroyed; they will go down to the depths of the earth. They will be given over to the sword and become food for jackals.
But the king will rejoice in God; all who swear by God will glory in him, while the moths of liars will be silenced."

The men of Ziph, who informed Saul of their new hiding place, then betrayed David and his army. Even though the Ziphites were Judahites, they did not want David and his army in the area, and even conspired with Saul to help him locate David's whereabouts.

Pearl: David wrote **Psalm 54** *in response to the betrayal by the Ziphites.*

Psalm 54: The LORD Upholds My Life

" O God, save me by your name, and vindicate me by your might.
O God, hear my prayer, give ear to the words of my mouth.
For strangers have risen against me, ruthless men seek my life; they do not set God before themselves.
Behold, God is my helper, the LORD is the upholder of my life.
He will return the evil to my enemies; in your faithfulness put an end to them.
With a freewill offering I will sacrifice to you; I will give thanks to your name, O LORD, for it is good.
For he has delivered me from every trouble, and my eye has looked in triumph on my enemies."

Over the next months to years, David continuously moved to avoid Saul, who relentlessly sought David.

But God did not give David into Saul's hand **(1 Samuel 23:14).**

Pearl: Saul's greater army and authority could not triumph over God's protection of David. Continuously on-the-run, David and his army of men and their families went wherever they could go, fully trusting in God's guidance.

Once again on-the-road fleeing Saul and his powerful forces, David and his men traveled about five miles south to the wilderness of Maon.

Meanwhile, Saul and his men continued to hunt David night-and-day.

Pearl: We will read how a messenger came to save David from Saul's clutches **(1 Samuel 23:27-29).**

In the desert of Maon, Saul determinedly pursued David until he found them on the mountainside of Mount Kohled.

David and his troops had headed to the eastern slope of Mount Kohled to attempt to escape towards the Dead Sea. Running out of time as Saul's forces quickly encroached upon David and his men, they were forced to take refuge on the mountain.

Saul and his forces diligently observed David's army and when they discovered David and his men on the mountain, Saul realized he could block David's escape route.

In order to gain military advantage, Saul divided his forces into two flanks, sending his divided troops north and south until they completely encircled the mountain.

In doing this maneuver Saul had succeeded in strategically blocking all avenues of escape off the mountain for David and his army!

The outcome looked ominous for David, as Saul and his men were quickly closing in on David and his army from all directions.

The end seemed near for David and his army...until the Lord intervened with a diversion.

At the last minute while David and his army were under siege, the Lord sent a messenger to Saul.

◆◆◆◆◆◆◆◆◆◆◆

P*earl: This 'mystery-messenger' told Saul information that would cause him to give up his pursuit of David. What could have been so important that Saul would give up the pursuit of the man that he had been trying to kill for years?*

◆◆◆◆◆◆◆◆◆◆◆

The 'mystery-messenger' told Saul that the Philistines were making a raid against Saul's land in Israel *(1 Samuel 23:27).* Saul was left with no other choice but to return home!

With this critical information given to him by the messenger of the Lord, Saul made the radical decision to return to his country to fight off the Philistines. Relinquishing his pursuit of David and his army on Mount Kohled to return home, Saul allowed David's troops escape from their inevitable capture.

◆◆◆◆◆◆◆◆◆◆◆

P*earl: In the ESV this notable place on Mount Kohled is called the 'Rock of Escape'. In the Masoretic text of the Hebrew bible it is translated to read as the 'Rock of the Divisions' (1 Samuel 23:28).*

117

The Rabbis' interpretation of David's experience at the Rock of Divisions from the Midrash is that David recognized that the messenger was an angel sent from heaven. This seems likely as David wrote about his experience in **Psalm 18,** when he described an angel from Heaven sent from above **(Psalm 18:16-17).**

Excerpts from Psalm 18:1-3, 16-17
A Psalm of David
Song to the LORD on the day when the LORD rescued him from the hand of Saul

"I love you, O LORD, my strength.
The LORD is my rock and my fortress and my deliverer, my God, my rock, in whom I take refuge, my shield, and the horn of my salvation, my stronghold.
I call upon the LORD, who is worthy to be praised; and I am saved from my enemies.
He sent from on high, he took me; he drew me out of many waters.
He rescued me from my strong enemy and from those who hated me for they were too mighty for me."

Another example of a faithful servant of God recognizing a visitor of divine manifestation was with David's ancestor, Abraham.

In **Genesis 18** it states that the Lord appeared to Abraham in the form of three men,

"And the LORD appeared to him by the oaks of Mamre, as he sat at the door of his tent in the heat of the day.
He lifted up his eyes and looked, and behold, three men were standing in front of him.
When he saw them, he ran from the tent door to meet them and bowed himself to the earth and said, O Lord, if I have found favor in your sight, do not pass by your servant."
(Genesis 18:1-3)

Abraham is said to have recognized that one of his visitors was a divine manifestation. As noted by his words "O Lord" in **Genesis 18:3,** Biblical scholars point out in the ESV that the original Hebrew word Abraham used in the Hebrew text of the Torah was translated as "Adonay", a distinctive term for God used in the Old Testament. A slight change of spelling of Adonay results of in the word "adoni," which in Hebrew translates to "my lord" indicating a polite term of respect, but not necessarily a term used for God himself.

The ESV uses the words "O Lord" in **Genesis 18:3** (which may also be translated as "O My Lord") to emulate the Hebrew word that Abraham used, being Adonay. This term emphasizes that Abraham used a specific word that was distinctive for God, indicating that he recognized that the Lord had manifested himself to him as one of the visitors appearing at his tent.

From their narrow escape on Mount Kohled, David and his men fled to live in the strongholds of Engedi, an oasis on the western shore of the Dead Sea, due east of Ziph.

Pearl: In Engedi we will see an example of David's spiritual depth and passion in his heart for God as he turns away from the temptation of killing Saul. David, as a warrior of God, had already killed many of the Lord's enemies, but never considered killing Saul, even though Saul was relentlessly trying to kill him.

In spite of Saul's obsession to murder him, David had respect for God's appointment of Saul as king.

David is willing to wait for God's timing for him to take the throne, and for God's action for justice to be served.

Scene 4: God's "Test"

1 Samuel 24:1-22
Pre-reading Exodus 22:28

Playlist: "The Same God" by Paul Baloche, "Lay Me Down" by Chris Tomlin

Saul is still in pursuit of David and thinks of nothing but hunting David down, day and night.

Hearing that David went to the wilderness of Engedi, Saul proceeded to ramp-up his efforts to seek and ultimately kill David.

Choosing three thousand of the best fighting men from all Israel to join him, Saul headed to Engedi to find David.

Pearl: The fact that Saul chose three thousand men, which was nearly five times as many men, as were in David's army, exemplifies his paranoia and obsession to kill David.

"Saul took three thousand chosen men out of all Israel and went to seek David and his men in front of the Wildgoats Rocks. And he came to the sheepfolds by the way, where there was a cave, and Saul went in to relieve himself.
Now David and his men were sitting in the innermost parts of the cave."
(1 Samuel 24:2-3)

Arriving in the area of Engedi, Saul wandered away from his troops temporarily into a cave with the intent to 'relieve himself'.

__P__earl: In order to understand this passage and create an effective, realistic word picture in your mind, it is helpful to understand the context of the culture of the ancient Jewish people. Let's look at what the words "and Saul went in to relieve himself" really mean.

In the Masoretic text of the Hebrew bible, the text is translated to say that Saul came to a cave and went in to __"cover his feet"__. The Midrash commentaries explain that this is a commonly used euphemism reflecting the modesty of the Jewish people, and is used to describe the act of covering oneself while passing stool during a bowel movement.

Considering the context of the day, Saul, being a modest Jew, completely covered himself with his garments like a __sukkah__ while passing stool.

The Hebrew word sukkah is translated as a temporary shelter or hut.

Taking this into consideration one can deduce that when Saul went to find a cave with the intent of relieving himself, he was squatting in the front part of the long, dark cave while he covered himself with his garments in the form of a sukkah.

Saul therefore must have wrapped his robe around him to form a hut concealing himself while he relieved himself.

Ironically, seeking out the privacy of a cave in the wilderness of Engedi, Saul thought he had found a location that was secluded. For even added cover, Saul furthermore formed a shelter out of his garments to completely surround himself to ensure his privacy.

Little did Saul know that he was not alone in the dark cave.

The caves in the wilderness of Engedi are known to be large and very long, which can make perfect hideouts for an army of men. Dark and secluded, David and his men chose one of these caves to hide out from the enemy, being Saul and his army of thousands.

The cave that Saul chose to "cover his feet" just happened to be where David and his men were taking cover from their enemies.

Even though David and his men were at the end of the long cave, they could easily see Saul at the front of the cave, as he had the light of the sun shining in through the opening to illuminate his presence.

However, Saul was unable to see David and his men, as they were deep in the cave hiding in the darkness. Besides, Saul was under the cover of his robe which he used as a sukkah, and wasn't exactly exploring the area.

120

Seeing Saul come into the cave and wrap himself under the cover of the sukkah, David's men nudged David to take action saying,

"Here is the day of which the LORD said to you, Behold, I will give your enemy into your hand, and you shall do to him as it shall seem good to you."
(1 Samuel 24:4)

Carefully observing Saul at the front of the cave in which they took cover, David emerged from his hiding place from the innermost depths of the cave and stealthily crept up behind Saul.

Taking slow, soundless steps, David came within inches of Saul. With his back turned and enveloped completely by his large robe, Saul was unaware of David's presence.

Gripping his sword, David prepared for the strike.

Saul, with his back turned and crouched to the ground with his robe draped around him like a tent was the perfect target for David.

David's men watched from the depths of the cave, holding their breath in anticipation of the final moment of justice.

With one move of his sword, David could take Saul's life making David's trouble with Saul a distant memory.

Visions of a stable life, with no more running from place to place, and actually being able to take his place as the rightful king, were vividly churning in David's mind.

Finally, David thought, he could seek revenge. Fingering the handle of his sword in its sheath, David began to calculate his next move.

Drawing his razor-sharp sword and striking with lightning-quick accuracy, David stealthily severed a corner of Saul's robe.

What? David severed Saul's robe? What about severing Saul's head from his neck?

At the last nanosecond, David had changed his mind and decided to spare Saul his head and his life. In the blink of an eye, history had been determined by David's act of faith in God.

Retreating into the darkness, David soundlessly returned to the innermost depths of the cave to rejoin his men.

Surprisingly, David immediately suffered remorse for his actions of cutting off a piece of Saul's robe. Even though he had spared Saul's life, David felt the guilt of the minor incident of severing the robe of his nation's king.

121

Admitting to his men, David said,

"The LORD forbid that I should do this thing to my lord, the LORD's anointed, to put out my hand against him, seeing he is the LORD's anointed."
(1 Samuel 24:6)

◆◆◆◆◆◆◆◆◆◆

P*earl:* Why was David remorseful? Cutting off a piece of Saul's robe seems like a minor offense, especially since David could have just as easily cut off Saul's head.

◆◆◆◆◆◆◆◆◆◆

Again the context of the culture must be considered.

*David respected Saul as the Lord's anointed, and therefore his lord. Saul was still on the throne as king of Israel **(1 Samuel 10:1),** and must be respected as such. Even though David had been anointed as the future king, David is respectful that Saul still retains the status of king, as this was God's will.*

David does not want to ascend to the throne through violence or disloyalty to God.

Going even deeper into the context of the Jewish culture, David's remorse in cutting off a piece of Saul's robe was because the robe of the king is the symbol of royal authority.

Therefore, David actually showed Saul contempt in severing his robe.

Even though David did not kill Saul as he could easily have done, he still felt as though he had disrespected the position that Saul occupied.

*The Rabbis of the Midrash explain that David was remorseful as he began to listen to his conscience. Of significance is that if David had severed a corner of Saul's robe taking with it the '**zizith'** or ritual fringes, it would be equivalent to severing the king's head.*

*David, a faithful servant of God, was well aware of His Word, as stated in **Exodus 22:28,***

"You shall not revile God, nor curse a ruler of your people."

After cutting the piece of Saul's robe, David then persuaded his men to not attack Saul.

Eventually Saul rose up from his makeshift sukkah, repositioned his robe, and left the cave to rejoin his army.

Watching Saul leave the cave, David jumped up and hurried after him calling,

"My lord the king!"
(1 Sam 24:8)

Startled by David's words, Saul turned around quickly to look behind him. Right in front of his eyes was the very man he had been hunting for so long!

But this was not how Saul had expected to see David.

To Saul's surprise, David was bowed with his face to the ground, paying homage to his king.

David then spoke to Saul,

"Why do you listen to the words of men who say Behold, David seeks your harm?
Behold, this day your eyes have seen how the LORD gave you today into my hand in the cave. And some told me to kill you, but I spared you.
I said I will not put out my hand against my lord, for his is the LORD's anointed."
(1 Samuel 24:9-10)

David then went on to prove to Saul that he could have killed him if he had wanted to.

Holding up the corner of Saul's robe as proof, David said,

"See the corner of your robe in my hand!
For by the fact that I cut off the corner of your robe and did not kill you, you may know and see that there is no wrong or treason in my hands.
I have not sinned against you, though you hunt my life to take it."
(1 Samuel 24:11)

Saul quickly reached down around his feet to pull up the edge of his robe. Staring at the cut corner in disbelief, Saul began to shake uncontrollably.

Looking back at David as he continued speak, Saul felt his heart pounding within his chest.

David went on to say,

"May the LORD judge between me and you, may the LORD avenge me against you,
but my hand shall not be against you.
As the proverb of the ancients says, Out of the wicked comes wickedness.
But my hand shall not be against you."
(1 Samuel 24:12-13)

At this point, Saul is trembling with fear and overwhelmed with emotion. He realized that David could have easily beheaded him moments ago in the darkness of the cave, while he was relieving himself and not on his guard.

David finished with,

> *"May the LORD therefore be judge and give sentence between me and you, and see to it and plead my cause and deliver me from your hand."*
> *(1 Samuel 24:15)*

Saul had been reduced to tears in his fear. With his whole body trembling he found the words,

> *"Is this your voice, my son David? You are more righteous than I, for you have repaid me good, whereas I have repaid you evil."*
> *(1 Samuel 24:16-17)*

Saul eventually calms down, as it is evident that David is not going to fight him. Saul then acknowledged that David would be king one day saying,

> *"I know that you shall surely be king, and that the kingdom of Israel shall be established in your hand."*
> *(1 Samuel 24:20)*

But then shifting gears to take a self-centered opportunity, Saul pleads with David saying,

> *"Swear to me therefore by the LORD that you will not cut off my offspring after me and that you will not destroy my name out of my father's house."*
> *(1 Samuel 24:21)*

David swore this to Saul, and the two parted ways.

◆◆◆◆◆◆◆◆◆◆◆

*P**earl:** reconciliation had been reached, but as before (**1 Samuel 19:7**), Saul's calming-down towards David will be very short-lived. We will see as we follow David's story that Saul's reconciliation toward David was only temporary.*

However, Saul most likely reached one permanent decision that day - being to never again enter a cave to relieve himself.

P*earl: David proclaims his faith in the Lord as is shown in his writings of Psalms*

*After David showed Saul mercy and spared his life in the Wilderness of Engedi, David faithfully prayed to the Lord. In Psalms he composed that exemplify how the faithful followers of the Lord should pray when malicious people are seeking to harm them, David wrote **Psalms 35, 57, and 63.***

*David ended-up writing many prayers to the Lord that arose from his angst during Saul's persecution. Some examples of these are seen in **Psalms 34, 52, 54, 56, 59, 108 and 142**.*

*Some excerpts from **Psalms 35, 57 and 63** are included below.*

"Contend, O LORD, with those who contend with me; fight against those who fight against me!
Let them be put to shame and dishonor who seek after my life! Let them be turned back and disappointed who devise evil against me!

For without cause they hid their net for me; without cause they dug a pit for my life. Let destruction come upon him when he does not know it!

And let the net that he had ensnare him; let him fall into it – to his destruction! Let not those rejoice over me who are wrongfully my foes, and let not those wink the eye who hate me without cause.

You have seen, O LORD, be not silent! O Lord, be not far from me! Awake and rouse yourself for my vindication, for my cause, my God and my Lord!

Vindicate me, O LORD, my God, according to your righteousness, and let them not rejoice over me!"
(Psalm 35:1,4,7,8,19,22,24)

"Be merciful to me, O God, be merciful to me, for in you my soul takes refuge; in the shadow of your wings I will take refuge, till the storms of destruction pass by.

I cry out to God Most High, to God who fulfills his purpose for me.

He will send from heaven and save me; he will put to shame him who tramples on me. God will send out his steadfast love and his faithfulness!"
(Psalm 57:1-3)

"My soul clings to you; your right hand upholds me.

125

But those who seek to destroy my life shall go down into the depths of the earth;

They shall be given over to the power of the sword; they shall be a portion for jackals.

But the king shall rejoice in God; all who swear by him shall exult, for the mouths of liars will be stopped."
(Psalm 63:8-11)

Summary Pearls: *1 Samuel 24*

So what might have been going in inside of David's heart as he spoke to Saul?

David did not take the opportunity to kill Saul, however he did use this opportunity to be able to talk with him. David was able to get a lot off his chest as he spoke, and through his words we can get a better insight of David's character and his heart for God.

With full intention and passion in his heart, David faithfully stayed obedient to God's Word and did not take revenge upon Saul.

Some insight into David's heart as seen in 1 Samuel 24:

1. **A balance between justice and mercy:**
    o   David showed mercy to Saul, rather than taking justice into his own hands.
    o   David believed that Saul should be punished for his wrongdoings, but not by him. David chose to turn that over to God, and let Him do justice.
    o   David, being true to God's Word and putting his full trust into Him, acknowledged that God is the only one who should avenge Saul.
    o   David was following God's Word.
    o   In the Song of Moses *(Deuteronomy 32:35*) we read God's Word,

    "Vengeance is mine, and recompense, for the time when their foot shall slip; for the day of their calamity is at hand and their doom comes swiftly."

Relevant New Testament verses concerning vengeance:

The apostle Paul wrote in *Romans 12:19-21,*

"Beloved, never avenge yourselves, but leave it to the wrath of God, for it is written, Vengeance is mine, I will repay, says the Lord. To the contrary, if your enemy is hungry, feed him, if he is thirsty, give him something to drink, for by so doing you will heap burning coals on his head.
Do not be overcome by evil, but overcome evil with good."

Paul was alluding to both Mosaic Law from **Deuteronomy 32:35** and to Jesus's words in the Beatitudes from the Sermon on the Mount written in **Matthew 5:11-12,**

"Blessed are you when others revile you and persecute you and utter all kinds of evil against you falsely on my account.
Rejoice and be glad, for your reward is great in heaven, for so they persecuted the prophets who were before you."
(Matthew 5:11-12)

In **Matthew 5:44-45** we read Jesus' words concerning vengeance,

"Love your enemies and pray for those who persecute you, so that you may be sons of your Father who is in heaven.
For he makes his sun rise on the evil and on the good, and sends rain on the just and on the unjust."

2. **David was tested and refined by God**:

David passed the test given to him by God through showing his awareness and discernment to not fall into the temptation of seeking justice on his own, and killing Saul when he had the chance.

David's men even remarked to him,

"Here is he day of which the LORD said to you, behold, I will give your enemy into your hand, and you shall do to him as it shall seem good to you."
(1 Samuel 24:4).

In other words, David's men were saying that Saul, coming into the cave where they were hiding, was a *'gift of God'*.

Was it really *a gift of God,* or did the men in David's army just want to think that it was?

✦✦✦✦✦✦✦✦✦✦✦

Pearl: This can be relevant to us as well, as how many times do we say, *'it is a gift of God'* when we <u>want</u> to think that because it serves us well?

Even when it seemed like God delivered Saul right into David's hands to receive the justice that he no doubt deserved, David resisted the temptation.

Instead of killing Saul, David exhibited mercy.

Through resisting the temptation of doing justice on his own, David demonstrated his obedience to God to let Him ultimately do the work that belongs to Him.

Instead of vengeance, David showed mercy to his enemies.

In other words, David realized that doing justice is God's job, and not his.

3. **David chose to improve from God's discipline**: David realized that God set his trials, and were all part of God's discipline to allow David to mature into the person that God had intended.
    o   *"My son do not regard lightly the discipline of the Lord, nor be weary when reproved by him. For the Lord disciplines the one he loves, and chastises every son whom he receives." (Hebrews 12:5-6)*

4. *The small things matter*: David **listened to his conscience** about the *small things,* and therefore felt remorse even after the minor offense of cutting off a piece of Saul's robe.
    o   David could have justified his actions by saying to himself that at least he didn't kill Saul, instead he felt bad about even thinking about killing him and cutting a piece of his robe.
    o   In *Luke 16:10* when reading Jesus' parable of the dishonest manager, Jesus cautions us in saying,

    "One who is faithful in a very little is also faithful in much, and one who is dishonest in a very little is also dishonest in much."

David as the foreshadow of Jesus

D avid was a foreshadow of the ultimate Messiah, Jesus Christ, in many ways. Jesus was the ultimate, and the better David, but in many ways David, in his latest experience exhibited characteristics that exemplified Jesus.

David therefore was a character from the Old Testament that pre-empted Jesus Christ, the Messiah.

Ways in which David foreshadowed Jesus:

✦   Both were falsely accused of sins that they did not commit

✦   Both had the opportunity to seek revenge on their enemies

    o   David with his army of over 600 people against Saul

128

- o Jesus with his army of angels, as he was crucified on the cross

✦ Neither gave their enemies what they *deserved* ~ both David and Jesus left that up to the sovereignty of God. Recognizing the supreme power of the Lord, they surrendered their will to His way.

✦ Both exhibited grace and mercy to their enemies
   - o David could have killed Saul, but instead he took a piece of his robe and told Saul of his intentions
   - o Jesus absorbed the sin of humanity, redeeming us in realization of God's greater purpose for His suffering
   - o Both David and Jesus were obedient to God, realizing His greater purpose
   - o Neither David or Jesus took justice into their own hands, but obediently left justice to God

✦ Both were willing to leave it to God to avenge their enemies
   - o David believed that Saul should be punished for his wrong doings, but leaned on God to avenge him *(Deuteronomy 32:35)*
   - o Jesus walked in obedience to God, and left it up to Him to avenge the ultimate enemy, the Devil

✦ Neither took the action of revenge, which served to set an example for their followers
   - o David did not kill Saul, nor did he allow his army of men to kill him
   - o Jesus, as he was crucified on the cross, provided the ultimate example of forgiveness for all believers who would follow him as the Messiah, the Son of God.

"Father forgive them, for they know not what they do."
(Luke 23:34)

Scene 5: David Marries Two Women

1 Samuel 25

In the opening of this scene, we find that Samuel, the prophet and last judge, has died.

After Samuel's death and the mourning of all of Israel, David headed to the wilderness of Paran. Soon he traveled back to the wilderness of Maon, south of Ziph, where he had been previously.

Traveling throughout the land with his faithful army of men and their families, David was still evading Saul.

Even though a 'truce' had been established between the two, David does not trust Saul.

Hearing that a man named Nabal from Carmel, a Judahite town between Ziph and Maon, was shearing his sheep, David sent ten of his young men to seek him out.

With the intention of acquiring food for his army during Nabal's festivities of sheep shearing, David sent his men with a message to Nabal,

> **"Let my young men find favor in your eyes, for we come on a feast day.**
> **Please give whatever you have at hand to your servants and to your son David."**
> **(1 Samuel 25:8)**

Nabal answered David's polite request with refusal and contempt, belittling David and his men.

In anger, David summoned his troops to descend upon Nabal with swords.

Intercepting on her husband's behalf, Nabal's wife, Abigail, calms David's anger with her kind words and gifts of food for him and his soldiers.

Ten days later, the Lord struck Nabal dead **(1 Samuel 26:38)**.

Hearing of Nabal's death, David took Abigail as his wife.

David also took Ahinoam of Jezreel to become his wife.

✦✦✦✦✦✦✦✦✦✦✦

P*earl: Some of the ancient Rabbinical scholars exegete that Ahinoam of Jezreel was King Saul's wife, and that David married her to secure his position as the anointed, soon-to-be king.*

✦✦✦✦✦✦✦✦✦✦✦

*The tie to the interpretation that Ahinoam was King Saul's wife is a passage in **2 Samuel 12:8,** where Nathan, the prophet, rebukes David after his sin with Bathsheba.*

Nathan communicated to David the words of the LORD saying,

> **"And I gave you your master's house and your master's wives into your arms and**
> **gave you the house of Israel and of Judah.**
> **And if this were too little, I would add to you as much more."**
> **(2 Samuel 12:8)**

Biblical scholars in the ESV say that there is no other record of David marrying Saul's wives, but that he was in the position to do so considering the culture of the day.

Act 5: David Joins "Team Philistine"

1 Samuel 27

Ca. 1013 B.C.

Playlist: "Somewhere in Your Silent Night" by Casting Crowns, "Keep Making Me" by Sidewalk Prophets, "Burn the Ships" by King and Country

Introduction: *Just when you think that Saul has come to his senses and has put his hunt for David behind him, the page-in-life is turned and conflict arises once again.*

With the zeal of a madman, Saul continues his maniacal hunt and travels throughout Israel along with his army of thousands. In spite of their previous reconciliation and truce that was struck between David and Saul, the obsession to find David is Saul's only priority.

With brewing anger and extreme mood swings, punctuated with overwhelming jealousy towards David, Saul is consumed with the idea that he must kill David.

At this point, it seems as if Saul's behavior is bordering on insanity.

What started as jealousy and fear of losing his power and identity as the king of Israel has morphed into behavior that is detrimental to the nation of Israel, as Saul does nothing but seek David.

David, on the other hand, is worn out.

David is emotionally spent, and physically exhausted from his escapades of continuously having to flee from Saul and his armies.

Living like fugitives, David and his army of loyal followers and their families have spent the last six years on-the-run from Saul, the raging lunatic.

Finally, David thinks that the only way he can escape death from the hand of Saul is to leave Israel.

David rationalized that if he came to live in enemy territory, Saul would cease to pursue him.

David is now considering living with the enemy. He and his army are going to change 'teams'.

✦✦✦✦✦✦✦✦✦✦✦

Pearl: *David has had a 'faith swing'.*

David, just like all of us, was not perfect in his faith and following of the Lord.

Similar to the bob at the end of the rod of a pendulum, David's faith in the Lord oscillated from extreme trust, back through an equilibrium period of leaning on others, and finally ending the cycle by trusting only in himself.

Typically in his faith swings, David would then recoup and repent, with his faith in God swinging back to be restored. Exhibiting full trust in God, David then would once again be the obedient servant, and walk worthy doing His will.

In David's current faith swing, he decided to completely give up trust that God would protect him from Saul's hand. Instead of staying put with faith in the Lord, David decides to flee his beloved Israel, the nation God has promised him to lead.

With his lack of trust in God, David has also emotionally swung away from asking the Lord for guidance.

Instead, David has put his trust in others, and depended on them and on his own doings to get out of his unwanted circumstances.

What David temporarily forgot was God's promise to him to be the king of Israel.

But God did not forget.

Scene 1: The Crossing-Over

The night was dark, the blackest of black, but not as devoid of light as the depths of David's soul.

Sitting alone in the darkness, David could feel the doubt and despair creeping into him, spreading like a metastatic cancer throughout his entire body.
Hanging his head in his hands, David dwelled on the failures of his life.

Thinking how he had once celebrated that he was destined to be the King of Israel, he has instead lived the last six years running like a fugitive.

Fighting a battle that wasn't his to fight, David was tired of waiting for God to serve justice.

Exhausted both emotionally and physically, and knowing that he had failed his army of faithful men and their families, David made an unwise decision.

Coming to a conclusion fueled by doubt and despair, David thought to himself,

> *"Now I shall perish one day by the hand of Saul.*
> *There is nothing better for me than that I should escape to the land of the Philistines.*
> *Then Saul will despair of seeking me any longer within the borders of Israel,*
> *and I shall escape out of his hand."*
> *(1 Samuel 27:1)*

This decision was not made after consulting with the Lord, in fact David had not even asked the Lord for guidance. Knowing his sin, David decided to take matters into his own hands anyway.

David's decision was to leave his homeland – he must flee Israel.

This decision was not without consequence, as by leaving Israel David would forfeit his right to become king.

Going even further in his unwise plan, David decided to not only flee Israel, but to join forces with Israel's archenemy, the Philistines.

Developing his strategy to crossover his alliances with the enemy, David drew out a list of things in his mind that he must do to accomplish his goal.

First, it was imperative that David make contact with the King of the Philistine city of Gath, Achish. Second, David needed to make King Achish think that he would be gaining something by David and his army moving to Philistia.

David must first notify the King of Gath, Achish, with his problem. But knowing the odds of the king believing him, David knew that he must also present the king with a solution that would be a "win-win" situation for each of them.

David knew that he had to let the king know that the Philistines would gain valuable allies.

◆◆◆◆◆◆◆◆◆◆◆

*P**earl: David's Solution:** In light of the fact that David had previously feigned insanity in front of Achish to escape his angry men's clutches, David's wisdom in considering this step must be questioned.*

◆◆◆◆◆◆◆◆◆◆◆

However, this time David has a band of six hundred men to accompany him. He must also need to make it clear that he and his army are hostile to Saul, and the nation of Israel.

Even though David is leaving Israel, our Sovereign God's power is not limited to Israel's borders.

The Lord will begin His work in Philistia, directing the moves of Philistia leaders. Of significance is that David, even though he is not seeking God's direction, will continue to worship Him while in Philistia.

Confiding in Achish and telling him that he now had become hostile to King Saul, David informed him that and he and his army of 600 able-bodied warriors would like to dwell in Philistia.

In addition, to sweeten the deal, David made it clear that they would aid the Philistines with attacks on the Israelites.

Achish was elated but skeptical, as he knew of David's allegiance to Israel and to his God.

However, knowing that David would be accompanied by his army of 600 men with their families in-tow, helped gain his trust.

After all, men that came with their families would not be planning on raiding the land and its occupants, then fleeing back to Israel.

Hearing David's plan to aid the Philistines in battle, Achish agreed to David and his men and their families coming to Gath.

After David, his army, and all of their families arrived, David asked King Achish for a place outside of Gath for them to live,

> **"if I have found favor in your eyes, let a place be given me in one of the country towns, that I may dwell there.**
> **For why should your servant dwell in the royal city with you?**
> **(1 Samuel 27:5)**

Achish, in response to David's request, presented him with a nearby country-town.

◆◆◆◆◆◆◆◆◆◆◆

Pearl: *Achish was careful to choose a town which did not have surrounding walls, guaranteeing that David and his army would not fortify themselves within the walls and rebel against him.*

The "deal" worked well for David as he actually intended to be in a town away from Gath.

David's intent was that he and his men could conduct warfare as they chose, without Achish having knowledge of with who, and where they waged their raids.

The town that Achish gave to David was called Ziklag in the country of the Philistines. It was about 20 miles south of Gath on the Philistia border, just north of Amalek.

David, his army, and their families settled into their new home in the country town of Ziklag. The families were happy to have a permanent place to live in, as they had previously dwelled in tents in the wilderness as they followed David in his plight from Saul.

At this point David had taken two wives, so he and his wives and his army of men and their families took up their new home address of Ziklag, Philistia.

They were now part of *Team Philistine!*

> *"So that day Achish gave him Ziklag.*
> *Therefore Ziklag has belonged to the kings of Judah to this day.*
> *And the number of he days that David lived in the country of the Philistines was a*
> *year and four months."*
> *(1 Samuel 28:6-7)*

Importantly, David did not have to flee from Saul while he lived in Ziklag.

> *"And when it was told Saul that David had fled to Gath, he no longer sought him."*
> *(1 Samuel 28:4)*

◆◆◆◆◆◆◆◆◆◆◆

Pearl: *David, the future king of Israel has exiled himself from his own land and had taken residence among his nation's archenemy, the Philistines.*

The king of Gath undoubtedly thought that David would be a great asset to him due to his skills as a commander and warrior.

Besides, at this point David has gained a skilled army of over 600 men, who would also be part of 'Team Philistine'. All of David's men, and their families had settled in the town of Ziklag, Philistia.

However, David had deceived King Achish.

The Philistine king mistakenly thought that he had gained an army that would join their forces and fight against their 'now-common enemy', the Israelites.

Contrary to what King Achish thought, while living in Ziklag David and his men did not fight the Israelites.

Who did they fight?

Instead, they went and raided the Amalekites, who lived south of them towards Egypt, as well as the Geshurites and the Girzites.

During the raids, David and his army would leave no one alive to tell the truth about the attacks.

"David and his men went up and made raids against the Geshurites, the Girzites, and the Amalekites, for these were the inhabitants of the land from of old, as far as Shut, to the land of Egypt."
(1 Samuel 28:8)

✦✦✦✦✦✦✦✦✦✦

Achish was satisfied however with David, as David deceptively brought back the livestock and riches from their raids to share with the Philistines.

When Ashish asked David whom he and his army had raided, David lied, telling the king that they attacked Judahite, Jerahmeelite, and Kenite settlements in the area.

The king of Gath trusted David, thinking that he had become a true convert of the Philistines and was fighting their common enemies, including those of Judah.

Ashish completely trusted David, thinking that David had truly crossed-over to Team Philistine.

Thinking that David had cut his ties with Israel due to his raids on what used to be his beloved nation, Ashish commented about David saying,

"He has made himself an utter stench to his people Israel; therefore he shall always be my servant."
(1 Samuel 28; 12)

✦✦✦✦✦✦✦✦✦✦

Pearl: *David had weaved a very complicated tangle of lies, and was essentially living a life of duplicity. Consequently, his mind must have been a cluttered mess, with his conscious writhing in anguish. With one deception after another, David began believing his own lies.*

Not long before, he had been the trusted, obedient servant of the Lord, upholding His Word and fighting for God's glory. Now David has been reduced to a lying, deceptive man who was living the epitome of a life ruled by sin.

David had forgotten the promises of God, being that he was the anointed king of Israel. He had given into his fear of Saul, thinking that his problems were bigger than the one and

136

only Almighty God. The same God that had brought the Israelites through the Red Sea, the same God that had miraculously saved David multiple times before.

David had given into sin and turned his back on God. He had taken the easy-way-out and given into the "fleeting pleasure" of sin **(Hebrews 11)**.

Interestingly, during David's time of his disobedience to God he did not write or compose a single Psalm. The gift of creativity given by God to David as the 'best-ever worship director' was no longer burning inside of him.

God had extinguished David's creative flame.

David's duplicate life will therefore unravel before his eyes.

The lies continued, and David's life unraveled more and more. Living with the Philistines for over a year, David continued to deceive Ashish that he was loyal to the people of Philistia.

One day to David's dismay, he learned that King Ashish planned to go full-force against the Israelites in battle, who had encamped at Jezreel.

Preparing for war, Ashish gathered his forces at Aphek, which was about 30 miles north of Gath and requested that David and his men accompany him to aid in battle against the Israelites. The king desired to make David his personal bodyguard, as he respected his ability in warfare.

Ironically, the future king of Israel has now been asked to serve as the Philistine king's personal bodyguard as they fought against the Israelites. Having misgivings about his new role, David agreed and summoned his army of loyal men.

David was indeed living a duplicate life.

The Philistine commanders however did not approve of Ashish's assignment of David and became angry at their king's decision. Thinking that David would have loyalty to his fellow Israelites, the Philistine commanders did not trust David to fight along their side in battle against the Israelites.

Ashish's men did not trust David to fight with honor on 'Team Philistine'. They suspected that David would turn on them in the heat of battle against his own people, and told Achish,

"Send the man back, that he may return to the place to which you have assigned him.
He shall not go down with us to battle, lest in the battle he become an adversary to us.
For how could his fellow reconcile himself to his lord?
Would it not be with the heads of the men here?

Is not this David, of whom they sing to one another in dances,
Saul has struck down his thousands, and David his ten thousands?"
(1 Samuel 29:4-5)

✦✦✦✦✦✦✦✦✦✦✦

Pearl: *Apparently, Ashish's men knew David better than he knew himself! They knew that in the end, David would not be able to fight against Saul and his army and feared that he would turn on the Philistines. After all, David had killed many thousand Philistines in the past!*

✦✦✦✦✦✦✦✦✦✦

In compliance with his men, King Ashish dismissed David and his men with honor, as he trusted David fully.

✦✦✦✦✦✦✦✦✦✦

Pearl: *Consequently, due to Divine intervention David and his men did not participate with the Philistines in the battle against the Israelites. Instead, they headed back to their home and families in the town of Ziklag in Philistine. What they found upon returning to Ziklag was heartbreaking!*

✦✦✦✦✦✦✦✦✦✦

The next morning, the Philistine army went up to Jezreel to prepare for battle against the Israelites. Instead of heading out with them, David and his men set out for the three-day journey back home to Ziklag.

With mixed emotions, David and his army of men traveled home.

On one hand, David felt relieved that he was not faced with fighting his own Israelite countrymen, as he knew that would displease the Lord. Besides, David looked forward to seeing his wives and to the comforts of home.

On the other hand, David worried about the longevity of being able to continue living in Ziklag. How long could he continue to deceive the king with his lies of attacking the enemies of Philistia?

Settling into the long journey home, David looked around and saw the various emotions of relief and joy emanating from his army. Seeing the faces of his trusted men lit with smiles and hearing their laughter, David knew that they were looking forward to being united with their families.

Scene 2: Rising From the Ashes

1 Samuel 30

Playlist: "God of All My Days" by Casting Crowns, "The God Who Saves" by Matthew West, "Thankful for the Scars" by I Am They

The morning of the third day of travel, David and his men drew near to their hometown of Ziklag. They had encamped near Gath the previous night, and left well before daybreak in anticipation of the final-leg of the journey home.

Thinking they would soon be home with their families, the men began to sing and joke among themselves. The mood was lively and jubilant.

David however was not so jubilant.

Sensing something was wrong, David diligently watched for any signs of motion along the horizon, thinking that they were being stalked by an enemy. His senses heightened for any sign of danger, David was on high alert.

Picking up on the smell of smoldering wood, David's eyes scanned the horizon against the early morning sun. Suddenly, he visualized smoke as it drifted up from the land ahead.

Keying into the location of the smoke, with gripping fear David realized it originated from Ziklag, their home city!

Alerting his men, David and his army urged their donkeys to travel the terrain as fast as they could the rest of the miles home.

Coming up on the remains of the smoldering town, they surveyed the damage. Sadly, David and his men realized Ziklag had been burned-to-the-ground.

Scanning the fray, David frantically searched for signs of his wives and his men's families.

The silence was overwhelming as they realized that not a single soul was left in the town. Ziklag had become a ghost town.

David then realized that the Amalekites had burned Ziklag to the ground, and had taken captive all who had resided there.

"Now when David and his men came to Ziklag on the third day, the Amalekites had made a raid against the Negeb and against Ziklag. They had overcome Ziklag and burned it with fire and taken captive the women and all who were in it, both small and great.
They killed no one, but carried them off and went their way."
(1 Samuel 30:1-2)

The Amalekites had taken the wives and families of David's entire army captive.

✦✦✦✦✦✦✦✦✦✦

Pearl: *Taking advantage in knowing that the Philistia army had gone off to battle in the north, the Amalekites raided Ziklag and then burned it with fire. The Amalekites had also raided other cities in the surrounding area of the Negeb, south of Judah. Taking valuables, flocks, and herds of animals along with all those in the town of Ziklag hostage, the Amalekites absconded into the wilderness.*

✦✦✦✦✦✦✦✦✦✦

David and his men were devasted, and wept aloud until all of their strength was gone.

Thinking that their families were taken captive and possibly even killed by the Amalekites, the strong men of David's army were beyond consoling. The men were exhausted and without hope, thinking that they would never again see their wives and children.

David's loyal men, bitter with sorrow, even talked of stoning David as they put the blame on him for the loss of their loved ones.

✦✦✦✦✦✦✦✦✦✦

Pearl: *David turns back to God.*

The burning of Ziklag turned out to be a major turning point for David. As a result of experiencing this horrendous event, the pendulum of David's faith oscillated to re-align with God. Putting his trust in the Lord once again, David asked for direction. Receiving the word from God, David gained the courage needed to pursue the raiders.

"And David was greatly distressed, for the people spoke of stoning him, because all the people were bitter in soul, each for his sons and daughters.

141

But David strengthened himself in the LORD his God.
(1 Samuel 30:6)

David asked Abiathar, the priest, to bring him the ephod.

David then asked the Lord two questions,

"Shall I pursue after this band? Shall I overtake them?"

The LORD answered him saying,
"Pursue, for you shall surely overtake and shall surely rescue."
(1 Samuel 30:7-8)

✦✦✦✦✦✦✦✦✦✦✦

Pearl: *What is an ephod, and what function did it serve in ancient Jewish culture?*

An ephod is an ornate, sleeveless linen garment worn by a Jewish priest. In the Midrash, the Rabbis comment that David, in his state of emergency, made his two inquiries of the Urim and Thummim and received a reply from the Lord to both. The Urim and Thummim are elements of the Hoshen, which is the breastplate worn by the High Priest attached to the ephod. In the Hebrew bible, the Urim and Thummim symbolize knowledge, and are used to communicate with the Lord.

✦✦✦✦✦✦✦✦✦✦✦

After the answer given by the Lord, David and his army of six hundred men set out to rescue their families.

They went as far as the brook Besor, where two hundred men stayed, as they were too exhausted to cross the brook. These men did not return home, but encamped at the brook, which was about 12 miles southwest of Ziklag. Guarding the luggage and therefore lightening the load of those who were fit to proceed in battle, these two hundred soldiers stayed behind. These men waited earnestly for the four hundred to return from the pursuit of the captors of their families.

Before David and his four hundred men had gone any great distance from the camp, some men from those who remained behind at the brook found an Egyptian man wandering in the area.

Bringing him to David, the men hoped the Egyptian could provide some information concerning the whereabouts of the band of raiders who had kidnapped their families.

The young Egyptian man was near collapse from lack of food and water, but after being fed by David and his men, he was revived and cooperative.

David then questioned the man, asking him from what nation he came from. The man explained that he was a young Egyptian who was the slave of an Amalekite man. He went on to tell David that the Amalekites had raided several tribes in the southern desert plain, and had burned the city of Ziklag to the ground, taking hostage all those who were in the city.

With this information the young Egyptian supplied, David was hopeful that he could find the whereabouts of the Amalekite band of raiders.

Striking a deal with the Egyptian, David negotiated with the man to take him to the Amalekite hideout in the wilderness. In exchange, David promised to keep the informant safe and out of hands of his Amalekite master.

Proceeding with the young Egyptian slave as their guide, David and his army of four hundred men set out through the desert plain.

Not having to travel far, they came upon a hilltop where they could scan the valley below.

Looking out across the wilderness from their vantage point, David saw the Amalekite band in the valley below celebrating their victory.

"And when he had taken him down, behold, they were spread abroad over all the land, eating and drinking and dancing, because of all the great spoil they had taken from the land of the Philistines and from the land of Judah."
(1 Samuel 30:16)

David and his army had successfully found the band of Amalekites who held their families' hostage!

Now they must make their move against the enemy.

Knowing that the Amalekites were celebrating with music, food, and drink, David calculated that the time was perfect for him and his men to move to attack.

The Amalekites would be unsuspecting of any danger, as they were too preoccupied with their celebration. The music was loud and the wine was flowing, so they were most likely drunk and off their guard.

"And David struck them down from twilight until the evening of the next day, and not a man of them escaped, except four hundred young men, who mounted camels and fled.

David recovered all that the Amalekites had taken, and David rescued his two wives. Nothing was missing, whether small or great, sons or daughters, spoil or anything that had been taken.
David brought back all."
(1 Samuel 30:17-19)

◆◆◆◆◆◆◆◆◆◆◆

P earl: *The Hebrew Bible is translated to read a slightly different version of 1 Samuel 30:17*

◆◆◆◆◆◆◆◆◆◆◆

Of interest is the Masoretic text of the Hebrew Bible (translated to English text) reads:

"And David smote them from evening until evening to their morrow and no man of them escaped except four hundred young men who rode on camels, and fled."
(1 Samuel 29:17; Hebrew Bible – New English Translation)

The Talmudic and Midrashic explanation of 'from evening until evening to their morrow' in the Hebrew Bible is significant and of deeper meaning than 'from twilight until the evening of the next day' as is read in the ESV version.

The Rabbis explain that in the phrase 'their morrow,' the word 'their' refers to the Amalekites, and insinuates that they were capable of winning against David only with a sneak attack, being powerless when an extended battle ensued.

What leads to this interpretation?

The Rabbis comment on the phrase 'evening until evening to their morrow' homiletically, and point out that the Amalekites were 'victorious today', meaning in this world, but 'tomorrow' (their morrow) refers to their future in the Messianic era, where they are destined to meet their downfall.

Parallels to the New Testament ~ *Taking this concept further, one can see the parallels with the proposed battle of Armageddon, or global combat zone, where the final conflict between Jesus Christ, the Messiah, and Satan occurs in the Revelation given to Apostle John **(Revelation 16:16, 19:17-21, and 20:7-10).***

Similarities can be drawn between the Amalekites and Satan and his evil crew, who were both victorious in this world, but not in their morrow in the Messianic era, where they will perish and be destroyed by God.

From their victory over the Amalekites, David and his soldiers recovered stolen goods from several raids of the Amalekites on many cities in the desert plains of Judah. Additionally, they re-captured all of the livestock that the Amalekites had stolen. The spoil of war recovered from the victory over the Amalekites was very lucrative.

> *"David also captured all the flocks and herds,*
> *and the people drove the livestock before him, and said,*
> *This is David's spoil."*
> *(1 Samuel 30:20)*

David and his four hundred men then headed back to join the two hundred men who had stayed behind at the brook.

Seeing David and his army approach from a distance, the two hundred soldiers ran towards them with joy. Seeing his men, David welcomed them with open-arms.

In contrast to David, some of the soldiers who had accompanied David into battle against the Amalekites were not so welcoming of their fellow soldiers who had stayed behind.

Some of the men who had gone into combat, in their greediness and disobedience to David, wanted to penalize those who had stayed behind by not sharing the spoils they had recovered from the Amalekite band of raiders.

Addressing the disobedient soldiers with discretion and humility, rather than anger and rebuke, David explained that their victory was the Lord's doing, not theirs. David explained that the soldiers should therefore share the wealth recovered equally among them.

David said,

> *"You shall not do so, my brothers, with what the LORD has given us. He has*
> *preserved us and given into our hand the band that came against us.*
> *Who would listen to you in this matter?*

For as his share is who goes down into the battle, so shall his share be who stays by the baggage.
They shall share alike."
(1 Samuel 30:23-24)

♦♦♦♦♦♦♦♦♦♦♦

Pearl: David acknowledged that God was responsible for winning the battle against the Amalekites. The victory did not belong to David, nor to his army.

The Midrashic Rabbis point out that David realized that the Lord delivered the enemy, and that the Lord gave the enemy to all of them, not only to the combatants. No casualties were suffered and the women and children were returned safe and sound, all being accomplished by the Lord's power, not by the power of David and his men.

David recognized that God waged the battle on behalf of those who put their faith and trust in the Him.

The Rabbis go on to say that in dividing the riches between all of the soldiers equally, David was following the Torah, as this precedent had been set in **Genesis 14:24** and **Numbers 31:27**.

Unfortunately, over time this ruling in the Torah had been forgotten, and David therefore renewed the law following the ancient precedent set by God through Abraham and Moses.

By renewing the Mosaic Law, David is honored by having the ruling accredited to his name.

"And he made it a statute and a rule for Israel from that day forward to this day."
(1 Samuel 29:25)

David also gifted his friends and elders of Judah with part of the spoil, repaying those in all the places where David and his men had roamed over the last several years. In doing so, David demonstrated that he would soon reign as a just, righteous king.

♦♦♦♦♦♦♦♦♦♦♦

After reuniting with the soldiers who stayed behind at the brook of Besor, David and his entire army, along with their wives and families encamped for the night. Together again, the people joyously celebrated their victory, sharing a meal and singing songs of praise to the Lord.

As they sat around the campfire that night, David's heart was filled with exultation as he watched his loyal men reunited with their wives and children.

The last few days had been fraught with emotional ups and downs, and David now took the time to remember some poignant moments. As he sat around the campfire eating a meal and celebrating with his men and their families, David's mind drifted back to the past few hours.

One incident in particular stood out in David's mind.

Recalling how he had seen one of his mighty-men, Eliam, step-in to rescue his wife and young daughter during the heat of battle, David's heart throbbed with pride and joy for his people.

Thinking back to the warfare during the raid on the Amalekites, David recalled seeing a brave, young girl clutching her mother's hand during the fray and commotion. The girl was faithfully waiting and watching for her father to come forth from the hundreds of soldiers to rescue her and her mother from their plight.

The child was beautiful! Not more than five or six years old, her eyes were deep mahogany-brown, taking in every detail. Her stance was one of courage, as she bravely waited with faith in the Lord for her rescue.

David now knew who the brave, young girl was – she was Eliam's daughter, and her name was Bathsheba. Admiring her faith in God, David etched the scene of this brave little girl standing firm in the name of the Lord into his memory.

Remembering the scene in vivid detail, David thought back as one of his most trusted men, Eliam approached the woman and child. Observing his strong, mighty-man who was one of his most-trusted 'Thirty' warriors *(2 Samuel 23:34)*, David watched the fierce warrior Eliam lovingly scoop his child up into his arms. David's heart filled with joy as he saw Eliam embrace his wife and child with thanksgiving for the Lord in his heart.

Unbeknownst to David at this time, the young girl, Bathsheba, will come to hold a very unique and special place in his life.

♦♦♦♦♦♦♦♦♦♦♦

Pearl: *David has once again become a person of faith, not fear. God has molded David into the person he was meant to be through overcoming obstacles that had been placed in his life.*

After the raid on Ziklag and being assured of the safety of the wives and families of his soldiers, David wrote a Psalm of Thanksgiving to the Lord. We don't know for sure which Psalm that might have been, but **Psalm 4** is likely.

"Answer me when I call, O God of my righteousness! You have given me relief when I was in distress. Be gracious to me and hear my prayer!

You have put more joy in my heart that they have when their grain and wine abound.
In peace I will both lie down and sleep;
For you alone, O LORD, make me dwell in safety."
(Psalm 4:1,7,8)

Interestingly, God seems to place unwanted circumstances into the lives of people who He most wants to develop for His glory.

David is a perfect example of this, as God took the time to mold David into the great king that He had destined David to be.

However, this molding of David took time.

Time, which was on God's time-line, not David's.

Time has indeed gone by for David, much of which has been full of hardship. Fighting for his life and fleeing from Saul for over six years has not been an easy road for David to negotiate.

David must hold tight to God's promises, as seven years after being the young shepherd-boy who was anointed as the next King of Israel, he has not yet taken the throne.

During the past six years plus, while David has been on the run from Saul, God has been grooming David to ascend to being the King of Israel.

Not just any king, but the King that the Lord has destined David to become.

Meanwhile, Saul entered the scene once again.

Act 5: Finally...the Throne

Ca.1011 B.C.

Introduction: *Unlike David, Saul is turning further and further from God. He is frustrated, as God is not communicating with him, neither directly nor through prophets. Samuel the prophet has since died, but Saul wants desperately to communicate with Samuel's spirit, as he thinks that he can benefit from Samuel's guidance on tactics of war against the Philistines.*

War between the Israelites and the Philistines was imminent, and Saul desperately feared defeat.

Scene 1: Desperately Seeking Samuel
1 Samuel 28

Saul had gathered his army to fight battle against the Philistines. The Israelite soldiers encamped at Gilboa, and the Philistines were already at Shunem, north of the Jezreel Valley from Mount Gilboa.

Seeing the army of Philistines who were prepared to fight, Saul trembled with fear. Filled with doubt, Saul became indecisive of how to proceed.

Complaining that the Lord had not answered him after he asked for direction, Saul became desperate. As a result, he despairingly consulted a medium that claimed she could conjure Samuel up from the dead.

"When Saul saw the army of the Philistines, he was afraid, and his heart trembled greatly. And when Saul inquired of the LORD, the LORD did not answer him, either by dreams, or by Urim, or by prophets.
Then Saul said to his servants, Seek out for me a woman who is a medium, that I may go to her and inquire of her.
And his servants said to him, Behold, there is a medium at En-dor."
(1 Samuel 28:5-7)

Pearl: The Hebrew Masoretic text is slightly different, and is translated to read,

"And Saul said to his servants, seek for me a necromanceress, and I shall go to her, and inquire of her."
(1 Samuel 28:7)

♦♦♦♦♦♦♦♦♦♦♦

Pearl: What is a necromancer (female: necromanceress)?

According to the Midrash, a necromancer (necromanceress) was one who by magic powers was able to conjure a corpse from the grave into their armpit, where it would speak to them in a low voice.

The Rabbinic scholars of the Midrash state that the Mishnah (oral tradition of the Jewish law and first part of the Talmud) points out that the Torah forbade this type of 'divining'.

God forbade the Rabbis comment in the Midrash that after the death of Samuel, prophecy was scarce and many people resorted to the practice of consulting a necromancer for advice, in spite of knowing it.

The Hebrew Bible said that Saul knew that the Lord forbade contact with the dead, and that he had put the necromancers out of the land **(1 Samuel 28:3).**

However, Saul had fallen into disfavor with the Lord and was not answered when he asked God for direction. In his distress, Saul contacted a necromanceress and instructed her to conjure up the dead prophet, Samuel, so Saul could seek his advice concerning the war with the Philistines.

Once again, Saul was disobedient to the Lord when he contacts a necromanceress, in spite of knowing that it was forbidden.

The sin of necromancy turned out to be the final blow to Saul.

God will not protect Saul against the Philistines in the day to come. Nor will He protect the Israelite people against the enemy.

God will allow the necromanceress to conjure the prophet Samuel from the dead.

However, to Saul's extreme disappointment, Samuel provided no answers, only dismal news.

The Lord allowed the necromanceress to summon Samuel from the dead, and acting as if he was startled and not appreciative of being woken from his sleep, Samuel said,

> *"Why have you disturbed me by bringing me up?"*
> *(1 Samuel 28:15)*

✦✦✦✦✦✦✦✦✦✦

Pearl: *The ancient Rabbis exegeted from this verse that Samuel was startled and not pleased, as he perceived it was as if he was being risen from the dead for the Judgement Day in front of God, the Almighty.*

✦✦✦✦✦✦✦✦✦✦

When Samuel found out why he had been disturbed from his sleep, he went on to inform Saul that the Philistines will be victorious against the Israelite army.

Furthermore, Samuel informed Saul that he and his sons would die tomorrow on the battlefield, and would join him in the realm of the dead.

Samuel told Saul,

> *"The LORD will give Israel also with you into the hand of the Philistines, and tomorrow you and your sons shall be with me.*
> *The LORD will give the army of Israel also into the hand of the Philistines."*
> *(1 Samuel 28: 19)*

Falling to the ground as if paralyzed, Saul was consumed with fear after hearing the words of Samuel.

Unable to rest, Saul had a fitful night with no sleep, which ended the next day with disaster for him and his sons

Scene 2: The Death of Saul and Jonathan

1 Samuel 31
Ca. 1011 B.C.

Playlist: "Burn the Ships" by King and Country, "Strength Will Rise" by Lincoln Brewster

Introduction: As the prophet Samuel had warned Saul, the Philistines fought against Israel and overtook the Israelites on Mount Gilboa (Hebrew: Har HaGilboa).

In the beginning of the grisly battle against the Philistines, Jonathan and his two brothers were slain.

The fighting pressed on, and Philistine archers pursued Saul up the slopes of Mount Gilboa, badly injuring him with their arrows.

Near death and unable to fight back, Saul expected that he would be captured and tortured to avenge all the Philistines he had slain in battle. Saul knew that he could not escape and that his death was certain.

Aware of his dismal outcome, Saul took his own sword and fell upon it, taking his own life.

"Therefore Saul took his own sword and fell upon it."
(1 Samuel 31:4)

Saul and his three sons, Jonathan, Abinadab and Malchishua all died that same day during the battle on Mount Gilboa.

Sadly, the Philistines returned to the scene of battle the next day, cut off Saul's head and stripped his body of his armor. Putting Saul's armor in the house of Ashtaroth, the Philistine God of Sheep, they then nailed Saul's body on the wall of Beth-shean to mock all of Israel.

Pearl: *A slightly different account is given in **1 Chronicles,** stating that the Philistines put Saul's armor in the temple of the gods and impaled his skull in the house of the Philistine god, Dagon **(1 Chronicles 10:10).***

The inhabitants of Jabesh-gilead, a city that Saul had once saved from a Philistine take-over, took the bodies of Saul and his sons and buried them under the oak tree in Jabesh *(1 Chronicles 10:11, 1 Samuel 31:8-13).*

David later reburied their bones in the land of Benjamin in Zela in the tomb of Kish, Saul's father *(2 Samuel 21:14).*

Pearl: Jonathan, Saul's son, had a son who was crippled in both feet. The boy was injured when he was five years old.

The story of Jonathan's son's injury was that when the news about Saul and Jonathan came from Jezreel concerning the battle on Mount Gilboa, the Israelite people became terrified and fled their towns as they feared the Philistines.

Upon hearing the horrific news about the deaths of Saul and his sons, Jonathan son's nurse picked the boy up to flee. As she hurried to leave while carrying the five-year-old, she tripped and she and the boy both fell to the ground. The fall was very severe and the boy became disabled in both his feet. The boy's name was Mephibosheth *(2 Samuel 4:4).*

We will pick up Mephibosheth's story later after David takes the throne.

David lamented over the death of Saul and Jonathan. He wrote a lamentation, which was taught to the people of Judah. David's lamentation is written in the Book of Jashar, as well as in *2 Samuel 1:19-27.*

From David's heartbreaking words one can tell his anguish in the loss of Saul and his son, Jonathan, who was his dear friend.

David's Lament
"A gazelle lies slain on your heights, Israel.
How the mighty have fallen!
Tell it not in Gath, proclaim it not in the streets of Ashkelon, lest the daughters of the daughters of the uncircumcised rejoice.
Mountains of Gilboa, may you have neither dew nor rain, may no showers fall on your terraced fields.
For there the shield of the mighty was despised, the shield of Saul – no longer rubbed with oil.
From the bold of the slain, from the flesh of the mighty, the bow of Jonathan did not turn back, the sword of Saul did not return unsatisfied.
Saul and Jonathan – in life they were loved and admired, and in death they were not parted.

They were swifter than eagles, they were stronger than lions.
Daughters of Israel, weep for Saul, who clothed you in scarlet and finery, who
adorned your garments with ornaments of gold.
How the mighty have fallen in battle!
Jonathan lies slain on your heights. I grieve for you, Jonathan my brother; you were
very dear to me.
Your love for me was wonderful, more wonderful than that of women,
How the mighty have fallen!
The weapons of war have perished!"

Pearl: David's lamentation is included in the Book of Jashar. What is the Book of Jashar?

*The Book of Jashar is a Jewish, non-biblical written source which also included **Joshua 10:12-13** and Solomon's poem in **1 Kings 8:12-13**.*

Jashar is related to the Hebrew words, 'sing' or 'upright'. The book appears to have contained poetic accounts and songs of the deeds of heroes.

Saul had suffered a deficiency of his spiritual condition, and failed to serve the Lord with his whole heart. Therefore, the Lord put Saul to death and turned the kingdom over to David, the son of Jesse *(1 Chronicles 10:13-14)*

Scene 3: The Anointed One Takes the Throne

2 Samuel 2-6
Ca. 1011 BC

Introduction: *After fleeing Saul for the last seven years, David's plight finally ended with Saul's death. With mixed emotions of sorrow over Saul and Jonathan's death, but also with relief that he no longer must flee for his life, David knows that finally the responsibility of the kingship will be his.*

Unsure of what the future held for him, David turned to God and inquired of the Lord about what he was to do next.

In response to David's inquiry, the Lord sent David to Hebron in Judah to continue to mature before becoming King of Israel.

In Hebron, David will be anointed as King of Judah, but his kingship over all of Israel is still another seven-plus years away.

Of significance is that David's faith had matured and he turned to the Lord for guidance. Seeking direction from the Lord was one of many traits, which made David a great leader for God's people.

When David moved to Hebron he was thirty years old.

Sent to Hebron to mature, God recognized it would not be in David's, or the people of Israel's best interest for him to immediately take over as King of the entire nation of Israel.

David needed time to adjust to governing as king. After all, he had just spent the last several years running from Saul, fighting battles and leading an army of soldiers throughout the wilderness. David has developed leadership and combative skills, but the traits needed for a great king must still be developed.

God will hone these important skills that David is still lacking. For His Glory, God will cultivate these skills in David, his obedient servant.

Importantly, time was also needed for the nation of Israel to recover after the end of Saul's leadership.

Recovering from civil conflict, the Israelite people were still reeling from unrest that was rampant in the land. Under the poor leadership of Saul in the past years, there was divergence and turmoil among the people of Israel, which would not immediately end after Saul's death.

While Saul had been king he had significant influence over the northern tribes of Israel, but because of his obsession to kill David, he had never attempted to conquer Jerusalem in Judah.

A Jebusite tribe occupied the city of Jerusalem; therefore the Israelites never had gained control of Jerusalem (2 Samuel 5:6-15).

One of David's first and most significant moves, as king will be the conquest of Jerusalem.

Conquest of Jerusalem will be a tremendous feat for the Israelites, and the victory will be David's, under the guidance of the Lord.

In contradistinction to Saul, David will make God the primary focus of his kingship.

To Jerusalem, which will become known as the City of David, David will return the sacred ark of God, and make plans to build a permanent temple, both of which symbolize the presence of the Lord.

For all of his faith and efforts, God will assure David that his descendants will be blessed, as God will proclaim to David what is known as the 'Davidic Covenant.'

With Saul no longer pursuing David, and all of their homes in Ziklag burned to the ground, David prayed to the Lord asking His Divine guidance of where he should go from here.

David longed to return to the Holy Land. Thinking that it was most likely safe for him to return, now that Saul was no longer alive, David still was reluctant to proceed without Divine sanction.

Wanting to return to his homeland and provide a permanent home for all of his faithful army of men and their families, David inquired of the Lord,

"Shall I go up into any of the cities of Judah?"
(2 Samuel 1:1)

The Lord answered David by saying *"Go up"*, and when David asked where to go, the Lord told him to go *"to Hebron" (2 Samuel 1:1)*.

◆◆◆◆◆◆◆◆◆◆◆

Pearl: *David showed great humility to not immediately occupy the throne; even though he knew he was destined to reign after Saul's death. Even though God anointed him, David knew that he still needed to gain the support of his own tribe of Judah before venturing further.*

Being from the lineage of Judah, David also understood the deeper meaning of Jacob's blessing on his son Judah.

"Judah is a lion's cub; from the prey, my son, you have gone up. He stooped down;
he crouched as a lion and as a lioness; who dares rouse him?
The scepter shall not depart from Judah, nor the ruler's staff from between his feet,
until tribute comes to him, and to him shall be the obedience of the peoples."
(Genesis 49:9-10)

David was well aware that Jacob meant that the kingdom coming from Judah's lineage would have a small beginning, similar to a lion's cub, then grow and mature into the full stature of a ferocious, full-grown lion.

Accordingly, David was prepared to grow his kingdom by starting small like a lion's cub. Recognizing that he needed the support of his own tribesmen of Judah, David began the growth of his kingdom by gaining their confidence. The move to Hebron would prove to be very strategic, and of good judgement.

✦✦✦✦✦✦✦✦✦✦✦

At the Lord's direction, David brought his two wives, Ahinoam of Jezreel and Abigail, the widow of Nabal of Carmel, and all of his loyal army of men and their families from Ziklag to Hebron.

> **"And David brought up his men who were with him, everyone with his household, and they lived in the towns of Hebron. "**
> **(2 Samuel 2:2)**

It was in Hebron where David was anointed King over the tribe of Judah by the men of Judah **(2 Samuel 2:1-4).**

> **"And the men of Judah came, and there they anointed David king over the house of Judah."**
> **(2 Samuel 2:4)**

✦✦✦✦✦✦✦✦✦✦✦

P*earl: Even though God had anointed David, the tribe of Judah's anointment symbolized his acceptance by the citizens of Judah. Dual acceptance of both God and the people was necessary according to Jewish law for David to become king.*

David began his rule over Judah, symbolizing that the kingdom of Judah was separate from the kingdom of Israel.

The kingdom of Judah was under the rule of the house of David, but other tribes in Israel accepted Ish-bosheth, the last living son of Saul, as their ruler.

Ish-bosheth therefore reigned over all of Israel, while David reigned over the tribe of Judah in Hebron.

David had more influence over the southern tribes of Israel, and therefore had the support of all of the people in Judah.

In Hebron David grew in his maturity and was groomed by the Lord to eventually take over kingship of all Israel. David was king in Hebron over Judah for seven years and six months.

◆◆◆◆◆◆◆◆◆◆◆

In Hebron David took four more wives, and eventually had six sons from his six different wives.

David's firstborn was Amnon, the son of Ahinoam; his second was Chileab, the son of Abigail. The third son was Absalom, the son of Maakah. The fourth was Adonijah, the son of Haggith. The fifth son was Shephatiah, the son of Abital. The sixth was Ithream, the son of Eglah *(2 Samuel 3:2-5; 1 Chronicles 3:1-4).*

"Six were born to him in Hebron, and he reigned there seven years and six months, and thirty-three years he reigned in Jerusalem."
(1 Chronicles 3:4)

◆◆◆◆◆◆◆◆◆◆◆

Pearl: **David's greatest sin**
        The fact that David took six wives gives us insight into what will become David's greatest sin. David, against the will of God, was a polygamist who could not control his sexual appetite. Eventually, this sin led him further down an even greater path of sin.

◆◆◆◆◆◆◆◆◆◆◆

After Saul's death, Saul's only surviving son, Ish-bosheth, stepped-in as the King of Israel, ruling from Mahanaim, which was northeast of Hebron by about fifty miles and across the Jordan River.

For the next seven-and-a-half years there was a long war between the house of Saul, with Ish-bosheth at the head, and the house of David.

However, over time David's influence grew stronger with the people, while the house of Saul weakened *(2 Samuel 3:1).*

With the assassination of Saul's son, Ish-bosheth, the house of Saul finally fell.

Soon after the death of Saul's last surviving son, all of the tribes of Israel came to David in Hebron and acknowledged that he should be King of all of Israel. The people of Israel knew that David was a proven military leader, and that the Lord had intended for him to be king *(2 Samuel 5:1-5).*

✦✦✦✦✦✦✦✦✦✦✦

P*earl: The people now stood with David, and he was anointed King of Israel (2 Samuel 5:1-3, 1 Chronicles 11:1-3, Ca. 1005 B.C.)*

"So all the elders of Israel came to the king at Hebron, and King David made a covenant with them at Hebron before the LORD, and they anointed David king over Israel."
(2 Samuel 5:3)

✦✦✦✦✦✦✦✦✦✦✦

Finally, after approximately fourteen years from first being anointed as the future king of Israel by Samuel under God's direction, David became King of the entire nation of Israel and Judah. David's years of power struggles with Saul and his one remaining son, had finally come to an end.

✦✦✦✦✦✦✦✦✦✦✦

P*earl: Multiples of seven ~ Interestingly we come upon a recurring theme of the importance of numbers in the Bible. As seven is considered by the ancient Hebrew culture to be the number of completeness, this number is significant in David's epic rise to his kingship.*

Fourteen years, a multiple of seven, was the amount of time that God honed and trained David to become the King of Israel. Signifying completeness, this number is significant in light of Hebraic culture.

The number seven will continue to be prominent in the Hebrew Bible as well as in the New Testament. Especially significant in the Revelation given to John by Jesus Christ, the number seven is part of a central theme woven throughout the unfolding of events.

"David was thirty years old when he became king, and he reigned forty years. In Hebron he reigned over Judah seven years and six months, and in Jerusalem he reigned over all Israel and Judah thirty-three years."
(2 Samuel 5:4-5)

David accomplished many things during his reign over all Israel and Judah, which covered a cumulative time span of forty and a-half years.

Under King David's reign Israel's borders were significantly expanded. The nation of Israel grew from approximately 6000 to 60,000 square miles, and became a powerful monarchy with major trade-ways.

Importantly, under David's reign, the people of Israel became prosperous and unified as a nation.

David's first action as King of Israel was to conquer Jerusalem. His aim was to move the capital of the nation of Israel from Hebron to Jerusalem.

At the border of Judah and Benjamin, Jerusalem had previously not been controlled by any Israelite tribe and therefore was both symbolically and geographically well suited to be the capital of all Israel.

♦♦♦♦♦♦♦♦♦♦♦

earl: Jerusalem was called the stronghold of Zion, and was held by the Jebusites. The Jebusites were Canaanites, and were considered to be among the Amorites. Being not only a pagan society, the Amorites were known for extreme, evil practices such as child sacrifice. The city they had constructed, and their fierce armies were considered too strong to have been conquered at the time of Joshua (Joshua 10:5; 15:63, Judges 1:21). Remaining as a pocket of 'incomplete conquest' by the Israelites, the Jebusites had therefore persisted to exist in Judah.

Defensive walls, steep hills and valleys surrounded the stronghold of Zion, so it had been impenetrable throughout the ages. Zion was located on the western slope of the Kidron Valley on a hill known as Ophel, above the spring of Gihon, which provided an excellent source of water. To utilize the water source of the spring of Gihon, an extensive network of tunnels had been excavated leading from the spring into the city.

*Jerusalem as a city was first mentioned in **Genesis 14:18** where Melchizedek, priest of 'God Most High,' and king of Salem brought out bread and wine and blessed Abram. His blessing attributed Abram's victory of his rescue of Lot to the power of God.*

*'Salem' was an abbreviated version of 'Jerusalem' and is related to **shalom,** the Hebrew word for peace (**Hebrews 7:2, Psalm 76:2**).*

With the mention of Melchizedek, the priest-king of Salem, there appears to be an expectation and standard set in scripture for later kings of Jerusalem to resemble him, as he was both a priest and a king *(Psalm 110:4)*.

✦✦✦✦✦✦✦✦✦✦

Psalm 110, "Sit at My Right Hand" (A Psalm composed by David) is a Royal Psalm. It's theme deals with the role of the House of David in the life of God's people. Importantly, it looks forward to the Messiah, who is the final king.

Excerpts from Psalm 110: verses 1,2, and 4 (A Psalm of David)

"The LORD says to my Lord, sit at my right hand, until I make your enemies your footstool.

The LORD sends forth from Zion your mighty scepter, rule in the midst of your enemies!"

"The LORD has sworn and will not change his mind, you are a priest forever after the order of Melchizedek."

This Psalm is often cited in the New Testament, where authors integrate the idea that the risen Lord Jesus is the reigning Messianic king seated at "God's right hand."

The prophet Zechariah foresaw a merger of the two offices of priest and king (as was Melchizedek) in the person of the Messiah, or "The Branch" *(Zechariah 6:9-14)*.

Zechariah reiterates Jeremiah's promise *(Jeremiah 33:15)* of a coming king who will flourish, branch out and build the temple of the Lord, reflecting the authority and legitimacy of the King's rule.

The book of **Hebrews** presents Jesus Christ, from the royal line of David as belonging to the order of Melchizedek, and therefore is superior to the Levitical priests. "God Most High" in Hebrew is 'El 'Elyon, as 'El' is the common Jewish term for God *(Hebrews 5:5-10, 6:20-7:17)*.

The author of Hebrews cited **Psalm 110:1**, using this verse to explain to Jewish-Christians why Jesus, the now-reigning heir of David is also the ultimate priest.

Scene 4: The City of David ~ A Symbol of Hope

Pre-reading: 2 Samuel 5, 1 Chronicles 11
Ca. 1005 B.C

Playlist: "I Raise A Hallelujah" by Bethel Music

Introduction: As one of David's first conquests as King of Israel, he overcame the impenetrable city of Jerusalem. With the strategic move of utilizing the extensive water tunnels excavated to capture the water supply of the spring of Gihon, David sent his men up a water shaft to capture the city.

◆◆◆◆◆◆◆◆◆◆◆

Pearl: *This water shaft is identified as "Warren's Shaft", which is directly over the water channel near the Gihon spring. Victorious, David renamed the Stronghold of Zion, also previously known as Jerusalem, the "City of David".*

"And David lived in the stronghold and called it the city of David.
And David built the city all around from the Millo inward.
And David became greater and greater, for the LORD, the God of hosts, was with him."
(2 Samuel 5:9-10)

◆◆◆◆◆◆◆◆◆◆◆

Pearl: **What is the Millo?**
The millo is a Hebrew word for "the fill."

Built on a steep slope, Jerusalem was constructed with a series of terrace walls supporting the fill behind it in order to create level areas. Houses were built on these artificial platforms that were connected by narrow staircases.

These terrace walls required regular maintenance in order to ensure that they would provide support of the fill during heavy rainfall.

It was one of the king's duties to oversee that maintenance was done on the walls to keep the people and the houses of the city safe.

◆◆◆◆◆◆◆◆◆◆◆

162

Pearl: History of Jerusalem and takeover by King David

About 1000 years before, Jerusalem was called Salem with its king being Melchizedek *(Genesis 14:18).* Salem was taken over by the Jebusites around 1850 B.C., who built a wall with massive towers around the city, making it impenetrable by invaders. The Jebusites called their city Jebus *(1 Chronicles 11:4).*

The Jebusites were so confident of their fortification that they taunted King David, saying that even the lame and the blind would prevent him from capturing their city *(2 Samuel 5:6).*

At David's direction, Joab (David's commander-in-chief) secretly entered the city through the water system and opened the gates for David and his army to enter and take control *(1 Chronicles 11:6).* The Jebusite citadel was then destroyed and replaced by the stronghold of Zion, also known as the city of David *(2 Samuel 5:7).*

Later on, David would build an altar to God on the threshing floor of Araunah the Jebusite, which stopped a plague sent by God upon Israel from reaching Jerusalem *(2 Samuel 24:18-25).*

Araunah's threshing floor was located on the top of Mount Moriah, which according to Jewish tradition is the same place where Abraham built an altar to sacrifice his son Isaac *(Genesis 22:2, 2 Chronicles 3:1).*

King Solomon, David's son, built the Most Holy Place of the temple on the top of Mount Moriah, called the Rock *(2 Chronicles 3:1).*

✦✦✦✦✦✦✦✦✦✦

After the conquest of Jerusalem, David's next move would be to move the capital of Israel to this strategically located city.

The move of the capital of Israel from Hebron to Jerusalem was a tactical one on David's part. Hebron had been the seat of power for the southern tribes, but with the conquering of Jerusalem and making it the capital, this served to unify the entire kingdom of Israel.

✦✦✦✦✦✦✦✦✦✦

Pearl: Jerusalem, also known as the City of David, became a symbol of hope to the Israelites for a reunified kingdom of Israel.

David moved his family and all of his loyal following of men and their families from Hebron to Jerusalem.

Moving to Jerusalem to reign as King Of Israel, David needed a house for all of his family and servants. David needed a palace fit for a king!

Realizing David's need, the King of Tyre, Hiram, sent cedar trees, carpenters and masons, who built David a grand palace of Phoenician style. The men Tyre sent to Jerusalem also constructed well-structured walls surrounding the city *(2 Samuel 5:11)*.

◆◆◆◆◆◆◆◆◆◆◆

*P**earl**: According to the ancient Rabbis, Hiram, the King of Tyre, was of Phoenician origin whose people had long-standing political and economic ties with the Israelites. Tyre was a trading empire, and it was in the king's interest to keep the inland trade routes through Israel to Egypt open to merchants. The cedars of Lebanon were famous throughout the Near East and in great demand, so it was therefore a strategic move on the part of Hiram to have a good relationship with King David of Israel.*

◆◆◆◆◆◆◆◆◆◆◆

Filling his palace with family, David took more concubines and wives, and over the years of his rule produced many sons and daughters *(2 Samuel 5:13-14)*.

"And these are the names of those who were born to him in Jerusalem: Shammua, Shobab, Nathan, Solomon, Ibhar, Elishua, Nepeg, Japhia, Elishama, Eliada, and Eliphelet."
(2 Samuel 5: 14-16)

◆◆◆◆◆◆◆◆◆◆◆

*P**earl**: The ancient Rabbis held a Midrashic tradition that David took eighteen wives, the maximum number allowed under the commandment placing a prohibition on the Israelite monarch from taking an excess of women (Deuteronomy 17:17).*

◆◆◆◆◆◆◆◆◆◆◆

According to Halachic opinion, this number does not apply to include concubines, only wives. The definition of a concubine is a woman taken without betrothal (formal engagement), or a 'kethuba' (Jewish marriage contract).

Two of these sons who were born in Jerusalem are significant in Christian history, as they are in the ancestry lineage of Jesus Christ. These two unique sons were Nathan *(Luke 3:23-38)* and Solomon *(Matthew 1:6-7).*

The Gospels of Luke and Matthew differ on which son actually was Jesus' ancestor, but both Gospels agree that David was an ancestor of Jesus, which was passed on through either Nathan or Solomon.

Importantly, during David's reign as king, his main goal was to restore the presence of God to Israel. Jerusalem was now called *"David's City,"* being the unifying symbol of a united Israel. However, as a man of God's heart, David had even greater plans for the reunified nation of Israel.

David's aim was to make Israel a great nation, in which God was the King.

"And David knew that the LORD had established him king over Israel, and that he had exalted his kingdom for the sake of his people Israel."
(2 Samuel 5:12)

David set out to achieve his goal with humble confidence, as he acknowledged and gave full credit for his being chosen to reign as King of a nation under God.

From his beginnings as the "shepherd boy who defeated Goliath", David was the *champion* that always gave the credit and glory to God for his successes. David recognized that all of his blessings were directly from God's presence.

Upon finally being anointed King of Israel, David's prime objective was to restore the worship of God as being of utmost importance among the Israelite people.

In order to accomplish his goal of prioritizing worship of God in Israel, David knew he needed to restore the *presence of God* to the people of Israel.

❖❖❖❖❖❖❖❖❖❖

Pearl: *To restore the presence of God in Israel, David needed to bring the Ark of the Covenant to its rightful place, being Jerusalem, the capital of Israel* **(2 Samuel 6).**

❖❖❖❖❖❖❖❖❖❖

David's objective was for Jerusalem not only to be the political capital of a united Israel, but to be the spiritual center as well. With returning the Ark to Jerusalem, David knew that the people of Israel would be in the presence of God.

◆◆◆◆◆◆◆◆◆◆◆

Pearl: The Ark of the Covenant signified the presence of God in the context of the day.

David had to reclaim the Ark for the Israelites and move it to the capital, as it had been in the house of Abinadab for the last twenty years.

Prior to this, the Philistines had captured the Ark (1 Samuel 4) from the Israelites and held it for seven months in Ashdod, next to their idol, Dagon (1 Samuel 5:1-7). After taking it to Gath, then to Ekron, the Philistines sent the Ark to Beth-shemesh to finally return it to the Israelites. After God terrified the Philistines while the Ark was in their hands, they returned it on a cart to the Israelites with a guilt offering (1 Samuel 6:10-15).

The Ark was the visible sign of the holy presence of God (Numbers 7:89). The Lord's real throne was above the heavens, but the Ark served as the focal point of God's presence among his people. The Ark was considered to be the tangible place of God for His people (1 Chronicles 16:27).

God commanded that the Ark was only to be carried by those of the tribe of Levi (Deuteronomy 10:8), using poles placed through the rings on the sides of the Ark (Exodus 25:14-15).

Due to his lack of leadership and obsession of hunting David, during Saul's reign the Ark had been ignored and remained in the house of a man named Abinadab in Baale-judah.

◆◆◆◆◆◆◆◆◆◆◆

David wrote several Psalms concerning the theme of God's covenant with the House of David, with Jerusalem being the resting place of the ark.

Psalms 132, 122, and David's Song of Thanks in 1 Chronicles 16, conflate this theme.

<u>Excerpts from Psalm 132 (verses 4,5,8,13)</u>
"I will not give sleep to my eyes or slumber to my eyelids until I find a place for the LORD, a dwelling place for the Mighty One of Jacob."

"Arise O LORD and go to your resting place, you and the ark of your might."

'For the LORD has chosen Zion, he has desired it for his dwelling place."

<u>Excerpt from David's Song of Thanks (1 Chronicles 16:27)</u>
"Splendor and majesty are before him, strength and joy are in this place."

Scene 5: In Search of the Ark

2 Samuel 6
Pre-Reading: Hebrews 10, Psalm 110, and Psalm 40

In preparation to bring the Ark back to Jerusalem, David gathered thirty thousand chosen men from the Israelites. He and his men traveled to Baale-judah, where the Ark was kept in the house of Abinadab, with his two sons Uzzah and Ahio *(2 Samuel 6:1-3)*.

Arriving in Baale-judah at the house of Abinadab, David and his men loaded the Ark on a ritually clean cart that was pulled by oxen to bring it to Jerusalem.

Ahio walked ahead of the cart, while Uzzah walked beside it, guiding the oxen *(2 Samuel 6:3-4)*.

David and all of the House of Israel were celebrating. There was music, singing and much merriment. People were having fun and the party was joyous!

"And David and all the house of Israel were making merry before the LORD, with songs and lyres and harps and tambourines and castanets and cymbals."
(2 Samuel 6:5)

But the celebratory mood of the people suddenly came to a screeching halt!

God struck down Uzzah, who had been walking by the oxen-drawn cart carrying the Ark. His dead body lay lifeless in the dirt by the cart.

What happened?

The oxen had stumbled, and Uzzah had reached out to steady the ark. He, a sinful man like all of us, had touched the Ark. Uzzah had tried to steady the Ark from falling, as the cart started to tilt.

An angered Lord struck Uzzah down *(2 Samuel 6:5-7)*.

"And the anger of the LORD was kindled against Uzzah, and God struck him down
there because of his error, and he died there beside the ark of God.
And David was angry because he LORD had burst forth against Uzzah.
And that place is called Perez-uzzah to this day. "
(2 Samuel 6:7-8)

✦✦✦✦✦✦✦✦✦✦

Pearl: What does Perez-uzzah mean?
Perez-uzzah, in English is translated to mean "Breach of Uzzah".

As we remember from the birth of Perez, the son of Judah and Tamar, Perez is the Hebrew word for 'breach.'

Perez was so-named because he breached the contract with his twin brother during birth. Of the twins Perez was the second, not the first child to enter the birth canal. Pulling himself past his brother so he could be birthed first, Perez dishonestly claimed himself to be the first-born, cheating his brother out of his birthright.

*Therefore Perez breached the contract of his brother, Zerah, and thus became the 'first-born" with all of its rights and privileges. Because of this incident, Perez received his name, meaning, "breach" **(Genesis 38:27-30)**.*

Of significance is that the line of Perez descending from Judah becomes the branch of the tree of ancestry that leads to Jesus Christ.

Pearls to Ponder about 2 Samuel 6: 7-8 ~ the death of Uzzah

1. *Why did God strike Uzzah dead?*

- *Even though Uzzah's motive was to prevent the Ark from hitting the ground, touching the Ark was a violation of God's law **(Numbers 4:15)**.*

- God was also angered by the way the Ark had been transported. The Ark was not to be transported on a cart pulled by oxen. It was His command that it be carried on the shoulders of members of the Levite tribe, using the poles placed through the rings on the sides of the Ark **(Exodus 25:14-15, Deuteronomy 10:8, 31:9, 1 Chronicles 15:15).**

- Furthermore, a sin sacrifice had not been given. A sin sacrifice was a specific command of God, as given in the Torah. David had not followed God's guidelines or wishes **(Leviticus 10:1-7)** in the way that the Ark was being transported.

2. What can we learn from this passage of scripture?

First and foremost, God is Holy and Almighty. Sin separates man from God, and God looks upon sin as a deadly, serious matter. Sin was therefore an issue that mankind had to acknowledge about himself, and reckon with **prior** to coming into the presence of God.

A sin offering must therefore be made before approaching the presence of God, as it acknowledged the sinful nature of humanity.

While transporting the Ark, David and the people had been feeling festive and were celebrating! But their worship was not what God wanted or intended during the transport of the Ark.

God had given very detailed instructions about transporting the Ark in the Torah, and David had not followed them.

Pearl from the Midrash: The scholars of the Midrash point out that the merry-making of the people while moving the Ark had numerous transgressions.

Of importance, the music was to be provided only by Levites, who were officially assigned in the Torah to do this task. Music was also to be played on instruments specifically designed for such an occasion.

Secondly, the Rabbis point out that the people celebrated in a frivolous manner, when a more serene form of rejoicing would have been more appropriate.

Summary Pearl: This scripture brings home the point that not even our best, well-intended efforts cannot bring us into the presence of the Almighty, Holy God!

The actions of sinful man had desecrated the Ark.

The celebration was over folks.

How did David handle God's reproach?

David was afraid, so he left the Ark in the House of Obed for the next three months **(2 Samuel 6:11).**

Pearl: David was not only afraid, but he was angry for what God did. David had mistakenly reasoned and believed that just because he was moving the Ark to Jerusalem, that everything would be great with God.

Upon further examining what had happened, David came to the realization that God was Holy, and many transgressions were made by sinful men who could not come into the presence of God by just doing what they 'felt' or 'believed' was right.

David was reminded of God's Holiness, and of the necessity of approaching God according to His instructions in the Torah, not according to what we think or feel.

David then turned to the Lord for guidance and asked,

"How can the Ark come to me?"
(2 Samuel 6:9)

David had to regroup and plan to transport the Ark according to God's plan. He didn't go to Plan B of his own doing; he went instead to Plan G, God's Plan.

David was successful and eventually did bring the Ark to Jerusalem after 3 months of preparation. This time he followed the Lord's guidelines *and did what God instructed* **(2 Samuel 6:12-15).**

What was God's plan for transport of the Ark? (1 Chronicles 15:12-15,26; 2 Samuel 15:24)

- *First, David performed a sin sacrifice prior to approaching into God's presence.*

  - *Upon taking six steps with the Ark, David stopped to sacrifice an animal to the Lord. Why six steps? Seven steps represented forward progress, so David performed a sin sacrifice at six steps* **(2 Samuel 6:13; 1 Chronicles 15:26).**

- *Secondly, David carried the Ark as God instructed.*
  - *He had Levites carry the Ark by the poles on the Ark's side, not on a cart drawn by oxen. The Levites bore the Ark of God upon their shoulders with the staves, as Moses commanded according to the Word of God.*

- According to the Hebrew Bible and the ancient Rabbis, David performed a sin sacrifice after six steps while wearing an ephod, which is a linen robe worn by priests.
- The instrument that was played during the procession was a shofar, which generates a pensive, somber sound *(Amos 3:6)*.

✦✦✦✦✦✦✦✦✦✦✦

Pearl: The Rabbis of the Midrash point out that this scripture gives tremendous insight into David's character. The mighty warrior, the slayer of Goliath and the Philistines, surrenders to God's wishes. David demonstrated his obedience to God, and became a devout servant.

✦✦✦✦✦✦✦✦✦✦✦

Summary: What can we learn from this valuable story?

✦ God is Holy
✦ Man is sinful
✦ Man cannot ever earn his own way to God
✦ Man's "good" can never earn his way to God
✦ Our "good" can never outweigh our bad, as we all are sinful and God is Holy
✦ In order to be right with God, we need a *'sin sacrifice'* to atone for our sins
✦ Before we can come into the presence of God, we must first deal with our sin

✦✦✦✦✦✦✦✦✦✦✦

Pearl: What is a Sin Sacrifice in ancient Mosaic Judaism?

God gave strict instructions to Moses about how His people must deal with their sin *(Leviticus 4, 5)*.

In Mosaic Law, the ritual purification of the people in God's sanctuary of worship required the death of an animal and its blood to be shed. Under the law, almost everything was purified with blood from an animal. Without the shedding of blood there is no forgiveness of sins *(Hebrews 9:22)*.

Sin needed an atoning blood sacrifice *(Leviticus 17:11)* and these sacrifices served as a vivid, horrific reminder to the person who committed the sin, and of God's Holiness.

The people therefore needed to preemptively perform a sin sacrifice to purify themselves of their sins **prior** to coming into the presence of the Ark of the Covenant, as it represented the Holy presence of God.

Throughout the Old Testament, God required repeated animal sacrifices to be performed by His people as the bloodshed only provided temporary covering of sins. It therefore was impossible for the blood of animals to take away our sins forever **(Hebrews 10:4).**

Why were repeated sacrifices needed?

The animal sacrifices symbolized the payment for sins, but did not accomplish it in entirety, as no animal was worthy of paying the price for us before a Holy God.

These animal sacrifices were not permanent either, as the last sacrifice made for a sin did not cover the next sin. This meant that sacrifices had to continually be given.

~Jesus, the Ultimate Sin Sacrifice~
Playlist: "Love Moved First" by Casting Crowns

The shedding of blood in Mosaic Law served as a foreshadow for the perfect and complete sin sacrifice, the sacrifice of Jesus Christ.

A ritual sacrifice of animal blood can never make a person perfect, but did only our Savior do Jesus Christ a shadow of the true form of sacrifice for us.

"We have been sanctified through the offering of the body of Jesus Christ once for all." (Hebrews 10:10)

"By a single offering, He has perfected for all time those who are being sanctified." (Hebrews 10:14)

A Psalm by David, Psalm 40, applies to our Messiah, Jesus Christ, who is descended from the Davidic line. As quoted in **Hebrews 10,** the author states: When Jesus Christ came into the world, he said,

**"Sacrifices and offerings you have not desired, but a body have you prepared for me; in burnt offerings and sin offerings you have taken no pleasure.
Then I said, behold I have come to do your will, O God as it is written of me in the scroll of the book.
I delight to do your will, O my God; your law is within my heart." (Hebrews 10:5-7 quoting Psalm 40:6-8).**

David's psalm highlights his awareness that God desires a person's heart, faith, and obedience, and not just the performance of rituals.

Psalm 40 *can also be taken to have prophesized the coming of the Messiah who will do God's will.*

~The Ark; what did it represent~

In Mosaic Law, the Ark represented the presence of God, and allowed people access to God.

We, as Christians, have access to God through our Savior, Jesus Christ.

What we can take away from the story in **2 Samuel 6** *is that the Ark was a foreshadow that pointed to the substance of Jesus Christ.*

We can also draw a parallel from David to Jesus in **2 Samuel 6.**

The Scripture showed us that David essentially acted out the Gospel of Jesus. David knew he could not bring the Ark to Jerusalem alone; he had to ask God for direction. With humble obedience, David followed God's instructions, and acknowledged that he and all of God's people are sinners.

David found out that all people had to become right with God before entering into His Holy presence, symbolized by the Ark.

We, as Christians, do not need to perform ritualistic animal sacrifices, nor do we need an Ark as a symbol of God's presence.

The Ark, which was lodged in the Holy of Holies in the temple Solomon built, was behind a veil so that no one other than Jewish priests of the most high could access it.

When Jesus died on the Cross, the veil in front of the Holy of Holies was torn by God, symbolizing that Jesus had died so that all believers could access God and His Kingdom.

The veil was torn, meaning that we can access God through His Spirit, who lives in us.

All of this was possible because of Jesus' death on the cross, and His resurrection.

We, as Christians are thankful for what Jesus Christ did for us on the cross, as He made the ultimate sin sacrifice.

Jesus drank our sin, absorbing it, so that we can approach God in His Holiness.

Jesus gave us the opportunity to enter into the **presence of God for eternity.**

Sorry 'Indiana Jones', but you can stop looking for the Ark of the Covenant.

It would be an awesome find and an interesting relic, but we, as Christians don't need it.

Thank you Jesus!

Additional New testament verses of relevance:
- ✦ **Romans 6:10**
- ✦ **Hebrews 10:2**
- ✦ **Hebrews 10:11-18 (Psalm 110)**
- ✦ **1 Peter 3:18**
- ✦ **John 15:3**

Scripture Summary: 2 Samuel 6, Chronicles 16

*David and all the people of Israel celebrated the arrival of the Ark in Jerusalem **(2 Samuel 6:17-19, 1 Chronicles 16:1-6, 37-43**). David appointed the Levite, Asaph, the chief to minister before the Lord.*

*Regular worship was established to minister regularly in accordance with the Law of the LORD which had been given Israel **(1 Chronicles 16**).*

*David gave praise to the Lord with **Psalms 105 and 96.***

"Oh give thanks to the LORD, call upon his name, make known his deeds among the peoples!
Sing to him, sing praises to him, tell of all his wondrous works!
Glory in his holy name; let the hearts of those who seek the LORD rejoice!"
(Psalm 105:1-3)

"Oh sing the LORD a new song, sing to the LORD, all the earth!
Let the heavens be glad and let the earth rejoice, let the sea roar, and all that fills it, let the field exult, and everything in it!
Then shall all the trees of the forest sing for joy before the LORD for he comes for he comes to judge the earth.
He will judge the world in righteousness, and the peoples in his faithfulness."
(Psalm 96:1, 11-13

174

Act 7: The Davidic Covenant ~ The Eternal Throne

2 Samuel 7:1-29, 1 Chronicles 17:1-2

Playlist: "The Way" by Jeremy Camp

After David became settled in his palace in Jerusalem, the LORD had given him rest from his enemies.

King David then proceeded to ask Nathan, the prophet about building a house for the Lord.

"See now, I dwell in a house of cedar, but the ark of God dwells in a tent."
(1 Samuel 7:1)

Nathan replied to King David,

"Go, do all that is in your heart, for the LORD is with you."

That same night, the Lord spoke to David through the prophet, Nathan,

"Would you build me a house to dwell in?
I have not lived in a house since the day I brought up the people of Israel from Egypt to this day, but I have been moving about in a tent for dwelling in all places where I have moved with all the people of Israel, did I speak a word with any of the judges of Israel whom I commanded to shepherd my people Israel saying
"why have you not built me a house of cedar?"
(2 Samuel 7:5-7)

"I took you from the pasture, from following the sheep, that you should be prince over my people Israel.
And I have been with you wherever you went and have cut off all your enemies from before you.
And I will make for you a great name like the name of the great ones of the earth."
(2 Samuel 7:8-9)

"When your days are fulfilled ad you lie down with your fathers, I will raise up your offspring after you, who shall come from your body, and I will establish his kingdom.
He shall build a house for my name and I will establish the throne of his kingdom forever.

I will be to him a father, and he shall be to me a son.
When he commits iniquity, I will discipline him with the rod of men, with the stripes
of the sons of men, but my steadfast love will not depart from him as I took it from Saul
whom I put away from before you.
Your house and your kingdom shall be made sure forever before me.
Your throne shall be established forever."
(2 Samuel 7:12-17)

David gave thanksgiving and praise to the Lord *(2 Samuel 7:18-29, 1 Chron 17:16-27).*

◆◆◆◆◆◆◆◆◆◆◆

P*earl: Known as the **Davidic Covenant**, the Lord promised to make one family, that of David, the representative of His people forever.*

This scripture points to Jesus, the descendant of David, who will sit on the Throne for all eternity. The Messiah, Jesus Christ, will therefore establish David's throne forever.

*In what is known as Isaiah's first of four Servant Songs **(Isaiah 42:1-9)**, Isaiah makes reference to the servant of the Lord, fulfilled in Jesus Christ.*

*In the **Davidic Covenant,** David's heirs represent and embody the people as a whole, as Israel is God's son **(Exodus 4:22-23)** and the king becomes God's son on his coronation **(2 Samuel 7:14; Psalm 89:26-27)**.*

*The servant that Isaiah speaks of **(Isaiah 42:1-9)** follows the pattern of David's heirs, and also foreshadows the Messiah. The servant achieves the expansion of his rule throughout the Gentile world, which is the work of the Davidic Messiah **(Isaiah 42:1-4; 52:13-15)**.*

*Later, prophets describe an heir of David as the servant Isaiah speaks of, with him being the messianic figure **(Ezekiel 34:23-24; 37:25; Haggai 2:23; Zechariah 3:8; Jeremiah 33:21-22,26)**.*

Isaiah 42:1,4
"Behold my servant, whom I uphold, my chosen, in whom my soul delights; I have put my Spirit upon him; he will bring forth justice to the nations.
He will not grow faint or be discouraged till he has established justice in the earth;
And the coastlands wait for his law."

Isaiah's Four Servant Songs: Messianic prophecy of an heir of David fulfilled in Jesus Christ:

+ *First: Isaiah 42: 1-9 (The Lord's Chosen Servant)*
  - *"Coastlands" is a term that uses the lands surrounding the Mediterranean Sea as the image, designating the most remote people, being the Gentiles of the earth*
+ *Second: Isaiah 49:1-13 (The Servant of the Lord will restore Israel and save the Nations)*
  - *Salvation of the servant applies to the whole world – again using the terminology of 'O Coastlands'*
+ *Third: Isaiah 50:4-9 (The Lord's Servant Taught, His People Attentive)*
  - *These verses focus on the servant as a rejected prophet*
+ *Fourth: Isaiah 52:13 – 53:12 (The Lord's Servant: The Exalted Sin-Bearer)*
  - *The Messiah removes the guilt of all sinners before God, as He drinks the sins of the world*

"Behold, my servant shall act wisely, he shall be high and lifted up, and shall be exalted.
As man were astonished at you – his appearance was so marred, beyond human semblance, and his form beyond that of the children of mankind – so shall he sprinkle many nations, kings shall shut their mouths because of him;

for that which has not been told them they see, and that which they have not heard they understand."
Isaiah 52:13-15

❖❖❖❖❖❖❖❖❖❖

D uring this period of respite from his enemies, David asked the Lord if he was to build a house, or a temple for the Lord. God directed that David should build a house for himself, but not for the Lord.

God chose Jerusalem to be His dwelling place on earth, but David was not to build the temple.

According to *1 Chronicles 22:8*, God said that David was a man of war with blood on his hands, so he was not to build the temple for the Lord.

Instead, Solomon, David's son, would be charged with building the temple for the Lord *(1 Chronicles 22:9).*

*As part of God's **Davidic Covenant,** the Lord instructed David to build his 'own house' instead.*

✦✦✦✦✦✦✦✦✦✦✦

Pearl: What is the meaning behind David's 'House'?
The terminology God used of David's house had tremendous meaning, as God had made His Covenant with David to bring about a house in his name.

*This phraseology was meaning to use David's 'house', **or his offspring**, to bring forth the Messiah.*

Of significance was that God's own son would come from the lineage of David, and would be born to redeem humanity.

Meanwhile, David continued on to find victory in battle against Israel's enemies.

"And the Lord gave victory to David wherever he went."
(2 Samuel 8:14)

"So David reigned over all Israel. And David administered justice and equity to all his people."
(2 Samuel 8:15)

Importantly, ever the warrior in battle, David the king of Israel had time to do God's work in other ways that were equally important.

We will see how David exhibits God's ultimate love for His people – His Chesed

Act 8: David's Chesed

2 Samuel 9

Playlist: "Come to the Table" by Sidewalk Prophets

Introduction:

D avid was a man of his promise, and he remembered his oath to his best friend Jonathan, son of Saul.

As often happened with a change in the leadership of a dynasty, the new king will destroy all of the living descendants of the ex-king. This is done to eliminate the threat of future take-overs by the ex-king's sons, who may have thought that the throne should have been rightfully passed on to them.

David had promised Jonathan that he would preserve his living offspring in the event that he took over as king. David swore to never sever his kindness from Jonathan's house (*1 Samuel 20*).

After becoming King of Israel, David had to inquire if there were any living relatives of King Saul, so apparently he was not aware of Jonathan's son. It is quite possible that Jonathan's son was in hiding from David, as he may have fled to obscurity after his father was killed, and David became king.

David asked,

> *"Is there still anyone left of the house of Saul, that I may show him kindness for Jonathan's sake?"*
> *(2 Samuel 9:3)*

✦✦✦✦✦✦✦✦✦✦

P *earl: Let's take a moment and put the word "kindness" into context in the Hebrew culture. The English translation of the verse, using the word kindness does not do justice to the original Hebrew word. The original Hebrew word was* "**chesed**."

*The Hebrew word 'chesed' literally means **"the kindness of God."** We, as Christians may interpret this all-encompassing word as **God's Grace**.*

The English translation of the Masoretic text of the Hebrew Bible of **2 Samuel 9:3** actually reads,

> **And the king said,**
> **"Is there none left from the house of Saul, that I may do to him the kindness of God?"**
> **(2 Samuel 9:3, Hebrew Bible)**

The kindness of God, or chesed, has been interpreted by Christian exegetes to mean **grace of God.** This is understandable, as the kindness of God is multifactorial, and can't even be comprehended by us, let alone be accomplished by mere humans.

Similarly, grace can be described as kindness shown to one who does not deserve, earn, or cannot possibly repay it. Grace has been described as kindness shown to a person, even though they are not considered 'worthy.'

In the author's previous book, "Cultivating the Christ", we first explored the meaning of chesed when we looked at the character of Boaz, as he demonstrated chesed to Ruth.

We will now take a look at how David showed chesed to Jonathan's son, Mephibosheth.

Scene 1: David finds Jonathan's Son

After the death of Saul and Jonathan, David searched for someone who may have known the whereabouts of any of Saul's descendants.

He found Saul's trusty long-time servant, Ziba, and asked him if anyone from Saul's house was still alive.

Ziba knew of Jonathan's son and replied,

> **"There is still a son of Jonathan, he is crippled in his feet."**
> **(2 Samuel 9:3)**

The author of **2 Samuel** had written previously that Jonathan's son had been injured the day that people heard the news of the deaths of Saul and Jonathan in battle against the Philistines.

On the horrific day of Jonathan's death, the boy had been dropped by his nurse after she heard the news that his father had been killed, as she was hurrying to flee the area.

The boy's nurse most likely knew that there would be a change of leadership after king Saul's death, and that the new king would very likely put to death all of Saul's descendants. Trying to flee with the boy in her arms, the nurse tripped and fell and inadvertently dropped the youngster, injuring him in the process.

Jonathan's son was permanently injured that day, and had since been in hiding, living in poverty in an obscure location.

Even though Ziba disclosed very little to David about Jonathan's son, he made sure that David was aware that the son had been permanently crippled, and was therefore considered to be 'unworthy' in the eyes of society. Undaunted by the information that Jonathan's son was crippled in both his feet, David persisted to find out his whereabouts.

David found out that Jonathan's son, Mephibosheth, was living in the house of *Machir, in Lo-debar.*

◆◆◆◆◆◆◆◆◆◆◆

P*earl: We are not told who Machir was, but the house was most likely not a five-star resort. The Hebrew meaning of Lo-debar is "without pasture." In other words, it was in a desolate, stark land, in the middle-of-nowhere.*

◆◆◆◆◆◆◆◆◆◆◆

Sure enough the boy had been exiled to a remote, desolate area after Saul's death, which at this time had been many years ago. By now, Mephibosheth is a young adult. However, with his disability he would be living in poverty, or possibly supported by someone who had taken pity on him and had taken him in.

David, determined to find Jonathan's son, traveled to *Lo-debar.*

David's entourage was probably the most unlikely thing that Mephibosheth had seen in his days in exile.

Seeing the grand procession, Mephibosheth feared the worst, being that the king was coming to execute him, as he was the last living descendant of Saul.

As the procession of David and his servants approached his house, Mephibosheth thought that his life would soon be ended. He could do nothing but wait and see.

Upon David's arrival, Mephibosheth came to David and humbly fell on his face.

David assured him,

"Do not fear, for I will show you kindness for the sake of your father Jonathan, and I will restore to you all the land of Saul and you shall eat at my table always."
(2 Samuel 9:7)

Pearl: In one instant, Mephibosheth had been lifted up from poverty to the wealth of a king.

In one instant of mercy, Mephibosheth was assured that all the land that Saul had owned as king would be his. After Saul's death, his land had eventually been passed on to David as the new King of Israel. From now on, David decreed that this land and all of its benefits would instead belong to Mephibosheth.

Plus, David offered to treat him as his own son, assuring him that he will always have access to his personal fields with abundant agriculture to support him. Mephibosheth's son, Mica, was also accepted by David, which guaranteed the preservation of the lineage of Jonathan, just as David had promised.

"Mephibosheth lived in Jerusalem, for he ate always at the king's table.
Now he was lame in both his feet."
(2 Samuel 9:13)

♦♦♦♦♦♦♦♦♦♦♦

*P**earl:** King David had shown God's kindness, or chesed, to Mephibosheth. The source of this astonishing kindness was Divinely inspired, and truly showed that David had a heart for the Lord. In this case, David's heart was manifested as obedience for how God wants us to treat others, especially those who are less fortunate.*

♦♦♦♦♦♦♦♦♦♦♦

The story of David and Mephibosheth has striking similarities to the theme of chesed we discussed in the Book of Ruth in *"Cultivating the Christ"*. The amazing kindness that Boaz heaped upon Ruth has parallels to David's treatment of Mephibosheth.

Study Points: Similarities between David and Boaz

Parallels between David and Boaz (David's great-grandfather) ~ Demonstration of Chesed, God's Grace

- Ruth (David's great-grandmother) and Mephibosheth were both considered 'unworthy' in the culture of the time.
  - Ruth was of Moabite heritage (a foreigner and an enemy of the Israelites). She was an outcast who was not accepted, and therefore would not able to sustain herself in Israel as a foreigner.
    - As a Moabite, Ruth was considered to be an enemy of Israel.
  - Mephibosheth was crippled and permanently impaired; therefore he was unable to sustain himself without the help of others.
  - Neither could ever 'earn,' nor change their way out of their particular un-wanted predicaments.

- David invited Mephibosheth 'to the table,' providing for him, and treating him as family.

- Boaz invited Ruth to his 'table,' when he invited her to dine with him and the reapers.
  - Both David and Boaz extended the invitation to people who could never possibly repay them. Plus, neither had the expectation of ever being repaid.

- Both Mephibosheth and Ruth were economically deprived, barely obtaining enough food to sustain themselves and their families.
  - Boaz provided for Ruth and Naomi with plenty of grain.
    - Allowed Ruth to glean freely in his field
    - Provided her protection from the other reapers
    - Gave gifts of grain to help sustain Ruth and her mother-in-law, Naomi
  - David provided for Mephibosheth and his family with harvest from Saul's and his own land.

- Both Boaz and David were 'kinsman-redeemers.'
  - Boaz purchased, and then redeemed the land to Ruth and Naomi that was owned by Naomi's deceased husband, Elimelech. The land was therefore kept in the family of Elimelech.

- David redeemed Saul's land (that he had acquired due to being King of Israel) to Mephibosheth, keeping the land in the family of Saul.

✦ Boaz and David were both powerful men that had great authority, yet had hearts that were capable of extraordinary kindness.
- As Jesus commanded of His disciples in **Luke 14:12-24**, both men showed extreme generosity toward those who were physically impaired and economically deprived.

✦ Boaz and David were spiritually similar in their manifestation of chesed, and can be considered as foreshadowing the ultimate kindness of God with the gift of His Son, Jesus to us.

Both David and Boaz foreshadowed Jesus, our ultimate redeemer - the One with the authority of God, and the kindness of the Lamb.

A relevant verse in the New Testament is found in **Revelation 19: 6-10, the Marriage Supper of the Lamb**. Though we are unworthy, Jesus has extended His invitation to dine at His table for eternity. Believers who belong to His beloved bride, the church, have been called through the gospel of grace.

"Blessed ae those who are invited to the marriage supper of the Lamb.
These are the true words of God."
(Revelation 19:9)

We as believers have been called to the table through the Grace of God.

The prediction of the Messianic banquet was anticipated in **Isaiah 25:6-9.**

Isaiah 25:6-9
"On this mountain the LORD of hosts will make for all peoples a feast of rich food, a feast of well-aged wine. Of rich food full of marrow, of aged wine well refined.
And he will swallow up on this mountain the covering that is cast over all peoples, the veil that is spread over all nations.
He will swallow up death forever; and the LORD God will wipe away tears from all faces, and the reproach of his people he will take away from all the earth, for the Lord has spoken.
It will be said on that day, Behold, this is our God, we have waited for him, that he might save us.
This is the Lord; we have waited for him; let us be glad and rejoice in his salvation.

Scene 2: David's Kingdom is Defended and Increased:

Even though David had become the king of Israel, he still had to constantly battle God's enemies in order to preserve the blessings promised to God's people.

Enemies of Israel included the Philistines, Moabites, Edomites and the Ammonites. In the course of time, David defeated the Philistines, taking Gath and surrounding towns from Philistine control.

✦✦✦✦✦✦✦✦✦✦

Pearl: *During this time, David composed* **Psalm 60**, *a Miktam of David, to the tune of "The Lily of the Covenant." The places David mentioned are all parts of the land that God promised to Israel, and therefore belong to the LORD* **(Exodus 19:5)**. *David viewed his military campaign in the context of Israel's mission and calling in the name of the Lord, not just as mere territorial expansion.*

"You have made your people see hard things; you have given us wine to drink that made us stagger.
You have set up a banner for those who fear you, that they may flee to it from the bow.
That your beloved ones may be delivered, give salvation by your right hand and answer us!

God has spoken in his holiness; With exultation I will divide up Shechem and portion out the Vale of Succoth.
Gilead is mine; Manasseh is mine; Ephraim is my helmet; Judah is my scepter. Moab is my washbasin; upon Edom I cast my shoe; over Philistia I shout in triumph.

With God we shall do valiantly; it is he who will tread down our foes."
(Psalm 60: 3-8, 12)

✦✦✦✦✦✦✦✦✦✦

With his God-given skills, David had successfully formed an army who was capable of *defeating the external forces* of Israel's enemies.

One of the hardest of battles during this time of defending the Davidic kingdom was when war broke out again between the Philistines and Israel. Fighting against his old, fierce enemies, David encountered a huge man, Ishbi-benob, who was one of the descendants of the giants (**Hebrew: Rapah**).

Ishbi-benob, armed with a gigantic spear and a new, technologically advanced sword, sought to kill David. Weary from fighting, David was thankfully aided by one of his loyal men, who fought and killed the Philistine.

David's men at this point swore to him that he should no longer accompany them in battle, as losing him would be a risk for the nation of Israel.

"You shall no longer go out with us to battle, lest you quench the lamp of Israel."
(2 Samuel 21:17)

◆◆◆◆◆◆◆◆◆◆◆

*P**earl:** Ishbi-benob was an offspring of the Rephaim, the ancient, pre-Israelite inhabitants of Canaan that had overwhelmed the spies sent by Moses to scope out the land. The spies brought back news of these huge men, which deterred the Israelites from settling the Promised Land under the leadership of Moses (**Genesis 14:5, 15:20, Joshua 12:4, 13:12, 17:15**). Several other Philistine descendants of the giants of Gath also fell by the hand of David and his loyal men (**2 Samuel 21:22**).*

*David was thankful to God for delivering him and his beloved Israel from the hand of their enemies. Composing his 'Song of Deliverance' (**2 Samuel 22**) as a personal song, David then also composed **Psalm 18** as a public hymn of thanksgiving to the Lord.*

"I love you, O LORD, my strength.
The LORD is my rock and my fortress and my deliverer, my God, my rock, in whom I take refuge, my shield, and the horn of my salvation, my stronghold.
I call upon the LORD, who is worthy to be raised, and I am saved from my enemies."
(Psalm 18:1-3)

◆◆◆◆◆◆◆◆◆◆◆

Over the past twenty years since David had first become king of Judah, and then king over all of Israel, God, who gave David many successes, defended his kingdom.

Acknowledging his success was due to the Lord, David also gave credit to the men in his loyal army. Naming his Mighty Men, thirty-seven in all, they came to be known as the 'thirty'. David was very close to his men, and rightly so, as these men had at one time or another saved his life in the throes of battle (*1 Samuel 23:8-39*).

David and his army of men had many successes, defeating the external forces against Israel.

But what about David's *internal enemies?*

In the middle of all of his successes during his reign of King of Israel, David falls victim to his own internal enemy. The internal enemy of the temptation of the flesh will come to plague David in his near future.

David's *pendulum of faith* will once again swing away from being the obedient servant of God. Like all of us sinful, broken humans, David will give in to the negative forces of the Devil.

As the Devil often works in the lives of those who love and try to be faithful servants of God, the Devil tempted David.

Tempting David with what turned out to be his greatest downfall, the Devil put an obstacle in the form of temptation of the flesh into David's life. On his own, David was not capable of resisting the temptation, and would submit to the schemes of the Devil.

Falling into the trap of the Devil, David submitted to his own desires of the flesh and became not only an adulterer, but also a murderer.

What started with a seemingly small sin, escalated into a massive cover-up that resulted in the abominable sin of killing an innocent man.

David's actions not only affected him, but also caused tremendous heartache in others and resulted in serious consequences.

The Lord however did not remove His sovereign Hand from David. Instead of abandoning David, God disciplined him, and guided him back to being His obedient servant.

Through God's mercy, David repented after his serious moral offenses. After tremendous emotional agony and remorse, David was re-routed back through God's grace to be a man after the Lord's heart.

Act 9: Bathsheba ~ Not Just the 'Other Woman'

2 Samuel 11, 12; 1 Kings 1-2, Psalm 51

Ca. 980 B.C.

Playlist: "God Only Knows", "Sink the Ships" by King and Country, "Symphony" by Switch

Introduction: Author's Pearl

*I*n contradistinction to what is often taught in Bible studies, Bathsheba was '**the** woman', not merely the '**other** woman.'

Why do I say this?

If one just casually reads the Bible, without delving completely into what God is trying to tell us, the reader may at first be lead to think that Bathsheba was the quintessential 'other' woman.

The 'other' woman who 'destroyed' David and led him into sin, disrupting his relationship with his other wives and children, as well as his career.

Not so. Things aren't always how they may first appear.

As we continue the story of David and his offspring, let's go deeper into how Bathsheba changed the course of the history of mankind, and the course of eternity.

At this point in his life, David had been the successful king of Israel for about twenty years. He had taken many wives and numerous concubines throughout the years. Various sources list as many as ten to eighteen wives, and a similar number, or possibly even more of concubines.

David had many sons and daughters from his many wives and concubines.

Of significance is that none of his original wives produced the offspring who is the direct lineage of Jesus Christ. None of his wives he had married were yet to be responsible for continuing the Davidic Dynasty and importantly, the legacy of the making of the Messiah.

In other words, even though David had taken many wives, he had not as of yet taken the wife that will produce the offspring that would spring forth the final branch in the growing Tree of Life, the Tree that will lead to Jesus, the Messiah.

The lineage of Jesus the Messiah, the ultimate Tree of Life, has yet to be determined. The One who through his sacrifice allowed us to have an eternal life with God, the Father.

Who will this 'mystery wife' of David's be?

Enter into the scene of God's Masterplan for the salvation of humanity, Bathsheba.

Through David and Bathsheba the Messiah will come.

It is through this seed of 'the woman,' being Bathsheba, that Jesus Christ our Savior is descended.

This is why the story of Bathsheba is so important.

And also so ironic.

Once again, we see how God uses the most unlikely people in His Masterplan to save humanity.

In David's story we will see how God took what started out as a mortal temptation, which then morphed into a horrific sin and tragedy, and then turned it back around to head straight into the glorious path leading to the Messiah.

The story of David and Bathsheba presents a very dark side of humanity, proving once again that we humans are all sinners. As always, the Bible is blatantly truthful and allows us to see even the 'heroes' of the Bible exactly as who they really are.

Were David and Bathsheba heroes? Not exactly. But even as sinful and imperfect as they were, we will see how their repentance and God's grace works for the good of those who love the Lord.

By looking deep into the Bible and learning about the people who God uses for His glory, it will serve to remind us that even 'good' people who follow the Lord can stray to the dark side.

Re-living the stories of God's people reminds us that we are all sinners, driving home the point that we are all in need of a savior.

Accompanying humanity's sinful, dark side, scripture also guides us to the light of redemption allowing us to receive God's blessing of forgiveness.

The sinful nature of humanity displayed in the ancestors of Jesus help us to fully understand God's grace, His chesed.

What led to David's temptation and resulting sin?

First, let's put things into context. Let's start with the time of the year.

It was spring.

Spring was the time of the year when kings fancied to enter into battle. David and his army had to continue to defend his kingdom from Israel's enemies, which they had done successfully over the past twenty years of David being king.

David was in mid-life and was enjoying the pinnacle of his success as King of Israel. He rejoiced in his victories and blessings, acknowledging that all that was given to him was a blessing from the Lord. It was the height of his career, and David reveled in his success as his people had come to respect and admire their king.

◆◆◆◆◆◆◆◆◆◆◆

P**earl: Why did kings lead their ensemble of warriors into battle during the spring?**

- ✦ Fair weather led to growth of stalks in the land, which enabled the warrior's horses and donkeys to find grain in the fields to eat.
- ✦ The warmer climate also meant that the men did not have to contend with the extremes of the cold weather, and could move about without the hindrance of storms that brought extreme rain and floods.

All of these factors pointed to spring being the customary time for the Israelite army, as well as the armies of their enemies, to head out to battle.

But not this spring. This spring David stayed home in Jerusalem.

David's loyal troops however, set out to fight battle against Israel's enemies.

Why did David stay home?

Biblical scholars exegete from Scripture that there were several potential reasons. For one, David was not a youth anymore; in fact he was in his late-forties to early-fifties.

At this point, David had supreme confidence in his power and authority over all of the people of Israel. He had proven himself to be a successful military commander, as well as a political and spiritual leader.

David, the most successful King of Israel, had lead the nation over the years to become a powerful monarchy, successful in defeating its enemies and expanding its borders far beyond what had ever been achieved or expected.

But yet this time David stayed home in Jerusalem while he sent his army out to battle the Ammonites without him *(2 Samuel 11:1)*.

At this point, we don't know why David avoided participation in the battle against the Ammonites.

What we do know is that things always happen for a reason.

Since the Bible makes such a point of telling us that David did not venture into battle with his troops, with no mention of illness or disability, we can possibly deduce that David may have become vulnerable to his own success.

In light of his accomplishments, David neglected his responsibility of leading his army of men and protecting his people against Israel's enemies. With all of his fame and success, perhaps David over time had succumbed to the sins of self-indulgence and arrogance.

Or maybe David was just tired. He was getting older, and had spent many years living a hard life of running from Saul.

We don't know exactly why David stayed home, but we do know that the Lord had it in his Masterplan for him to do so.

"In the spring of the year, the time when kings go out to battle, David sent Joab and his servants with him, and all Israel. And they ravaged the Ammonites and besieged Rabbah.
But David remained at Jerusalem."
(2 Samuel 11:1)

Scene 1: Late One Afternoon

The sun was beginning to descend slowly in the sky on this one particular beautiful spring afternoon.

The day was warm and David, idle and bored, had taken a long nap on the couch situated on his palace roof, overlooking the vast city of Jerusalem.

◆◆◆◆◆◆◆◆◆◆◆

Pearl: David's palace was built on the ruins of the Jebusite Citadel, at the most northern edge of the city of Jerusalem on the top of a hill. Located on the Eastern Hill, the city spanned between the Central Valley to the west and the Kidron Valley to the east. Jerusalem had an abundant water supply derived from the Gihon Spring.

From his palace roof David could look over the Millo, which was a terraced construction on a steep slope descending down from his palace on which the people's houses were built. The most northern-situated houses were directly below David's palace. The houses nearest to the palace were occupied by the people of David's court, such as the Mighty Men (the Thirty) of his army and their families.

◆◆◆◆◆◆◆◆◆◆◆

Upon waking, David lazily stretched and then decided to indulge in the beautiful view from the vantage point of his palace rooftop. Thinking that after his walk, he would then head inside his palace to enjoy a sumptuous evening meal by candlelight.

Slowly rising from his couch, David strolled to the edge of the roof to gaze over the vastness of his successful empire. Finally, he thought, it had all come to fruition!

After years of fleeing Saul and his army and successfully defending his newly formed kingdom, David felt relief and gratitude that those days were behind him.

Thinking back of the days and nights he spent running as a fugitive, David now embraced the life of a king, living in a palace with servants to tend to his every need.

Admittedly, David was tired.

Now in his late-forties, he had spent his entire life in the field, first as a lowly shepherd then later as an esteemed warrior who led an army of faithful men. Much of this time however, he and his army had lived as nomads, continuously running from Saul and his army of thousands.

After years and years of hiding from Saul and fighting battles for Israel, David the warrior was relieved that for once he was not at war.

However, David had doubts concerning his decision to stay behind while his men went off to battle. Shaking off pangs of guilt for not being at war against the Ammonites with his faithful army of men, David continued his leisurely walk around the palace roof.

Trying to cast off his guilt, and enjoy his idle stroll in the afternoon sunshine, David looked far-off over the spread of the city of Jerusalem. He took in the full expanse of its size, and noting the evidence of wealth he thought to himself that the city was indeed a symbol of his accomplishments.

Jerusalem, or the 'City of David' as David had re-named it upon conquering the Jebusites, represented his power and authority in all of the land of Israel.

Remembering the day of the conquest when the Jebusite Citadel was destroyed and replaced by the stronghold of Zion, Jerusalem, David thought back to his own name for the city, the 'City of David'.

♦♦♦♦♦♦♦♦♦♦♦

Pearl: *Sadly, David had once fully acknowledged that the City of David, also known as Jerusalem, represented the unified nation of Israel under God. Not attributing his successes to his own power, David had once given God all of the Glory for which He, the Almighty, was responsible.*

David's faith swing, described earlier as a pendulum, had again begun to swing away from God. Instead of attributing his success to the Lord, the temptation to think that he was responsible for his own success was beginning to surface.

♦♦♦♦♦♦♦♦♦♦♦

Among his accomplishments, David thoughts turned to his family with his many sons who would be heirs to his throne. Over the past years David had acquired many beautiful women to be his wives, producing many sons who would eventually inherit the amazing wealth he had created.

His wives had come from many places, securing pacts with leaders of far-off lands. Helping to build his empire, the deals David negotiated with leaders from afar secured his alliances with surrounding nations.

Besides, the women David acquired were all beautiful, and had given him many children.

However, In spite of the large flock of women at his beck and call, David's eyes still tended to wander when it came to the ladies.

David definitely had an eye for a beautiful woman. Now in his late-forties, he felt himself becoming bored with his many wives and concubines.

◆◆◆◆◆◆◆◆◆◆◆

*P**earl:** We had an inclination of David's tendency to sin earlier, as he had been disobedient to God's will in becoming a polygamist. Taking many wives was against God's will, but David had not heeded the Lord's commandment.*

*In **Deuteronomy 17:17** the laws concerning kings commands, **"And he shall not acquire many wives for himself, lest his heart turns away."***

Unable to control his sexual desires, David was disobedient to the Lord's Word and acquired multiple wives and concubines.

Now, made even worse with his faith turning further away from God as the pendulum swings, David has become discontented with the blessings bestowed upon him. Even though he had a whole household of women and many sons and daughters in his family, he yearned elsewhere for sexual excitement and pleasure. Call it boredom or seeking adventure, on that particular afternoon David's wandering eye scanned the women of the city who had been left behind as their husbands went off to fight in battle for Israel.

◆◆◆◆◆◆◆◆◆◆◆

In his boredom, David looked down upon the city and wondered what the townspeople of Jerusalem were doing. He observed several women meandering the streets of the market place, purchasing food to prepare for the evening meal.

He continued his stroll on his roof, but hesitated when movement from a house directly below suddenly caught his eye.

Taking a double-take, David stopped dead-in-his-tracks.

Savoring the moment as desire welled-up inside him, David's eyes took in the pleasures of the flesh.

In David's sights was the most beautiful woman he had ever laid eyes on. Like a cat on the prowl for a mouse, he watched her every move while calculating his.

Bathing in her house below his palace, David continued to observe the gorgeous woman's every movement. Then, as the woman gracefully rose from the water, he was taken aback with utmost pleasure.

Stepping out from her bath to briefly face him, the woman slowly pulled her robe around her naked, sumptuous form.

With David's birds-eye view from the roof of his palace, the woman was oblivious to his presence. Continuing to watch her, David knew that he was shielded from her sight.

Standing on the roof, unable to turn his eyes away from watching the woman, David knew he was in lust! Watching the woman disappear into the depths of her house, he yearned to be with her.

Who was this gorgeous woman, he wondered? Somehow, David thought she seemed vaguely familiar. Too far away to observe her facial features, he searched his memory for why he seemed to know this woman.

Immediately David turned on his heel and headed inside the palace to inquire about the woman. One of his many servants was sure to know who she is!

Inside the palace, David sent for a servant.

And David sent and inquired about the woman. And one said, "Is not this Bathsheba, the daughter of Eliam, the wife of Uriah the Hittite?"
(2 Samuel 11:3)

❖❖❖❖❖❖❖❖❖❖

Pearl: *This sentence in scripture is full of meaning, and the exact wording is important.*

First let's look at how the wording is in the ESV Bible. Of significance is the servant is assumed to be the 'one' who answered David's inquiry about the woman.

In this verse of the ESV, the servant was the one who carefully informed David that the woman he had asked about was married. The servant seemed to be aware of David's lust for women, and was making sure that David knew that the woman of his current desires was married. Not only did the servant disclose that she was a wife, but he mentioned the man's name. He also mentioned the name of the woman's father.

Why is this important?

Bathsheba was the wife of one of David's faithful army men, Uriah! Her father, Eliam, was also an esteemed warrior, and one of David's elite guards. Coming from a family of men who fought beside and protected King David, Bathsheba was well-known among David's court.

Of even more significance was that Bathsheba's husband, Uriah, was one of David's most trusted warriors, known as his Mighty Men or the "thirty"(2 **Samuel 23:39**). Bathsheba's father was also a trusted warrior and a member of David's 'mighty men' **(2 Samuel 23:34)**.

~ Are we interpreting the scripture correctly? How could David have NOT known who Bathsheba was? (See notes concerning the Midrash later in this pearl and later in the text)

Putting this into the context of the day, we must remember that the king had absolute authority and could act as the law. The king even served as the sole judge, deciding cases of dispute among his people which were brought to him to make a legal decision about who was right and who was wrong. Although David was in the position of being the all-powerful monarch, he had in the past known and had shown by his behavior, that he was not above God's law.

David had been different from the usual king, as his priority had been to be a Servant of God, protecting his people and looking out for the needy and afflicted. David had a heart for God and for those that he ruled.

This had been the case, but was about to change.

At least temporarily.

Pearl: But is this wording in the ESV capture the original meaning?

Of significance is the way that the Masoretic text of the Hebrew Bible reads differently from the ESV Bible translation.

The original Hebrew text (translated to English by Hebrew scholars) is listed below. Note that the ESV text differs from the Masoretic Hebrew text by one word.

2 Samuel 11:3 (Masoretic Text of the Hebrew Bible)
"And David sent, and inquired about the woman. And he said: 'Is this not Bathsheba, the daughter of Eliam, the wife of Uriah the Hittite?"

2 Samuel 11:3 (ESV Bible)
"And David sent and inquired about the woman. And one said, "Is not this Bathsheba, the daughter of Eliam, the wife of Uriah the Hittite?"

The Jewish Rabbi, Alschich, contends that the way the Hebrew scripture is worded indicated that it was David (being 'he' in the statement "and he said") that said the statement about Bathsheba. David not only noted Bathsheba's name, but also named her father and her husband.

In contrast, the ESV indicates that the statement about Bathsheba's heritage and marriage was communicated by the servant, as the text reads "and one said'.

What difference does this make?

If David said this, stating Bathsheba's name, as well as whom her husband and father were, he obviously knows Bathsheba.

In fact, David probably has known Bathsheba since she was a youngster, as her father was one of the loyal army members who accompanied David during his plight from Saul, moving from location to location with his family in-tow. It is well documented that David's trusty army moved with him from place to place, as they defended David's life against Saul.

Therefore we can deduce that if we take the Hebrew Bible verse in proper context, David knew Bathsheba personally.

*We will explore this further when we look at the Enigma of Bathsheba at the end of this session.

Scene 2: The Seduction

Introduction: Casting aside his priorities and responsibilities as servant of God and king of Israel, David gave in to his own sexual desires.

Thinking of nothing else but his own forthcoming pleasure, David promptly sent his guards to summon Bathsheba and escort her to his palace.

**"So David sent messengers and took her, and she came to him, and he lay with her.
(Now she had been purifying herself from her uncleanness).
Then she returned to her house."
(2 Samuel 11:4)**

Bathsheba's long hair, still damp from her purification bath, was ushered by the servants from her home to the side entrance of David's palace.

Walking through the palace, brilliantly illuminated by thousands of burning candles, Bathsheba was in awe of its splendor.

Bathsheba had known that David's palace had been expertly crafted by carpenters and masons sent from Hiram, king of Tyre. Never having been a guest to the palace however, she marveled at its beauty.

Built of cedar wood in Phoenician style, the palace roof was nearly sixty feet high, and the rooms immense and beckoning. There were many ornately carved, large wooden facades with sacred alcoves behind them adorning the hallways.

With tapestries and artwork covering the walls that were gifts from royalty from distant lands, the palace was not only structurally sound, but also beautifully decorated. Bathsheba marveled at the floors as she stepped, which were constructed of exquisitely carved limestone, hand-crafted by Hiram's personal masonry men.

A guard on each side of her, the two men guided Bathsheba away from the main part of the palace to a secluded corridor. Walking to the end, they came to two extravagantly carved cedar wood doors which towered above them stretching to the palace roof.

Within seconds after the guards knocked briefly on the closed doors, they expectantly flew open.

Standing alone behind the open doors was David, his face flushed with excitement and his beautiful green eyes gazing longingly at Bathsheba.

Greeting Bathsheba with open arms, David ushered her quickly inside his private quarters. Quickly dismissing the guards, David closed the doors behind them. The two stood alone in David's private quarters.

Briefly looking past David, Bathsheba took in the sights of his romantically prepared private room.

Aglow by the candlelight, the spacious room was warm and inviting. Bathsheba noticed a lavish spread of a culinary delight that had been laid out with care on a huge dining table. Several sofas surrounded a fireplace, and a large bed was off to the side. The décor was lavish, yet tasteful and comfortable.

With her heart beating wildly, Bathsheba turned her gaze back to intently look into David's intense green eyes. Sparkling like a multifaceted tsavorite gem, David's eyes danced flirtingly playing on her emotions. With her attention drawn to nothing else, she focused only on David.

The evening progressed, starting with small talk between them about their times during the past years, but soon climaxed with intimacy.

David and Bathsheba, enveloped with intense desire for each other, fell prey to temptation of the flesh and engaged in sexual relations.

In a matter of minutes, the course of human history was changed.

✦✦✦✦✦✦✦✦✦✦✦

Pearl: Behind the scenes in David's Palace Quarters- *The two engaged in sexual relations soon after Bathsheba was brought to the palace by David's messengers. We don't know how long they spent together, but apparently the encounter did not last longer than the one evening – the Bible states that she arrived to the palace, had sexual relations with David, and returned to her house. All of this was stated in the same concise verse.*

Why did their sexual encounter happen so quickly? Why was there was no courtship, or getting-to-know each other time?

The answer is simple.

David and Bathsheba already knew each other.

They had known each other for years. In fact, Bathsheba grew up idolizing David, as he became the handsome, fearless leader of the Jewish people. Her family was one of the many families who followed David during his plight from Saul and fought along with him.

Bathsheba had witnessed David's rise to power as king first-hand. She had experienced the emotions of adoration and reverence for David that was shared by the nation of Israelites.

Put very simply, the Israelites loved David!

With the virtues of the quintessential king, David was courageous, handsome, musically talented, and possessed the utmost of communication and leadership skills.

Most of all, the people of Israel knew God was with him!

Even though David was King and could command Bathsheba to lay with him, it makes more sense that since the two had known each other for years that their sexual encounter was consensual.

Putting David and Bathsheba's relationship into context it is apparent that their union on that one particular evening was much more than just a casual fling.

As we discussed, since Bathsheba's father was one of David's mighty warriors, it is highly likely that her father and his family accompanied David during his escapades of battle before he was actually king of Israel. David and his army had no permanent home, so they were forced to move their families from place to place as they fled Saul and fought for their lives.

Living in tents, the warrior's children grew up encamped in the wilderness. The men's families most likely experienced first-hand the leadership of David as he was growing his forces of men.

The children undoubtedly would sit around campfires in the evening with their warrior fathers and their mothers, listening to stories of battle, and worshiping the Lord as David played his lyre.

Known as the "sweet psalmist of Israel", David wrote many of his most passionate Psalms praising the Lord during these years that he shared with his followers while on the run from Saul.

As the 'ultimate worship director' David undoubtedly was responsible for converting and strengthening his men's and their families' faith in the Lord through the music and lyrics he composed.

Putting this into context, David undoubtedly knew Bathsheba as a young girl. In fact, since Bathsheba was a young girl living with her parents as they trekked across the wilderness with David, it is very likely that her faith was strengthened through hearing David's beautiful psalms composed to the Lord.

Losing track of her throughout the years after finally moving his people to Jerusalem after he had risen to the throne, David saw what a gorgeous woman she had become.

Seeing her bathing on her terrace below his palace would have jolted David into the reality that Bathsheba was no longer a child as he had remembered her.

David may have possibly even wondered why she was now the wife of one of his warriors, rather than his own wife. How could he have let her slip away from him?

David had many wives, many who were the daughters of kings and officials from neighboring nations, but we are unclear about their faith in God. The Bible never tells us.

We do know however, that Bathsheba, born into a devout Jewish family, was raised in the Mosaic Laws and with reverence to the Lord. David would have most likely admired Bathsheba's faith in the Lord that he so worshipped.

Undoubtedly, Bathsheba held David in the highest respect as she grew up living among his ranks, and may have even had a young girl's "crush" on him in year's prior. Of interest, is that in figuring out the difference of their ages, Bathsheba would have been twenty to twenty-five years younger than David. Therefore David may have actually have served as a mentor to Bathsheba as she grew up among his loyal followers.

The invitation ~ How did that night of David and Bathsheba's union unfold?

On the night of David and Bathsheba's original sexual encounter, David most likely had sent his messengers for Bathsheba with the invitation to dine at the palace as an honored guest.

After all, Bathsheba's father and her husband were two of David's most trusted warriors, and they had been away for quite some time at battle. David may have covered up his longing for her by his concern for her well being while her father and husband were away at war.

Showing Bathsheba and her family respect and dignity, David may have thought he was justified in preparing an elaborate dinner for the two to share privately. He may have even covered up his lust with thinking that his actions originated from the good intention of catching-up and checking on how she was faring while her men-folks were away.

However, one sin easily led to another, and soon the two became overwhelmed with emotion and desire for each other. And we know how that ended.

As far as who was the father of Bathsheba's unborn child, it is made implicitly clear in the Bible that Bathsheba was not pregnant from her husband at the time of her union with David.

*Scripture specifies that Bathsheba was taking a purifying bath to be cleansed after her menstrual period, which was in compliance of Jewish law **(Leviticus 15:19-24)**. According to the law, she had finished her menstrual period, and was considered unclean for seven days.*

After the seven days, Bathsheba then purified herself, and was then considered clean. At no time had Bathsheba been with her husband after her menstrual period, indicating that David was indeed the father of the unborn child.

We will explore these twists and more later in the text.

Scene 3: Nine Weeks Later

When the warm summer days enveloped Jerusalem, Bathsheba sent a concise message to David.

Sitting alone in her home, Bathsheba knew what had to be done. Nine weeks had passed since her sexual union with David. She had skipped two menstrual periods, and she knew she was carrying the king's baby.

Tearing off a piece of parchment from her husband's accounts, Bathsheba penned three words.

"I am pregnant."
(2 Samuel 11:5)

Sending her handmaiden to the palace with note, Bathsheba instructed her to enter the court where David would be deciding cases and deliver the scroll to him personally. The handmaiden did as instructed.

Emotions caving in around him, David's heart dropped like a stone falls to the bottom of a shallow pond as he read Bathsheba's message.

David realized that his little secret sin that he thought he had carefully kept hidden away would now become common knowledge.

The sin that started with coveting, then led to adultery, had now resulted in the unspeakable.

Bathsheba, a married woman was pregnant, and the child was not fathered by her husband.

David knew without any doubt in his mind that the unborn child was his.

To make matters worse, since Bathsheba's husband was living away from his wife while at war, it would be obvious to everyone that Uriah was not the father. There would be no hiding that fact!

Realizing that soon Bathsheba's slender form would change and start to show that she was expecting a baby, David knew he had to quickly improvise a plan. The townspeople and Bathsheba's relatives would soon recognize Bathsheba's baby bump, and their tongues would be on fire!

Realizing that everyone in Jerusalem knew that Uriah was off at war and Bathsheba, being the woman left at home while her husband was away was now pregnant, David became very worried.

David was worried for Bathsheba's life.

According to Jewish law, Bathsheba would be accused of adultery.

David's heart fell and his stomach twisted with anxiety and guilt knowing that adultery was punishable by death.

By Jewish law, the adulterous woman would be dragged from her house and stoned by her own family members in order to save their honor.

David knew that he would be forgiven, but Bathsheba would not. Perhaps he could change the outcome, he thought! After all, he was the king!

As king, David reasoned that he could pardon Bathsheba and prevent her death. However, he also knew her honor would always be tainted and her life ruined. Additionally, the family's honorable name would be tarnished forever.

David was torn with anguish. How could he possibly explain-away Bathsheba's resultant pregnancy?

Knowing that he was the guilty one, David realized that Bathsheba and her family would be the ones to suffer the consequences of life-long humiliation, shame, and possibly even Bathsheba's death.

Ripped apart with guilt, David took it upon himself to devise a plan.

Thinking through the motions, David suddenly came up with a 'brilliant' idea!

First of all, David needed to get Uriah back home to Jerusalem, and the sooner the better!

♦♦♦♦♦♦♦♦♦♦♦

*P**earl:** Notice at no time in his of tremendous need for guidance does David consult the Lord. Determined to take matters into his own hands, David rushed ahead with his self-conceive plan.*

As it will turn out, each sin David committed became exponentially larger.

Soon the devil will succeed in turning David away from doing the right thing, and even temporarily turn him away from God. The devil is no match for God, but the devil will however tempt and torment those who God loves.

♦♦♦♦♦♦♦♦♦♦♦

After thinking up his "brilliant plan", David sent word to Joab, his trusty commander on the battlefield. David instructed Joab to immediately send Uriah to the palace.

Doing as commanded, Uriah soon arrived at David's palace. Greeting the king with utmost respect, Uriah settled in as David began the conversation.

After some small talk about happenings on the battlefield, David deceitfully began to instrument his scheme by suggesting that Uriah go home to visit his wife.

David thought that if Uriah would go home, he would lay with his wife and everyone would then think that he was the father of the baby. It was early enough in Bathsheba's pregnancy that this plan could work, David schemed.

But to David's dismay, Uriah refused to go home.

Being a man of duty and feeling disloyal to his men who were still in the field of battle, Uriah refused to go to his house and take the pleasure of the comforts of home.

Instead, Uriah slept outside the palace with King David's servants.

"But Uriah slept at the door of the king's house with all the servants of his lord, and did not go down to his house."
(2 Samuel 11:9)

David kept Uriah in Jerusalem for two days, eating and drinking with him, hoping that one night Uriah would succumb to temptation and go to his house to seek pleasure with his young, beautiful wife.

Uriah still refused to go home to Bathsheba. When David asked Uriah why he would not go home, Uriah answered saying that he considered himself a warrior who was still on-duty.

Uriah explained his actions by saying,

"The ark and Israel and Judah dwell in booths, and my lord Joab and the servants of my lord are camping in the open field.
Shall I then go to my house, to eat and to drink and to lie with my wife?
As you live and as your soul lives, I will not do this thing."
(2 Samuel 11:11)

✦✦✦✦✦✦✦✦✦✦

Pearl: If you think about it, Uriah's words were actually somewhat disrespectful to King David. Uriah insinuates that he would never do such a thing as stay at home enjoying pleasures of his wife while his comrades were off at war.

Uriah is actually describing exactly what David had done!

David's first sin was that as king, he did not accompany his army into battle. Instead of being in battle with his men, David had stayed behind in Jerusalem to enjoy the pleasures of his wives and the luxuries of the palace.

A second consideration is if Uriah knew that David had summoned his wife to the palace?

Perhaps, after spending the night with David's servants, Uriah had heard from them about the whole ordeal.

Did Uriah suspect that something had gone on between David and Bathsheba? Is that why Uriah did not want to go home to face his wife?

Frustrated, and desperately feeling that all of his options to cover up Bathsheba's pregnancy were exhausted, David then sent Uriah back to battle.

Along with sending Uriah back into the field, David sent a letter with Uriah addressed to his commander, Joab.

"In the morning David wrote a letter to Joab and sent it by the hand of Uriah."
(2 Samuel 11:14)

The letter was Uriah's death sentence.

In the letter David wrote,

"Set Uriah in the forefront of the hardest fighting,
and then draw back from him, that he may be struck down, and die."
(2 Samuel 11:15)

As per David's instructions, Joab sent Uriah to the front lines of battle.

◆◆◆◆◆◆◆◆◆◆◆

Pearl: *David had told his commander to put Uriah in the worst possible circumstance that one could face in battle. He commanded that Uriah go to the forefront of the fighting, and then Joab was to draw his troops back so that Uriah would surely be killed (**2 Samuel 11:14-15**).*

Joab followed King David's orders, and the outcome was as expected.

Uriah was killed in battle, along with several other brave men fighting the enemy alongside of him *(2 Samuel 11:17).*

Joab sent word via messenger to David,

"So the messenger went and came and told David all that Joab had sent him to tell. The messenger said to David, The men gained an advantage over us and came out against us in the field, but we drove them back to the entrance of the gate. Then the archers shot at your servants from the wall. Some of the king's servants are dead, and your servant Uriah the Hittite is dead also."
(2 Samuel 11:22-24)

♦♦♦♦♦♦♦♦♦♦♦

Pearl: *Joab departed from standard military tactics, which called for an army, which is besieging a city to remain a safe distance from the city's wall, out of the range of the archers and slingers positioned atop the wall.*

♦♦♦♦♦♦♦♦♦♦♦

David was responsible for Uriah's death, as well as the death of several others of his loyal men who all had been placed in a horrific predicament because of his orders.

The news of the Uriah's death reached Jerusalem, and Bathsheba mourned her husband's death *(2 Samuel 11:26).* The relatives of the other loyal men also mourned the loss of their loved ones.

♦♦♦♦♦♦♦♦♦♦♦

Pearl: *We don't know how long after the incident, but it is clear that David then took Bathsheba as his wife. The mourning period was probably seven days, as was customary in ancient Jewish culture (**Genesis 50:10**). David most likely waited seven days before taking Bathsheba into his palace and making her his wife. Some months later, she delivered David's son.*

"And when the mourning was over, David sent and brought her to his house, and she became his wife and bore him a son."
(2 Samuel 11:27)

♦♦♦♦♦♦♦♦♦♦♦

The Lord sees everything and God, the Almighty, was angered. What David did was evil in the eyes of the LORD *(Psalm 51:4).*

"The thing that David had done displeased the Lord."
(2 Samuel 11:27)

The Lord was silently watching, and although David's actions failed to be displeasing to the people from whom David had successfully concealed the entire affair, it could not be concealed from God, from whom one cannot conceal anything.

✦✦✦✦✦✦✦✦✦✦✦

P*earl: How did David's sin of adultery escalate to murder?*

*David had started the downward spiral of sin by first breaking the tenth commandment (coveting; **Exodus 20:17**). This led to him then breaking the seventh commandment (adultery; **Exodus 20:14**), and then finally, the sixth commandment (murder; **Exodus 20:13**).*

Seeming as though the magnitude of the sin became increasingly worse, it appears that once a lesser sin was committed, each sin thereafter was greater, yet easier for David to carry out.

The Lord had watched David commit his multiple sins, and now called him to account for his actions. God sent the prophet Nathan to David to get him to acknowledge and confess his wrongdoings.

David had continued to run further and further from God, unwilling to face the consequences of his actions. It was time to face up to his sins, repent, and turn back to God.

Scene 4: Repentance

2 Samuel 12, Psalm 51

Playlist: "God Only Knows" by King and Country, "Holy Water" by We The Kingdom

The prophet Nathan, who served as David's counselor, came to David asking him for his judgement concerning a legal matter. The parable that Nathan described to David as a case for judgement was meant to point out to the king that his own actions did not match his judgement of others.

Essentially, without knowing it, David will be put in a position to cast judgement on his own case of his sins committed.

◆◆◆◆◆◆◆◆◆◆◆

Pearl: In the day, the King was often asked to issue judgement in legal disputes that would arise among the people. In this instance, Nathan brought forth a fictitious case to David that served as a parable to illustrate to David the sins that he had committed.

Parallels can be drawn to the way in which Jesus taught, using parables to communicate important points to His disciples and others.

◆◆◆◆◆◆◆◆◆◆◆

The case that Nathan presented illustrated that the king, as the Lord's representative, should have the responsibility and conscience to protect his people against abuse by the powerful.

In the parable Nathan described, there was a rich man who had many flocks of sheep. This rich man took a poor man's only lamb for his own feast, as he was unwilling to take a lamb from his own flock of many sheep.

The similarities to David taking Bathsheba were astonishing, but David at first did not make the connection.

Listening to Nathan's parable, David became very angry with the rich man because of his actions and quickly passed judgement against him. In an outburst of anger, David proclaimed that the rich man should not only restore the lamb to the poor man fourfold, but that he should die for his crime.

Nathan, realizing that David did not understand the deeper meaning and how it applied to him said,

"You are the man!"
(1 Samuel 12:7)

God then punished David for his sins. The Lord's punishment of David met the severity of the sins he had committed.

The Lord sent forth His dire news regarding the punishment of David through the prophet, Nathan.

In the words of the Lord, Nathan told David that because of his sinful acts, the following would happen,

"Therefore the sword shall never depart from your house,
because you have despised me and have taken the wife of Uriah the Hittite to be
your wife.
I will raise up evil against you out of your own house."
(2 Samuel 12:10)

In addition, because David had scorned the Lord, the child that Bathsheba will soon bear to David shall die *(2 Samuel 12:14).*

David acknowledged that he had sinned against the Lord. He exhibited sincere remorse and prayed for forgiveness.

God's amazing Grace accepted David's repentance. David's life was spared, but the Lord's punishment was not.

The son born to David died on the seventh day of his life *(2 Samuel 12:18)*.

During these times of trial, David responded to the Lord with repentance and praise. His response included his writing of *Psalm 51*. The psalm reinforces the view found in the Levitical system that the sacrifices bestow their benefits only on those who use them in humble and penitent faith *(Exodus 34:6-7)*.

Pearl: **Psalm 51** *in entirety has been included to embrace David's repentance. It is known as the Penitential Psalm, or the Psalm of Confession.*

Psalm 51 "The Penitential Psalm"
"Have mercy on me, O God, according to your steadfast love;
Bolt out my transgressions, Wash me thoroughly from my iniquity, and cleanse me from my sin!
For I know my transgressions, and my sin is ever before me.
Against you, you only, have I sinned and done what is evil in your sight, so that you may be justified in your words and blameless in your judgement.
Behold, I was brought forth in iniquity, and in sin did my mother conceive me.
Behold, you delight in truth in the inward being, and you teach me wisdom in the secret heart.
Purge me with hyssop, and I shall be clean; wash me, and I shall be whiter than snow.
Let me hear joy and gladness; let the bones that you have broken rejoice.
Hide your face from my sins, and blot out all my iniquities.
Create in me a clean heart, O God; and renew a right spirit within me. Cast me not away from your presence, and take not your Holy Spirit from me.
Restore to me the joy of your salvation, and uphold me with a willing spirit.
Then I will teach transgressors your ways, and sinners will return to you.
Deliver me from bloodguiltiness, O God O God of my salvation, and my tongue will sing aloud of your righteousness.
O Lord, open my lips, and my mouth will declare your praise. For you will not delight in sacrifice, or I would give it; you will not be pleased with a burnt offering.
The sacrifices of God are a broken spirit; a broken and contrite heart, O God, you will not despise.
Do good to Zion in your good pleasure; build up the walls of Jerusalem; then will you delight in right sacrifices, in burnt offerings and whole burnt offerings; then bulls will be offered on you altar.
Restore to me the joy of your salvation, and uphold me with a willing spirit."

David most likely out of anguish and remorse also wrote several other Psalms. In reading **Psalms 10, 31 and 32,** *parallels can be drawn to his experiences during this time of his life.*

"Into your hand I commit my spirit; you have redeemed me, O LORD, faithful God.
I will rejoice and be glad in your steadfast love, because you have seen my affliction: you have known the distress of my soul."
(Psalm 31: 5,7)

P *earl: The Midrashic commentaries point out that a major lesson to be derived from this incident is the enormous power of repentance.*

God will assure us a pardon. God will forgive, however we only receive His mercy through our repentance. More than mercy, we receive His grace, His cheshed.

However, we must sincerely be remorseful of our sin to truly repent. Only then will we be forgiven.

As Christians, we remember that Jesus, as the ultimate judge quickly took on our guilty verdict so that we are eternally pardoned from sin. All we have to do is embrace our sin, repent and receive the love of Jesus Christ. Through our savior, we are redeemed.

A reminder of who the Lord is, concerning his mercy, grace and justice can be found in the Word of the Lord himself as He spoke with Moses, written in **Exodus 34:6-7.**

"The LORD, the LORD, a God merciful and gracious, slow to anger, and abounding in steadfast love and faithfulness, keeping steadfast love for thousands, forgiving iniquity and transgression and sin, but who will by no means clear the guilty, visiting the iniquity of the fathers on the children and the children's children, to the third and fourth generation."
(Exodus 34:6-7)

✦✦✦✦✦✦✦✦✦✦✦

Nathan and Solomon are born

Bathsheba and David went on to have four sons after the tragic death of their firstborn. Their sons were Shammua, Shobab, Nathan and Solomon (*Shlomo* in Hebrew).

As we follow the lineage of Jesus Christ, the two sons Nathan and Solomon are of interest. Each are listed in the Gospels of being in Jesus' ancestry.

However, as we pointed out before the Gospel of Luke and Matthew differ, starting with these two brothers.

In the New Testament, the genealogy of Jesus is traced back to King David in the Gospel of Luke *(Luke 3:31)*, and Matthew *(Matthew 1:16)*. The two Gospels diverge after David, as Jesus' lineage is traced through the line of Nathan according to Luke, and through Solomon according to Matthew.

P *earl: No matter which son of David continued the line of Jesus, it is apparent that David's sins did not change God's Master plan to bring forth the Messiah through David's lineage.*

Through the offspring of David and Bathsheba, Jesus Christ will be brought forth and will bring salvation to humanity.

♦♦♦♦♦♦♦♦♦♦♦

Solomon, one of David's sons with Bathsheba, will become the next King of Israel after much conflict.

How was it that Solomon became the next king of Israel? This was out of the ordinary, as David had six sons from his other wives prior to any son being born from his union with Bathsheba.

♦♦♦♦♦♦♦♦♦♦♦

P *earl: According to the Midrash, Solomon's birth was symbolic of how the Lord informed David that his sins with Bathsheba had been forgiven (1 Chronicles 22:9-11).*

"Behold, a son will be born to you; he will be a man of peace, and I shall give him peace from all his enemies around about, for Solomon will be is name, and I shall give peace and quiet to Israel in his days. He shall build a House in my Name, and he shall be to Me as a son, and I to him as a father, and I shall prepare the throne of his kingdom forever."
(1 Chronicles 22:9-11 ~Hebrew Bible~)

♦♦♦♦♦♦♦♦♦♦♦

We will briefly describe events over the next two decades, leading to God choosing Solomon as the next King of Israel.

However, things for David in the meantime will not be easy – as the Lord is true to his Word, and David will therefore be disciplined.

Remembering the Lord's words to David,

"Now therefore the sword shall never depart from your house, because you have despised me and have taken the wife of Uriah the Hittite to be your wife."
(2 Samuel 12:10)

As the prophet Nathan had forewarned, violence and betrayal were the consequences of God's punishment on David's family.

These events, over the next several decades can be condensed as follows:
- David's firstborn son Amnon (by his wife Ahinoam of Jezreel), raped his half-sister Tamar *(2 Samuel 13)*
  - As a result, Amnon was later killed by his half-brother Absalom
- Absalom, David's third son (by Maakah) rebelled against David, and tried to take over his kingdom *(2 Samuel 14-18)*
  - David had to flee Jerusalem with his wives
  - Absalom took over David's kingdom and all of his concubines
  - Absalom died while trying to escape David's armies
- As David was dying, his fourth son, Adonijah (by Haggith) declared himself as the new King of Israel
  - God had other plans, as He had chosen Solomon, the son of Bathsheba to rule after David *(1 Chronicles 22:9)*
    - God granted Solomon wisdom and the blessings of peace and prosperity for his kingdom
    - Solomon was charged by God to build the House for the Lord, the Temple, as part of the transfer of leadership from David.
    - Solomon would have many accomplishments and demonstrate wisdom in his leadership, resulting in a *'golden age'* for Israel.
      - Israel's borders expanded and reached its largest size
      - Solomon wrote many of the Proverbs and several books that would become incorporated into the Bible
      - Solomon's construction projects included the temple in Jerusalem, the royal palace, and many cities
        - David chose the site for the temple and began to organize the project, making extensive preparations prior to his death *(1 Chronicles 22:2-5)*
        - David charged his son Solomon with building the temple.
        - David knew that he could not erect the edifice of worship as God had instructed David that his son, Solomon, would build the house in God's name *(1 Chronicles 22:6-16).*
        - King Solomon built the Most Holy Place (the Holy of Holies) of the temple on the top of Mount Moriah *(2 Chronicles 3:1).*
      - Israel's wealth increased through trade with other kingdoms

- Eventually, Solomon will rebel against God, going against what God described as the ideal king in **Deuteronomy 17:14-20**
- As a result of his rebellion against God, Solomon's rule ended with failure.
- After Solomon's death, the Kingdom of Israel would be divided into northern Israel and southern Judah.
- Eventually both northern and southern divisions of Israel would be destroyed *(1 Kings 11: 9,11; 1 Kings 12-14, 2 Kings 25).*

To delve deeper into the understanding of the people who make up Jesus' family tree and to better understand God's Word, we will take a slight diversion from looking solely at David.

We will now go behind the scenes to uncover some more interesting information about Bathsheba.

It turns out that Bathsheba is not just a beautiful woman who David lusted after. Bathsheba is much, much more.

Scene 5: The Enigma of Bathsheba

David's wife, and mother of Solomon and Nathan

Playlist: *"Be a Miracle" by Natalie Grant*

Background information and Introduction: While trying to understand Bathsheba and who she actually was, we run into some interesting twists and turns.

It turns out that the story of Bathsheba is like the cut face of an exquisite diamond, quite multifaceted. We definitely should not just associate her with her one sinful act of adultery with King David.

We don't know much about Bathsheba directly from Scripture, but upon reading deeper into the Bible and from reading the Rabbi's commentary in the Midrash, we can get a better insight about the **mystery and enigma of Bathsheba**.

For starters, Bathsheba is mentioned directly in _four incidents_ in Scripture:
- Her illegitimate sexual encounter with King David *(2 Samuel 11)*
- Her reaction to the death of her infant first-born son *(2 Samuel 12)*
- Her request for David to honor his oath of kingship to Solomon *(2 Kings 1)*

✦ Her request made to Solomon on behalf of Adonijah, concerning taking Abishag as his wife *(2 Kings 2)*

With so little information concerning Bathsheba, piecing things together concerning her character from what is said about her in the Bible is difficult.

Difficult, but not impossible!

Taking the challenge of finding out who Bathsheba really was, one needs to go deeper into the quest for information and consult several sources. As a reward for searching deeper, some interesting details concerning Bathsheba's lineage and character can be found.

Also of significance is the finding of some twists concerning the context of the culture during this time era.

With context in mind, this information can be applied to circumstances surrounding David and Bathsheba, giving further insight into who Bathsheba really was. Many of these insights are taken from the Jewish Rabbis' commentary in the Midrash.

Bathsheba's Ancestry and Marriage Ties

We do know a certain amount about Bathsheba's family, which gives us some insight into her background and cultural roots.

We know that she was from a prominent Israelite family, and had married a well-respected, loyal man that was a member of King David's elite army.

Let's take a look at the men in Bathsheba's life.

Bathsheba's father and first-husband:
Bathsheba's father was Eliam *(2 Samuel 11:3),* the son of Ahithophel of Gilo *(2 Samuel 23:34).* Bathsheba's first husband was Uriah the Hittite *(2 Samuel 11:3).*

Bathsheba's father and husband were both in prominent positions in David's kingdom, as they served in the elite palace guard. Both were mentioned as David's *'Mighty Men'*, part of the elite *'thirty' (2 Samuel 23: 32, 39)*. Both Eliam and Uriah were most likely very close and loyal to David to have had this honor bestowed upon them.

It was highly likely that to have such an honor to be listed among David's Mighty Men, both Bathsheba's father and her husband had at some point defended David's life to have been named in such an elite list.

Other Important Findings:

✦ Bathsheba's birth name was originally Bath-shua *(1 Chronicles 3:5)*. Her name was changed at some point early in her life to Bathsheba.

✦ It is not unusual among the Israelites to have a name change, which often occurs at the ceremony of Bar Mitzvah or Bat-Mitzvah.

✦ The child's birth name reflected on the feelings of the parents at the time of birth of the baby, while the second name was to reflect more of the child's own individual character.

    ○ Bathshua means 'daughter of my prosperity'.

    ○ Bathsheba signifies "daughter of an oath," and often refers to the oath or covenant God made with Abraham.

♦♦♦♦♦♦♦♦♦♦♦

P*earl: The name change is said by the Rabbis to be a positive thing, as rather than reflecting the material prosperity of her father at the time of her birth, it apprises spiritual growth.*

✦ Bathsheba's father was known as Eliam *(2 Samuel 11:3)*, also known as Ammiel *(1 Chronicles 3:5)*.

    ○ Eliam was a very prominent figure in Israel, and held a position in the elite guard of King David.

    ○ Seeing how Eliam named his daughter, she must have been born when he already held this position as David's guard.

    ○ Fittingly, this would put Bathsheba as a young woman of about twenty-something, when she and David had their illicit sexual encounter.

    ○ David most likely knew Bathsheba as she was growing up, as she would have accompanied her father as he was a member of David's elite guard as David moved his army to follow him to various places fleeing from Saul and fighting Israel's enemies.

        ■ Over the course of fourteen years the guards and their families devoutly followed David as he fled from Saul, living in the wilderness, then moving into the Philistine city of Ziklag. Eventually when David became king, his men and their families moved to Hebron and then on to Jerusalem.

        ■ In Jerusalem, Bathsheba became of marrying age and wed Uriah. Being a friend of her father's, Uriah was an excellent choice for her as a husband, as he was another prominent member of David's elite guard.

Bathsheba's Grandfather:

Ahithophel, the father of Eliam, was Bathsheba's grandfather. Ahithophel was also a prominent figure in David's court as he was king David's chief counselor, ranking above Jehoiada and Abiathar (*1 Chronicles 27: 33, 34*).

Ahithophel's counsel was considered very wise and,

> *"was if one consulted the word of God; so was all the counsel of Ahithophel esteemed both by David and Absalom"*
> *(2 Samuel 16:23).*

Ahithophel eventually turned against David, becoming Absalom's counselor when Absalom rebelled against his father. Giving strategic advice to Absalom to try to help him overthrow David, Ahithophel eventually committed treason against King David.

However, God was with David, and not Absalom and Ahithophel's advice was therefore rejected.

Ahithophel realized that the rejection of his advice meant the defeat of Absalom and his own ruin, which lead to him taking his own life *(2 Samuel 17:23).*

According to the Midrash, rather than dying the ignominious death of a traitor, Ahithophel chose a self-inflicted death and hanged himself.

David wrote of his own remorse concerning Ahithophel's treason in *Psalms 55:12-14.*

> *"For it is not an enemy who taunts me – then I could bear it; it is not an adversary who deals insolently with me – then I could hide from him. But it is you, a man, my equal, my companion, my familiar friend. We used to take sweet counsel together; within God's house we walked in the throng."*

We don't know the motive behind why Ahithophel turned against David.

The Rabbis of the Midrash theorize that Ahithophel's motive behind his treason was to avenge David for taking his granddaughter, Bathsheba as his wife and having her husband killed.

We do know for sure that David and Bathsheba were married at the time, and that Bathsheba remained a loyal wife to David throughout all of the tragic unfolding of events concerning her grandfather.

Going deeper ~ How did Bathsheba feel about her illegitimate sexual encounter with King David?

Scripture is silent concerning Bathsheba's feelings during the time of the illicit affair with David. However, we assume that like David, Bathsheba had the humility to repent for her sin of adultery.

We have several reasons to believe that Bathsheba repented after reading and digesting excerpts from Rabbis in the Midrash.

The Midrash spotlights the power of repentance. The Rabbis give prominence in their commentaries concerning God's forgiveness of both David and Bathsheba.

✦✦✦✦✦✦✦✦✦✦✦

Pearl: *The Midrash Rabbis emphasize that God forgave David for his sin due to his repentance, and thereby endorsed his marriage to Bathsheba. The Rabbis bring attention that through Bathsheba's son with David, Solomon, and the royal dynasty of the Davidic line was continued that indicated that both David and Bathsheba were forgiven.*

Was Bathsheba destined to become David's wife to continue the Davidic Dynasty?

The commentary of Rabbis in the Midrash indicates that Bathsheba had actually been destined to become David's wife.

However, David rather than being patient, chose to enjoy her as 'unripe fruit' (David did not wait until she was legitimately his before having relations with her).

The Rabbinic scholar, J.K. Alschich, further exegetes that David, endowed with the Divine Spirit, was aware of the role that Bathsheba was to play in his destiny. David was therefore surprised that she was given to another man when he found out her identity, and that she was married to Uriah.

As we touched on earlier, these interpretations are based on the way that the Masoretic text of the Hebrew Bible reads, which is as follows. The ESV, NIV and KJ version differs by one word.

2 Samuel 11:3 (Hebrew Bible)
"And David sent, and inquired about the woman. <u>And he said</u>: 'Is this not Bathsheba, the daughter of Eliam, the wife of Uriah the Hittite?"

2 Samuel 11:3 (ESV, NIV, KJV)
"And David sent and inquired about the woman. <u>And one said</u>, "Is not this
Bathsheba, the daughter of Eliam, the wife of Uriah the Hittite?"

Alschich contends that the way the scripture is worded, indicated that it was David that said this statement about Bathsheba after being informed of the woman's identity.

In contrast, the ESV (and NIV, and KJV) indicates that the statement about Bathsheba's heritage and marriage was communicated to David by the servant.

What difference does this make?

If David said this, he obviously knew of Bathsheba, of her heritage and of her marriage. David undoubtedly knew her personally, especially considering that Bathsheba's father and her husband were part of his elite royal guard and were part of the esoteric, loyal group of 'mighty men'.

The account of the sin between David and Bathsheba brings up some interesting questions:

Can they be answered?

The first question of whether David knew Bathsheba personally prior to their illicit affair has already been briefly discussed. A summary has been included here:

Through delving deep into scripture, ancient writings of the Rabbis and putting events into logical chronological order and context of the day, answers can be obtained. We looked at some of these before, and here a summary is provided for the reader. Additionally, some new information is provided concerning David and Bathsheba.

Here are some questions that arise after reading the biblical account of David and Bathsheba:

+ **Did David know her personally prior to their encounter?**
  - It actually would fit that David and Bathsheba knew each other prior to their first illicit encounter, knowing that Bathsheba's father and husband were both in prominent positions in David's kingdom serving in the elite palace guard. As previously mentioned, both were among David's 'Mighty Men', as each were one of the **thirty-seven (2 Sam 23:32 and 39) and were most likely close to David to have had this honor bestowed upon them.**
  - *Did David know Bathsheba as she was growing up?*

- Most likely he did. Looking at Scripture carefully and putting David's life in chronological order, it is very possible that David encountered Bathsheba as a young girl, as he knew her father and her family well.
- Seeing that Bathsheba's father was part of David's elite guard it would be highly likely that Bathsheba and her family were one of the many families of the loyal soldiers who followed David in his plight from, and in the conquest of Israel's enemies.
  - From the plight in the wilderness, to settling in Ziklag, Hebron then on to Jerusalem, David's royal army and their families followed David from place to place as he relocated his kingdom and his army.
- David's loyal troops and their families relocated depending upon David's direction that followed in obedience to God.
- Following their leader, David's loyal warriors, who continuously moved their families along with them in David's plight against his enemies, asked no questions.

The second question delves even deeper and helps put some additional ideas into context:

✦ **Was the fact that Bathsheba was a soldier's wife actually something that entered in to David's decision to pursue her, rather than deter him?**
- For some answers, let's turn to the Rabbinical Midrash. According to Rabbinical commentary, David as the King of Israel, had started the tradition that his soldiers who left for battle **would issue their wives a divorce.**
  - *Although this sounds cruel, it actually served an important purpose.*
    - *This was done to avoid a waiting period before the wife could remarry, in the case that the soldier was killed in battle.*
    - *With the dual purpose of protection of the woman who would be a widow and on her own, as well as allowing her to continue to produce children, this law was actually beneficial to the women whose husbands were part of the royal army.*
    - *Upon return from battle, the surviving soldiers would then re-marry their wives.*
  - Putting this information into context, this meant that Bathsheba and her husband Uriah were **legally divorced during the time of her illicit affair with David.**

- o   Did David rationalize that he could have sexual relations with Bathsheba, as she was not 'legally' a married woman? We don't know for sure, but if this law was in place as historians have suggested, David may have been justified in his own mind to pursue Bathsheba. Knowing that as a soldier's wife, Bathsheba's husband would have issued her a divorce prior to going off to battle.

◆◆◆◆◆◆◆◆◆◆◆

Pearl: An opinion in the Midrash offered by Rabbeinu Tam, the grandson of Rashi, argued that in keeping with the tradition of the time, Uriah would have given his wife a divorce when he left for battle. This held with the tradition that soldiers who left for battle on behalf of King David gave their wives a divorce.

The rabbis in the Midrash explained why this custom originated.

- *This allowed the wife to re-marry in the event of their husband's disappearance. These divorces stipulated that if the husband failed to return within a given time frame after the close of battle, the divorce would become valid retroactively.*
- *The husband left for battle with a strong promise to remarry his 'ex-wife' upon his return.*
- *If the soldier did return from battle and had been previously married, the couple would remarry upon the return of the husband.*

Pearl: Rabbeinu Tam said that after David inquired about Bathsheba, he knew that she had been granted a divorce by her husband; therefore David did not legally commit adultery.

However, the Rabbis don't mention that David himself was still legally married to six women.

Author's Pearl: Putting this fact into context, the Rabbis say that David and Bathsheba did not commit the sin of adultery. However, David was still married. Besides, if that was the case then why did David summon Uriah home from battle to try to cover up her pregnancy?

Note: Even though some of the Rabbis claim that they did not commit adultery, they definitely do not dispute the fact that David caused the death of Uriah, and the seriousness of his transgression.

✦ *Another question that often arises is that of Bathsheba's bathing on her porch. Scholars question whether Bathsheba was modest about her bathing?* **Why did Bathsheba bathe so publicly so that David could see her?**

Putting this question into context, we have to consider the architecture of the buildings and the ritual of a woman bathing in ancient Jerusalem.

- ○ ***Bathsheba probably did not consider that she was bathing publicly. Why?***
- ○ The houses in Jerusalem at the time had surrounding walls for protection and privacy. They were located in the Millo district, which was an area of Jerusalem that had a terraced construction. The protective walls around the Millo were made of earth and stone, and therefore were definitely not transparent.
- ○ The houses in the Millo district were located on a steep slope south of David's palace. David was looking down on the houses from his roof, which had a high vantage point so the walls around her house did not afford her total privacy from his view.
- ○ Bathsheba was undoubtedly unaware that she was being observed, as she thought that she had the privacy afforded by the surrounding walls. David may have actually only seen a vague view of Bathsheba, as it was late in the afternoon and the light was getting dim. Additionally, her house may have been a considerable distance from David's palace, making it difficult for David to see her in great detail.
  - ▪ David's palace was built on the ruins of the *Jebusite Citadel* north of the city, which placed it higher and at a distance from the city. David most likely was only seeing Bathsheba from a distance.
- ○ The Midrash comments that Bathsheba was partaking in a ritual bath connected with the uncleanness that was associated with a woman for seven days after her menstrual period *(Leviticus 15:25-33).*
  - ▪ This was most likely mentioned to not only describe her adherence to the Mosaic Law described in the Torah, but also to prove that she was not already pregnant at the time of her encounter with David.
- ○ Bathsheba is not presented in Scripture, or in the Midrash as being a seductress.
- ○ We don't know if she was a willing participant after David summoned her to his palace, although it is clear that David is the King and had started multiplying wives and concubines unto him, indicating that he had an eye for the ladies *(2 Samuel 5:13).*

- Bathsheba may have been under the impression that she too would become David's wife. Her husband had been gone to war for many months.
- Undoubtedly, Bathsheba was anxious to produce children, as having children in ancient Jewish culture was of high priority and of utmost importance to a Jewish woman.

✦ *And finally, the question of "How did the people of Israel look upon Bathsheba?"*

The astute reader has to wonder that even though God forgave David and Bathsheba, how did the people of Israel view Bathsheba? The people were known to have revered David, so they most likely looked the other way considering his sin with Bathsheba. But what were the feelings of the Israelites in regards to Bathsheba?

Was there the usual gossip and even slander concerning their marriage? Were there whispers among the servants and talk among the townspeople? How was Bathsheba received among David's other wives?

In doing the math and figuring out the time span involved from Bathsheba's note to David saying she was pregnant to her actually becoming his wife, one must figure that this could have occurred as soon as two to three weeks.

We know that Bathsheba mourned Uriah's death, and that the mourning period was probably seven days, according to Mosaic Law (**Genesis 50:10**). After that, Bathsheba became David's wife.

Scripture then stated that Bathsheba bore David a son. Interestingly, Bathsheba would have only been in the palace as David's wife for approximately six months before giving birth. Would this have raised some eyebrows among David's other wives, his servants, and the townspeople?

What did Bathsheba's family have to say about this time frame of her marriage to David to giving birth of six months?

Of significance is that the answers to these questions are not given in Scripture, nor do the Rabbis comment on this in the Midrash.

✦✦✦✦✦✦✦✦✦✦✦

Pearl: *We may consider that there most likely were those who condemned Bathsheba. What is important however is that with repentance, there is forgiveness. We are all sinners. God with His mercy, forgives.*

With Bathsheba and David's repentance, God gave His forgiveness. Not to say that their sins were left unpunished, as their first son died at a week of age. One can only imagine the heartache that both Bathsheba and David felt. But God did allow them other sons.

The remainder of David's reign was fraught with turmoil and anguish. After the first twenty years of building a kingdom, the next twenty years seemed as though it was becoming undone.

As it turns out, even though it seemed as if David's kingdom was falling apart, all was falling into place. Through the lineage of David and Bathsheba, the One perfect savior of humanity was ultimately created.

Using the most unsuspected, unworthy people, God fit Bathsheba and David perfectly into His Masterplan.

God's love motivated His plan of salvation through Jesus Christ and importantly, through Bathsheba, the lineage of Jesus Christ and His grace continued.

Romans 5:8
"God shows his love for us in that while we were still sinners, Christ died for us."

Other unanswered questions about the mystery of Bathsheba:

✦ *Bathsheba as a faithful mother?*
✦ *Her feelings about the first-born?*
✦ *What about her other sons born to David?*

In *1 Chronicles 3:5*, Bathsheba is mentioned as the mother of David's four children in Jerusalem.

"These were born to him in Jerusalem: Shimea, Shobab, Nathan and Solomon, four by Bath-shua, the daughter of Ammiel."

✦ Bathsheba was most likely David's only *wife* to bear him children in Jerusalem.

- o *1 Chronicles 3:6-9* recounts six sons born to David in Hebron from his original six wives. Scripture then states that thirteen other sons and one daughter (Tamar) were born to David in Jerusalem, where he reigned for thirty-three years. Four of these nine were from Bathsheba, but Scripture does not specify if the other nine sons were from David's other wives, or from his concubines. Tamar's mother is also not listed.
- ✦ Bathsheba's first son she bore to David, who was the product of their illegitimate union, died at seven days of age. This was prophesized by Nathan and part of God's punishment for David's sin *(2 Samuel 12)*.
- ✦ Bathsheba mourned the loss of her newborn son, as Scripture mentioned that she mourned and that David comforted his wife *(2 Samuel 12:24)*.
  - o When the child died, David worshipped the Lord and accepted the Lord's discipline, rather than being bitter *(2 Samuel 12:20)*.
  - o *There is no reason to think that Bathsheba felt any differently.*
- ✦ **Solomon** is mentioned as being the fourth son of David by Bathsheba *(1 Chronicles 3:5)*
  - o In the Gospel of Matthew, Jesus' lineage is traced to King David through the line of Solomon *(Matthew 1:6-7)*.
  - o Nathan, the prophet named him *Jedidiah,* meaning "*beloved of Jehovah*" *(2 Samuel 12:25)*.
  - o David named him Solomon, meaning *"peaceful" (2 Samuel 12:24)*.
- ✦ **Nathan**, listed as Bathsheba's third son with David, was named by Bathsheba herself in honor of the prophet Nathan, her counselor *(1 Chronicles 3:5)*.
  - o The naming of her son after the prophet, Nathan, shows insight into Bathsheba's character, as this was the man who carried the dire news of the Lord concerning her first-born son with David.
  - o Bathsheba must have humbly accepted Nathan's words of punishment for her to have honored him by naming her son with his name.
  - o In the Gospel of Luke, Jesus' lineage to King David is traced through the line of Nathan.
    - ▪ Jesus' lineage connects to Nathan through Heli, the son of Matthat *(Luke 3:31-32)*.
  - o Little is mentioned of Nathan in the Bible.
    - ▪ One instance is in *1 Kings 4:5* where Nathan's son, Azariah, is in charge of the district governors under the reign of Solomon.

Scene 6: Bathsheba ~ the faithful wife and mother

Pre-reading: 1 Kings: 1-4, 1 Chronicles 22-34, Psalm 23
Ca. 970 B.C.

Playlist: "Psalm 23" by Peter Furler, "Going Home" by Chris Tomlin, "Almost Home" by MercyMe, "Dear Younger Me" by MercyMe

Introduction: Bathsheba had a special standing with David, and was definitely one of his most favored wives. Scripture does not mention him consulting with any of his other wives during his marriage to them, as it does with Bathsheba.

Additionally, David fully acknowledged that Bathsheba's son, Solomon was to step into being the King of Israel upon his death.

This leads us to believe that Bathsheba had raised her sons under the guidance of God, which lead to David being able to trust them. One in particular, Solomon, was David's choice to be the next king of Israel.

Bathsheba sat outside of David's chambers with her head in her hands. Fighting back tears, she was faced with seeing her husband, the King of Israel, on his deathbed.

Once the strong, courageous man who had built Israel into an empire, David was now very ill and completely out of touch with what was happening in his kingdom.

At seventy years of age, David had prepared over the last few years to hand his kingship down to his son, Solomon.

Years before, David had charged Solomon as the son who should build a house for the Lord, the God of Israel.

Bathsheba recalled what David had said to their young son, Solomon,

"My son, I had it in my heart to build a house to the name of the LORD my God. But the word of the LORD came to me, saying,
You have shed much blood and have waged great wars.
You shall not build a house to my name, because you have shed so much blood before me on the earth."
(1 Chronicles 22:6-8)

Bathsheba thought back on the Lord's reasoning that Solomon would one day be King of Israel and that he importantly, he should be the one to build the temple.

Before Solomon was even born, David had told her that the Lord, with the Almighty saying, had instructed him,

> *"Behold, a son shall be born to you who shall be a man of rest. I will give him rest from all his surrounding enemies.*
> *For his name shall be Solomon, and I will give peace and quiet to Israel in his days. He shall build a house for my name.*
> *He shall be my son, and I will be his father, and I will establish his royal throne in Israel forever."*
> *(1 Chronicles 22:9-10)*

David had spent years helping to make preparations for the temple, as he wanted Solomon to be successful. Most of all, David wanted the Lord to be with Solomon in all that he did.

Bathsheba remembered how David had mentored Solomon with wise words, saying,

> *"Now my son, the LORD be with you, so that you may succeed in building the house of the LORD your God, as he has spoken concerning you.*
> *Only may the LORD grant you discretion and understanding, that when he gives you charge over Israel you may keep the law of the LORD your God.*
> *Then you will prosper if you are careful to observe the statues and the rules that the LORD commanded Moses for Israel.*
> *Be strong and courageous.*
> *Fear not; do not be dismayed."*
> *(1 Chronicles 22:11-13)*

With careful planning and follow-through, David had provided for the house of the Lord, setting aside great amounts of gold, silver, bronze, iron, timer, stone, and an abundance of skilled workmen and craftsmen. He had also commanded all the leaders of Israel to stand with his son, Solomon.

David's further preparations included the provision of religious, military and political leaders to help Solomon with staffing the temple with personnel and royal officials.

Bathsheba had seen this all unfold, feeling grateful to her husband for his planning, and for his mentoring of their son.

Now, years later, although Solomon was only in his early twenties, Bathsheba and her counselor, the prophet Nathan, felt that Solomon was ready to take on the challenge of the throne.

Unfortunately, David, who was once a strong man of war and authority, now is an old man on his deathbed who had grown out of touch with what is happening in his kingdom.

Unbeknownst to David, his oldest surviving son, Adonijah, son of Haggith, had already exalted himself as king saying,

"I will be king!"
(1 Kings 1:5)

Bathsheba was frustrated, as Adonijah was usurping both David's and the Lord's designation of Solomon being the choice to succeed David as King of Israel *(1 Chronicles 22:6-10)*.

Fighting back tears, Bathsheba thought back over the years and the trouble David's sons had caused.

If it wasn't enough that David's son Absalom had created a takeover that nearly tore the kingdom apart! Now, since Absalom's death, the handsome brother born after Absalom, Adonijah, was the oldest surviving son who thought himself to be the rightful heir to the throne upon David's death.

Like Absalom, Adonijah had also been indulged, and not held accountable for his actions by David throughout their childhood and adolescence.

Bathsheba blamed herself somewhat for David's inability to deal justly with his sons. Since his sin with her, it seemed that even as the head of the household, David had lost his moral courage when dealing with issues with his sons from his many other wives.

Time after time, David demonstrated that he was unwilling to punish his sons from his wives before Bathsheba for their disrespectful actions, which never ended well.

David's parental negligence had led to Absalom's rebellion when he tried to take over David's dynasty. The takeover was eventually unsuccessful, and tragically ended in Absalom's untimely death.

Now Adonijah, following in his brother's footsteps with extreme arrogance and disrespect, was also headed for disaster.

Bathsheba knew she had to counsel her husband, as she was aware that in his current state of illness he was not able to keep up with what was going on with his rebellious son, Adonijah.

David had been ill for quite some time and had lost touch with the inner-happenings of his beloved kingdom of Israel. Sequestered in his chambers day and night, David was no longer able to perform his duties as king.

This lack of awareness by David concerning Israel deeply saddened Bathsheba, as she remembered David in the height of his career with his reputation of having the **"wisdom of the angel of God to know all things on earth" (2 Samuel 14:20).**

Yes, Bathsheba knew she had to tell David what was happening. Not only for the sake of all of Israel, but also for her own sons' sake.

Bathsheba suspected that if David did not appoint Solomon as the next king of Israel prior to his death, that Adonijah would regard her and her four sons as rivals to the throne.

Bathsheba shuddered with fear as she remembered how things had unfolded in the past when a king felt threatened by a future rival. She had been a very young girl, but remembered how her father had defended David's life many times as he was hunted like a fugitive for years by then-King Saul, who knew that David was his replacement.

Bathsheba had grown-up living life with the loyal families who had supported David, running from crazed king Saul, who felt that David jeopardized his position as king. Saul was well aware that David was the Anointed One by the Lord, yet he tried for years to murder him.

Moving from place to place with her family to evade Saul's attempts on David's life, Bathsheba was all too familiar with how life can be when a king feels that he is no longer in power and in control.

Bathsheba's father had valiantly defended David's life from the deranged, out-of-control Saul, and had therefore earned David's utmost respect. David had bestowed upon Bathsheba's father the acclaimed, highest honor possible, being named one of David's elite, 'Mighty Men'.

Although she deeply respected her father and her husband as great warriors of Israel, Bathsheba certainly did not want this life for her sons.

Yearning for peace for her sons and for her native land of Israel, Bathsheba knew she had to talk with David about Adonijah's takeover as king.

✦✦✦✦✦✦✦✦✦✦✦

Pearl: *If Adonijah were allowed to continue his ruse of being the anointed king, Bathsheba and Solomon's lives, as well as the lives of all of her sons would be in danger. Solomon and his brothers, as well as his mother, Bathsheba, would be considered a threat to Adonijah's rule. Most likely, Adonijah would have Bathsheba and all of her sons murdered upon David's death and his take-over as king of Israel.*

✦✦✦✦✦✦✦✦✦✦✦

Right at this very minute, as Bathsheba was sitting outside of dying King David's bedchamber, Adonijah was pre-maturely celebrating his own victory as King of Israel!

Bathsheba could hear the cacophony of the merriment below in the garden. The guests at the feast Adonijah had thrown in his own honor of becoming king of Israel were jubilant, and their mood was fueled with flowing wine and the bountiful feast provided by the new king-to-be. The music and idle chatter of the celebratory atmosphere permeated the walls of the palace.

Ironically, as Bathsheba solemnly sat outside of David's chamber as he lay dying, Adonijah celebrated his self-proclaimed title of being the new King of Israel.

All of the royal officials of Judah had been invited by Adonijah to celebrate his joyous occasion, along with all of David's sons from his other wives. But of course, she and Solomon and her other sons had not made the guest list.

Nor had Nathan the prophet, nor had any of David's faithful, esteemed 'Mighty Men' been invited to Adonijah's celebration.

Nathan, the prophet, had served them many years as both she and David's counselor, and now she definitely needed his advice. After summoning Nathan, Bathsheba waited patiently for his arrival.

Finally, after what seemed an eternity to Bathsheba, Nathan arrived to sit with her outside of David's chambers. Huddled together and talking in hushed voices, the two discussed the dilemma concerning Adonijah proclaiming himself as the next king.

Together they arrived at the decision that Bathsheba should immediately inform David of Adonijah's ill-fated plan to become the new king of Israel.

Mustering her strength, Bathsheba rose to walk to David's chambers. Praying for the right words to communicate the situation to her dying husband, she slowly approached the large ornately carved wooden doors at the entrance of David's private chambers.

Having a flash from nearly thirty years prior as she stood at these same doors the night of her illicit affair with David, Bathsheba felt the guilt rise deep inside her once again. Praying to the Lord, she asked again for forgiveness for her past, and guidance for her and her son's future.

Jolted back to reality, Bathsheba heard the prophet Nathan speaking to her. As she stood outside the doorway to David's room, the prophet advised her to remind David of his oath that Solomon shall reign after him.

Nathan then reassured Bathsheba that he would come behind her, in support and confirmation of her words.

Bathsheba, with the confident assurance of knowing that she was doing the right thing in the eyes of the Lord, quietly knocked on the door, and then slipped through the open door into David's chamber.

David, weak and hypothermic from disease, but still cognizant and able-minded, recognized his beloved-wife, Bathsheba. Trying to prop himself up to see her better, David motioned Bathsheba to come sit next to him.

David had a young, beautiful woman by his side who his servants had found to attend him in his diseased state. Thinking this young woman could pull him out of his chronic hypothermia and severe illness, David's servants had charged her with caring for David during his dying days.

Neither Bathsheba, nor David paid the beautiful young girl any attention. Focusing intently on each other, the couple locked-eyes with loving-kindness emanating between them.

Bathsheba and David began their communications with the full respect and enduring love of husband and wife. The couple had been through many years of trials together, but the scars from these hurdles and tests-of-life only served to strengthen the bond of loyalty between them.

With utmost respect and honesty, Bathsheba explained to David the political situation of what had become of David's beloved kingdom of Israel. When she mentioned that his son Adonijah had proclaimed himself to be the new king, David's eyes darkened and his face twisted in anguish.

After listening to Bathsheba, David knew exactly what he needed to do.

David called Bathsheba to lean closer to him and he struggled to whisper in her ear. Swearing an oath on his deathbed, David used all of his strength to say to Bathsheba,

"As the LORD lives, who has redeemed my soul out of every adversity, as I swore to you by the LORD, the God of Israel, saying Solomon your son shall reign after me, and he shall sit on my throne in my place, even so will I do this day."
(1 Kings 1:28-30)

David then instructed that Solomon be immediately anointed King of Israel by Nathan, the prophet and Zadok, David's priest.

Adonijah's festivities were nonetheless ruined.

Hearing the news, the guests at Adonijah's party scattered like mice on a sinking ship.

Solomon was in his early twenties when he ascended to the throne in place of his father, David.

The Lord highly exalted Solomon in the eyes of all of Israel, and bestowed upon him royal splendor, such as no king before *(1 Kings 2:12, 1 Chronicles 29:23-25, 2 Chronicles 1:1).*

❖❖❖❖❖❖❖❖❖❖❖

Pearl: *The Midrash emphasizes that these verses can be interpreted as the Lord made Solomon exceedingly great in matters of the kingdom and in his spiritual uplifting. As Rashi explains, the LORD, his God, was with him. The Rabbis exegete that this meant that Solomon constantly kept God in mind, and thereby gained spiritual greatness. Essentially, Solomon at this point of his life chose to put God as center-focus of his life, and gave Him ultimate authority.*

❖❖❖❖❖❖❖❖❖❖❖

David died shortly thereafter.

"Then David slept with his fathers and was buried in the city of David."
(1 Kings 2:10)

Before his death, David advised Solomon to be strong and obedient to the Lord his God, walking in his ways, in accordance of the Law of Moses.

David had reigned over Israel forty years and died circa 970 B.C. He was known as the man after God's own heart.

◆◆◆◆◆◆◆◆◆◆◆

*Pearl: In preparation for his death, David recalled his writings of **Psalm 23**, the LORD is my Shepherd.*

Psalm 23
"The LORD is my shepherd, I shall not want. He makes me lie down in green pastures.
He leads me beside still waters. He restores my soul.
He leads me in paths of righteousness for his name's sake.

Even though I walk through the valley of the shadow of death, I will fear no evil, for you are with me; your rod and your staff, they comfort me.
You prepare a table before me in the presence of my enemies; you anoint my head with oil; my cup overflows.
Surely goodness and mercy shall follow me all the days of my life.
And I shall dwell in the house of the LORD forever."

◆◆◆◆◆◆◆◆◆◆◆

Bathsheba continued to be the faithful mother of her sons, and supporter of Solomon while he was king.

That brings us to the next enigma surrounding Bathsheba.

Scene 7: Bathsheba ~ Brains and Beauty!

Playlist: "Thankful for the Scars" by I Am They, "Dear Younger Me" by MercyMe

Was Bathsheba a wise prophetess? We have proof that Bathsheba was a prophetess with a tie to Proverbs, written by her son Solomon.

Bathsheba's grandfather was known for being a very wise man, who showed knowledge and good judgement. Her son Solomon, seemed to follow in his footsteps and became known throughout the land for his wisdom.

But did Solomon actually follow in his mother's footsteps, gleaning knowledge from her worldly wisdom and lessons from life?

Why was Solomon considered to be such a wise man?

Solomon was the author of more than 600 proverbs, poems and wise sayings and is attributed as being the author of several books in the Old Testament, such as most of the Book of Proverbs, the book of Ecclesiastes, and possibly The Song of Solomon.

Solomon was known to be exceptionally insightful, and exhibited a sense of worldly intelligence about daily living. He not only possessed knowledge, but he was able to apply his knowledge to life itself.

Most importantly, Solomon's proverbs distinctively acknowledge that all wisdom flows from Almighty God, and not from the culture of the day, or the knowledge of mere humans.

Solomon's proverbs center around wisdom, and one may wonder, that as part of his God-given gift perhaps some of his insight may have been passed down through the counsel of his mother.

We know that Bathsheba benefited from the constant counsel of Nathan, the prophet, and that she relied upon him for guidance and direction.

Bathsheba certainly had learned from her many trying life experiences. In her repentance, Bathsheba experienced God's great mercy. It therefore seems likely that as a caring mother, she would counsel her sons to live by the Word of God.

Bathsheba's Influence on her Sons

As Solomon was growing up, he most likely was curious, always questioning and pushing the edge for knowledge. It must have been a constant challenge for Bathsheba to make sure she provided the best education possible for her sons, especially Solomon with his extreme intelligence.

From talking with Jewish scholars, it is apparent that the Jewish woman had a tremendous role in the education of her children, both for worldly and spiritual knowledge. One can therefore insightfully deduce that Bathsheba played a prominent role in her beloved sons' education, both in the realm of worshiping the one true God of Israel, and in worldly knowledge.

Therefore, it is highly likely that Solomon, as he was growing up received guidance, advice and education from his mother.

Other things that may support this theory of Bathsheba's involvement with her son's education was knowing that Bathsheba's sons were considerably younger than their older half-brothers. They therefore would have received their education apart from their siblings, as their half-brothers were already adults when Bathsheba's sons were young boys.

Knowing that Bathsheba was much younger than David's other wives leads us to conclude that she provided for the education of her sons without their help. Bathsheba's sons would not have grown up around any of their half-brothers, as they were already grown men off doing battle.

Being dependent upon the help of her counselor, Nathan the prophet, but not dependent upon other women in the royal court or her sons half-siblings, Bathsheba held a tremendous responsibility for her sons' education.

Taken together, this would have most likely meant that Bathsheba would have served a central role in her sons' spiritual and worldly education.

◆◆◆◆◆◆◆◆◆◆◆

Pearl: *Not to discount the influence of David, and certainly not to discount the influence of God in Solomon's acquisition of education and ultimately wisdom, but one certainly can't discount the potential influence of Solomon's mother, Bathsheba.*

◆◆◆◆◆◆◆◆◆◆◆

Bathsheba undoubtedly influenced her young sons in their growing up to become men of God, especially considering that she must have, like her husband David, humbly repented for her sin of adultery.

From the above discussion we can assume that Solomon most likely received advice and education from his mother during his adolescence. Bathsheba certainly had her share of hard times during the years of being King David's wife, and like most mothers, would want her sons to benefit from her mistakes and worldly experiences.

Perhaps the life-experiences and counsel of his mother, Bathsheba, somehow impacted Solomon's poetic verses, which often contrast good and evil and emphasize that wisdom flows from God.

Through Bathsheba's own sin and repentance, she certainly would have been an excellent mentor for her sons. She had been through trials, and with her scars from the healed wounds of sin through repentance, Bathsheba would have been one who could have shared with her sons her story of God's grace and mercy.

All in all, Bathsheba was most likely a loving, God-fearing mother who raised her sons to be righteous men of the Lord.

❖❖❖❖❖❖❖❖❖❖

*P**earl:** With that being said, some scholars think that Bathsheba may actually have been linked to at least one, and possibly several of the Proverbs that Solomon may have authored.*

Which proverb is Bathsheba linked to? Interestingly, the last chapter of the book of Proverbs is said to have been written by a king named Lemuel.

Who was King Lemuel?

What was he the king of, and where was this said land?

❖❖❖❖❖❖❖❖❖❖

Of significance is that no one had or ever has been able to identify who Lemuel was, or where he was king!

Lemuel seems to be a fictitious king, who was admonished by his mother and in his mother's words, identified in the first verses of **Proverbs 31** what the 'ideal human king' should look like.

Whose viewpoint was this about this so-called 'ideal king'?

Was Lemuel, the supposed author of Proverbs 31, actually a penname of Solomon? And was he echoing the words of his own mother, Bathsheba?

Or did Solomon collect this particular proverb from another source, which he then attributed to a fictitious person he named 'Lemuel'?

Many Biblical scholars exegete that **Proverbs 31** of the book of **Proverbs** was written by Solomon in tribute to his mother, Bathsheba.

What brings scholars to agree and come to this conclusion?

For starters, **Proverb 31** begins with the heading, *"The words of king Lemuel. An oracle that his mother taught him."*

One thing for certain, this proverb is what **somebody's mother taught them**.

Who was this 'somebody'?

All scholars agree that no one knows who Lemuel was. Furthermore, they also have never heard of a king by that name, or where he could have served as a king.

In addition, this famous **Proverb 31** certainly fits with Solomon's writing style and theme.

Who was the 'mother that taught him'?

◆◆◆◆◆◆◆◆◆◆◆

Pearl: *If Lemuel was Solomon's pseudonym, then he is ascribing the chapter as a prophecy of his mother, Bathsheba.*

It would be logical to conclude that Bathsheba would teach her son who became king at an early age of twenty-something, some wise things that he could apply to his new job. It also would make sense that Bathsheba would warn Solomon not to make the same mistakes that she and his father, David, made in their younger years.

◆◆◆◆◆◆◆◆◆◆◆

Unfortunately, Solomon in the end did not heed his mother's advice.

We do know that Bathsheba courageously stood up for Solomon to become the next king of Israel, even though his half-brother was already clawing his way up the gilded throne.

It is only fitting that after all of the drama surrounding who was to follow in King David's footsteps, that Bathsheba would want her son, Solomon, to aspire to not just be a good king, but to be the-best-king-ever.

Unfortunately, in reading the verses, it seems as though that the king-in-question of **Proverb 31** may have already made some serious errors in judgement.

Pointedly, **Proverb 31** begins with a mother's reproach of her son, with the first part reading,

"What are you doing, my son?
What are you doing, son of my womb?
What are you doing son of my vows?"
(Proverbs 31:2)

Interestingly, in verses three through five, the author then zeroes in on what actually turned out to be Solomon's two greatest weaknesses, being women and wine!

"Do not give your strength to women, your ways to those who destroy kings.
It is not for kings, O Lemuel, it is not for kings to drink wine,
or for rulers to take strong drink, lest they drink and forget what has been decreed
and pervert the rights of all the afflicted".
(Proverbs 31:3-5)

The author of **Proverb 31** openly admonished the king for his mistresses, and for his drinking!

Could this have been Bathsheba's warning to her son? Did Bathsheba actually write this proverb?

The words of the proverb either warned or rebuked the king, or both. It definitely conveyed that involvement with mistresses is a waste of a man's strength.

These opening verses could possibly mean that anything other than a monogamous marriage will turn a man's heart away from God, and detract from his ability and energy for ruling well.

The proverb then describes that the ideal king should protect others through his wisdom, justice and compassion.

These characteristics were desired by the author of the proverb, but definitely in contradistinction to what the kings of the culture of day were like. The typical king in the ancient middle east were known to use his power for personal gain and riches, rather than ruling with justice, and defending the rights of the poor and needy.

*earl: The idea that Bathsheba is the 'mother who taught him' is actually appropriate to assume in **Proverbs 31**.*

◆◆◆◆◆◆◆◆◆◆◆

Bathsheba would have admonished her son, Solomon, in regards to his shortcomings, as she of all people, knew him best. Out of love for her son, Bathsheba would have wanted Solomon to succeed, and would have therefore counseled him accordingly.

*Proverbs 31 (verses 1-9) seems to parallel some of the comments of **Proverbs 8**, (especially verses 14-15), which refers to the comments of **'Lady Wisdom'** about how rulers are to rule justly.*

*This similarity between the two proverbs lends credence to believe that Solomon was the author of both **Proverbs 8 and 31**.*

> ***"I have counsel and sound wisdom; I have insight; I have strength.***
> ***By me kings reign, and rulers decree what is just."***
> ***(Proverb 8:14-15)***

*That brings us to contemplate, just who was **Solomon's 'Lady Wisdom'** in **Proverbs 8 (and 31)**?*

Did a woman inspire Solomon to personify the very fabric and innate quality of wisdom?

Was this inspirational woman possibly Solomon's mother, Bathsheba?

The second part of **Proverb 31 (verses 10-31),** describes 'womanly excellence'.

◆◆◆◆◆◆◆◆◆◆◆

earl: In the Masoretic Text of the Hebrew Bible, each verse begins with the successive letter of the Hebrew alphabet, emphasizing that this particular woman's character runs the whole range of distinction and highest quality.

◆◆◆◆◆◆◆◆◆◆◆

This second part of **Proverb 31** describes a woman who is married, and could possibly have been Bathsheba's description of a good wife that she would desire for her sons.

The ideal wife as described, realizes that although no wife is perfect, she importantly should honor God at all times.

In **Proverb 31,** the author describes that a woman should be strong, faithful, and endure hard times. She should realize that being faithful to God means that she should be willing to be obedient to God at all times and submit to His will.

Ultimately, the ideal woman should allow the Lord to reform and transform her into who she was meant to be. And always, she is worthy of God's Grace.

These insights would be indicative of a caring, God-fearing mother who desires the best for her child. They are also indicative of one who has been through hardships and trials, that have imparted wisdom, but also scars.

Perhaps these scars have allowed the author of **Proverb 31** to grow closer to the heart of the Lord.

Although we don't know a lot about Bathsheba directly, it is possible to infer quite a bit about her character from what we do know about the men who she influenced, and who also influenced her.

Unfortunately, most casual bible-readers may be overwhelmed by the story about her one sinful act of adultery with King David.

I personally think there is much more to Bathsheba to remember.

What can we learn from Bathsheba character and her trials, to draw us closer to God? Here are a few ideas:
+ The power of repentance
+ God's extreme grace and mercy
+ The chesed of God
+ Faithfulness
+ Care in raising of children
+ Loyalty to our spouse
+ Putting God first in our life
+ Honesty
+ Trust
+ Temptation ~ knowing it is the scheme of the enemy, being the Devil, and we must resist it and flee from it
+ Learning from our mistakes ~ taking the discipline of God in a positive way so that we may be changed
+ Allowing God to transform us into who we were designed to be

Of utmost significance is to remember that even though Bathsheba was not perfect, she repented and accepted God's gift of grace. She then allowed God to transform her into the woman of character that He had planned for her to be.

Bathsheba was indeed a fitting member of the puzzle of God's ultimate Masterplan.

From Bathsheba's life experiences, she gained wisdom. Bathsheba may have imparted pearls from her wisdom gained from the lessons learned from her mistakes in life to her son, Solomon.

Solomon, Bathsheba's son, became known as one of the wisest men who ever lived, and left a legacy of proverbs and wise writings.

Hopefully we can view Bathsheba from the perspective of looking not just at her one sinful act, but also as a humble, God-fearing woman who repented and allowed her life to be transformed.

Bathsheba grew in her faith, and became a loyal wife and trusted confidant, a faithful mother, and most likely, even as a wise prophetess.

By probing into the depths of understanding Bathsheba and her story, we are drawn closer to the heart of God.

Most important of all to remember is that through Bathsheba and David's offspring, God's promise of the Messiah will be fulfilled.

Through David and Bathsheba's life, we see God setting up his Master Plan for the coming of Jesus Christ.

Tribute to David: The Prophecies of David - The Messianic Psalms

David foreshadows Jesus with his prophecies, known as the Messianic Psalms. **David's Messianic Psalms** *include* **Psalms 2, 22, 27, 87, 110, 48, 47, 45, and 27.**

David has been credited to have written at least **73 of the 150 Psalms in the Bible.** Undoubtedly, more of the Psalms should be credited to him.

In nine of these Psalms, the coming Messiah is the paramount theme. These Psalms of David make predictions of the One who will come to save the world.

As we now know, that One is Jesus Christ, a descendent of David.

Not being a great political king, later events will show that the Messiah, fulfilled in Jesus Christ, comes as the Word of God being the spiritual leader of His people.

The most famous of these Messianic Psalms of Davidic origin is undoubtedly **Psalm 22,** where David accurately portrayed the happenings of Jesus as he was unjustly crucified on the cross.

Matthew 27:46 cites that at about the *ninth hour* of Jesus' crucifixion, His last words while on earth which were part of the seven sayings from the cross, included those of the opening verse of **Psalm 22:1**.

"My God, my God, why have you forsaken me?"(Psalm 22:1)

"Eli, Eli, lema sabacthani?" (Aramaic: Matthew 27:46)

Other parallels that Matthew uses from **Psalm 22** to Jesus' last hours on the cross are included as follows:

"they divide my garment among them, and for my clothing they cast lots."
(Psalm 22:18)

"And when they had crucified him, they divided his garments among them by casting lots." (Matthew 27:35)

"All who see me mock me; they make mouths at me; they wag their heads."
(Psalm 22:8)

"And those who passed by derided him, wagging their heads."
(Matthew 27:39)

"He trusts in the Lord, let him deliver him; let him rescue him, for he delights in him!"
(Psalm 22:8)

"He trusts in God; let God deliver him now, if he desires him, For he said, "I am the Son of God."
(Matthew 27:43)

*Below are excerpts from **Psalm 2 and 87**. **Psalm 110** has been included in entirety.*

Psalm 2: The Coming Messiah
(Verse 7) "I will tell of the decree; The Lord said to me, You are my Son; today I have begotten you."
(Verses 11, 12) "Serve the Lord with fear, and rejoice with trembling.
Kiss the Son, lest he be angry, and you perish in the way, for his wrath is quickly kindled. Blessed are all who take refuge in him."

Psalm 87:5-6: The Messiah to be Born in Zion
"And of Zion it shall be said, this one and that one were born in her; for the Most High Himself will establish her. The Lord records as he registers the peoples, This one was born there."

Psalm 110: Sit At My Right Hand
"The LORD says to my Lord; sit at my right hand, until I make your enemies your footstool.

The LORD sends forth from Zion your mighty scepter; rule in the midst of your enemies.

Your people will offer themselves freely on the day of your power, in holy garments, from the womb of the morning, the dew of your youth will be yours.

The LORD has sworn and will not change his mind, You are a priest forever after the order of Melchizedek.

The Lord is at your right hand; he will shatter kings on the day of his wrath.
He will execute judgment among the nations, filling them with corpses; he will shatter chiefs over the wide earth,

He will drink from the brook by the way; therefore he will lift up his head.

Pearl concerning Psalm 110: *Opening with an oracle from God (LORD: Hebrew: Yahweh) to the Davidic king (Lord),* **Psalm 110** *describes that the Almighty will subdue his enemies, making them subject to the authority of the Davidic king.*

David calls the king, 'my Lord', implying that the king is the Messiah, and much greater than David. This final king fulfils the prophecy of Zechariah who saw a merger of the office of both a priest and a king in the person of the Messiah (the Branch; **Zechariah 6:9-14**). *This psalm is about this final king, who is of the Davidic line, the Messiah who is fulfilled in Jesus Christ.*

Psalm 110 *also speaks of a warrior king who will be victorious over His enemies. Of significance is the wording is eerily similar to the happenings enveloping the Second Coming of Christ and the final judgement, as described in* **Revelation 19-20.**

In many ways, with the Psalms David wrote, his life pointed forward to, and foreshadowed Jesus.

Not to say that David was perfect, as he certainly was not, as he was human. David, although flawed, human and sinful, was a man after God's heart. Even with his imperfections, God loved David and made a covenant with him with His promises **(2 Samuel 7:11-16).**

Jesus was the 'perfect lamb,' and was the 'perfect David'. With His perfect love for humanity, Jesus made a New Covenant **(Matthew 26:28, Hebrews 12:24).**

Throughout the years, God protected David from his enemies, as he overpowered them with the Holy Spirit **(1 Samuel 19).**

Similarly, we as believers in Jesus Christ are also empowered and allow ourselves to be guided and controlled by the Holy Spirit.

In the words of Apostle Paul,

"For the love of Christ controls us,
because we have concluded this: that one has died for all, therefore all have died.
And he died for all, that those who live might no longer live for themselves but for
him who for their sake died and was raised."
(2 Corinthians 5:14-15)

David was tempted by evil, and fell to this temptation, leading to many bad decisions that culminated with further committed sins, and ultimately with the death of an innocent man.

In contradistinction, Jesus Christ, fully human, yet fully God, was tempted as was David, although Jesus did not fall.

"One who has been tempted in every way, just as we are, yet he did not sin."
(Hebrews 4:15)

God through His Grace, forgave and transformed both David's and Bathsheba's life. Through His all-encompassing chesed, God allowed children to be born to David and Bathsheba who would carry on the Davidic lineage. David and Bathsheba's son, Solomon, inherited David's throne, passing on the lineage of the Davidic Dynasty *(1 Kings 1:29-30)*.

God ultimately held true to His promise that a 'Son of David', (David's descendant) being Jesus Christ, would ultimately be born who would be the One, the Messiah.

Jesus, the Prince of Peace, holds David's throne forever *(Isaiah 9:6; Luke 1:31-33)*.

When we look at David's and Bathsheba's lives, we can see how God used broken, flawed, sinful people to tell a story that through His redeeming grace, brings us closer to Him.

Through God's own Son's obedience, crucifixion, death and resurrection, we see how God forgave humanity for their sins and allowed for us to live eternally in His Kingdom.

In Jesus Christ, the ultimate sacrificial lamb, all of God's promises come to fruition.

Thank you Jesus!

The Messiah's Birth

I n the Book of Isaiah, we also read about the Messiah's birth, who is to be born to a virgin. A woman will conceive without the seed of a man.

Isaiah 7:14
"Behold, the virgin shall conceive and bear a son, and shall call his name Immanuel"

Isaiah 9:6
"For to us a child is born, to us a son is given, and the government shall be upon his shoulders, and his name shall be called, Wonderful Counselor, Mighty God, Everlasting Father, Prince of Peace."

With these prophesies in mind, and knowing the cultural time in which Jesus was born, we return once again to Mary's story.

Finale: Mary ~ Seed of the New Covenant

Ca. 5 B.C.

Playlist: "Mary Did You Know" by Jeremy Camp, "How Many Kings" by Downhere, O Come, O Come Emmanuel" by Jeremy Camp, "O Holy Night" by David Phelps

Introduction:

Mary, the mother of Jesus
- *Date: **Ca. 5 B.C**.*
- *Setting*: The land of Palestine has been divided into the provinces of Judea, Samaria, Galilee, Perea, and Decapolis.
- The people of the land, including the Jews, are governed by Roman rule, under the auspices of Emperor *'Caesar Augustus.'*
- The Roman Senate has granted Herod the Great, the title "King of the Jews". He is King of Judea.
- Mary lived in Nazareth, which is in the province of Galilee, 75 miles north of Bethlehem in Judea.
- Mary, a virgin, is 3 months pregnant. She has miraculously conceived a son, by the Holy Spirit of God. He will be called Jesus.

Jesus, the Son of God, will soon come to earth in a humble manner. He will be born to a virgin, Jewish woman.

God of Creation, will send His Son, Jesus Christ, to die for the sins of humanity and conquer death and evil once and for all.

Jesus will give the hope of salvation to all who turn from their sin, and believe in Him.

Scene 1: Breaking the News

Mary has just spent the last three months with her wise, older cousin Elizabeth, but now has returned home to Nazareth. Mary is three months pregnant.

Elizabeth will also soon give birth, as she is nine months pregnant.

Pearl: **John the Baptist:** Elizabeth will also soon give birth to a baby boy, who will be named John. He will become *"strong in spirit, and live in the wilderness until he appeared publicly to Israel." (Luke 1:80)*

The boy will grow up to become **John, the Baptist**. He will become a prophet of God, **(John 10:40-41),** and preach to the people about the one, true God. Talking of repentance and turning from sin towards the Lord, he will bring people closer to God and baptize hundreds in the Jordan River.

A forerunner of Jesus, John the Baptist will proclaim that Jesus will become the sacrificial Lamb of God's New Covenant, and will attain final salvation for God's people.

John predicted that Jesus will fulfill the symbolism of the Passover lamb, and through His blood God's people will be redeemed from sin, death and the Devil.

John 1:29
"Behold, the lamb of God, who takes away the sin of the world."

John will baptize Jesus himself, as he begins his earthly ministry at approximately twenty-nine years of age.

This brings us full circle to the beginnings of time, and Jesus will ultimately fulfill God's prophecy of **Genesis 3:15.**

Some scholars note that even though John the Baptist denied being the ancient prophet, Elijah, Jesus saw John as fulfilling the prophecy about Elijah as a "voice" to carry the message of Jesus."

John the Baptist said about himself,

John 1:23
"I am the voice of one crying out in the wilderness. Make straight the way of the Lord, as the prophet Isaiah said."

Isaiah 40:3
"A voice cries in the wilderness prepares the way of the Lord; make straight in the desert a highway for our God."

The ancient prophet Elijah never died **(2 Kings 2:11),** and was expected by the Jews to return in the end times to restore all things **(Malachi 4:5; Matthew 17:11; Luke 1:17).**

Malachi 4:5
"Behold I will send you Elijah the prophet before the great and awesome day of the Lord comes. And he will turn the hearts of fathers to their children and the hearts of children to their fathers, lest I come and strike the land with a decree of utter destruction."

In the book of Malachi, it is prophesized that a future messenger would have a prophetic ministry similar to that of the historical Elijah. When John the Baptist denied he was Elijah, scholars agree that he was denying that he was Elijah in person, not that his ministry was similar to Elijah's.

As John the Baptist stated, he wanted to call the people back to God, and serve as a voice to carry the message of Jesus ***(John 1:23).***

✦✦✦✦✦✦✦✦✦✦✦

Mary and her older cousin, Elizabeth, had just completed their time together, visiting and studying the Tanakh. They had spent long hours recounting the stories of their ancestors that spanned over the last thousands of years, since the dawn of Creation. These stories had been passed on through each generation, and now had been passed to Mary from her older cousin, Elizabeth.

Mary had grown up attending the synagogue, hearing readings from the Tanakh in Rabbinic tradition. These stories she and Elizabeth shared had sprung to life and gave new meaning to Mary when the two women put them into perspective and in the context of the day.

Both women now realized who their ancestors really were through reading about the trials they had overcome with the help of the Lord. Elizabeth and Mary now realized that through the course of the last two thousand-plus years since Creation, their ancestors had been part of God's Masterplan for salvation of humanity.

Their studies took on a new light and meaning when they were put into the context that Mary is now faced with in her very own life. Through Identifying with her ancestors such as David and Bathsheba, Mary now had the hope and determination that she needed to remain a faithful and obedient servant of the Lord.

She, the mother of the coming Messiah, is the one who God himself prophesized would bring forth the One who would destroy the Devil once and for all.

Through her seed, Mary will play a pivotal role in God's Master plan. Mary, a humble teen-aged peasant, was the woman who would bear the seed of the Holy Spirit *(Genesis 3:15)*.

As all the pieces of God's mysterious puzzle come together during the chaos of the last thousands of years, Mary is the essential piece needed to complete the Lord's Masterpiece.

Mary and her wise, older cousin had also studied the prophecies about the birth of Christ, the Messiah. Piecing together the lives of David and Bathsheba, along with reading the Psalms David had written, Mary began to see how the events were unfolding in front of her very eyes. These events were fulfilling the specific proclamations of the Word of God!

Jesus, the Son of God, would descend from her seed and the seed of her ancestors, being from the lineage of Abraham *(Genesis 12:3)*, Isaac *(Genesis 26:4)*, Jacob *(Genesis 28:14)*, Judah *(Genesis 49:8-12)*, Jesse *(Isaiah 11:1)*, and David *(Isaiah 9:7)*.

Now, even though she was only a young woman of fourteen, she must somehow shoulder the weight of bearing and raising the *Son of God*. Mary was indeed faced with a very unexpected challenge, one that no one before or after her, had ever encountered.

She could scarcely believe the whole situation herself, let alone expect her betrothed husband, Joseph to believe her. Somehow she needed to muster the courage to tell Joseph of her pregnancy.

Joseph needed to understand that she was still a virgin, as she had miraculously conceived her baby through the Holy Spirit.

Mary thought that Joseph was unlikely to believe any of this.

Briefly, she thought back on how her life would have been if she were not pregnant.

♦ ♦ ♦ ♦ ♦ ♦ ♦ ♦ ♦ ♦ ♦

Pearl: *In keeping with the culture of the day, after coming of marrying age and engagement to a respectable Jewish man, there would be a waiting time of about one year. During this year, the Jewish young woman would have continued to live under the auspices of her father in his house. Then, after the official marriage to her betrothed, they would cohabitate and start a family in hopes of producing heirs.*

♦ ♦ ♦ ♦ ♦ ♦ ♦ ♦ ♦ ♦ ♦

This was the typical, ordinary thing to do for a young Jewish woman coming from a God-fearing, Law-abiding family.

However, now things were very different. Mary was no longer just an ordinary, Jewish girl.

Her life would not be expected to unfold in a typical, ordinary fashion.

She, who was once an ordinary girl, must now accomplish the extraordinary.

Now that Mary was back home she had work to do. She had to talk with Joseph, but how will she get him to believe her?

Matthew 1:18
"Before Mary and Joseph came together she was found to be pregnant through the Holy Spirit."

Pearl: *The Scriptures do not elaborate on how exactly Mary went about telling Joseph the news of her pregnancy, but considering the time and culture, it is doubtful that the two would have been able to meet alone. There may have been interruptions from family members, or perhaps a lack of detail and explanation during their discussion, as most likely parents or relatives serving, as chaperones would have been present.*

We do know however that 'the talk' happened, and things did not go well. Sure enough, Joseph did not believe her.

Mary felt that she had been obedient to God, and stood firm in telling her future husband that she was still a virgin, yet was pregnant. She explained that she had not conceived this baby in the usual way by being with a man.

The baby was the Son of God!

Mary thought back to the conversation.

She had been nervous, and somewhat at a loss for words. She felt that Joseph did not hear what she had to say. Joseph was a good man, but he was a firm believer in the Law.

One thing for certain, Joseph did not want to put her and her family to shame.

Being a righteous man, after the discussion about Mary's pregnancy, Joseph let Mary and her family know that he had come to the conclusion to quietly divorce her.

Pearl: *If Joseph's decision were carried through, it would cause Mary to be destined to remain single for the rest of her life. She would never be able to marry and have more children, and would have to live out her days as a single woman under the guardianship of her father.*

That is, If her father was willing to defend and honor her by letting her live under his roof.

Betrothment, which was a legally binding contract, could only be broken by a formal divorce.

Even though they were not legally married per se, If the man thought that his future wife had been guilty of adultery during the time of betrothment, according to the Law, the woman would be stoned to death by her own family. This was done to absolve the family of the shame the woman had bestowed upon them (Deuteronomy 22:13-21; John 8:4-5).

✦✦✦✦✦✦✦✦✦✦

After her talk with Joseph, Mary had obediently and quietly retreated to her home, carefully keeping her emotions in check. Back at home she found time to be alone, and sitting in the dark finally let her tears pour out.

Mary was devastated, as her worst nightmares had come true.

Joseph did not believe her. Who knows if her own father did either.

Actually, Mary's life was in danger. She realized that if her own family thought she had committed adultery, the law said she should be killed due to her shameful actions.

Feeling hopeless and alone, Mary was scared to death.

Thinking back on the conversation with Joseph, Mary had seen the look of despair in Joseph's eyes. She knew that he had felt betrayed, and he surmised that she had turned against him.

Mary was also very frustrated, as she had been unable to communicate with Joseph on a deeper level. Joseph had tuned her out, as he was too upset at hearing the news that she was pregnant.

He just didn't seem to be listening when she told him she had been visited and told the news by the angel sent by God, Gabriel.

Joseph could not grasp the concept that she had become pregnant without having sexual relations with a man.

Mary even got the impression that Joseph thought that she was crazy, or at least a very good liar. He just didn't understand that her baby boy would be Holy, as the Holy Spirit conceived him. He had even asked her, how did she know that it was going to a boy?

Even though scared and frustrated, Mary couldn't give up hope, as she truly was submissive to God's word and promise. Mary began to pray to the Lord for a solution. She trusted that the Lord would make things right.

No one ever said that faith makes things easy, but it makes them possible.

Luke 1:37
"For nothing will be impossible with God."

Soon, Joseph will have his own visit by an angel of God.

Mary prayed fervently all night. She obediently asked God for His guidance and help as she recognized that she could not possibly get through this whole ordeal without His Divine intervention.

Praying for a miracle, Mary took comfort knowing that she had been blessed by God as the woman chosen to bear His Son, the *Messiah*.

When all hope seemed lost, God stepped in to save the day.

As Joseph considered his decision in fitful sleep, an angel of the Lord came to him in his dream saying,

"Joseph, son of David, do not fear to take Mary as your wife, for that which is conceived in her is from the Holy Spirit. She will bear a son and you shall call his name Jesus, for he will save his people from their sins."
(Matthew 1:20-22)

Joseph was told that God had a Master plan. The son that his future wife had conceived would save God's people from sin, and be the Savior of the world.

This fulfilled what the Lord had spoken through the prophet, Isaiah:

"Behold, the virgin shall conceive and bear a son, and they shall call his name Immanuel, which means God with us."
(Isaiah 7:14)

When Joseph woke, he did as the angel of the Lord commanded and took Mary for his wife. But he knew her not until she had given birth to a son.

Relevant verse: Matthew 28:20; *God will be with his disciples in every age, to empower them in their commission to make disciples of all nations,*

"Behold, I am with you always, to the end of the age."
(Matthew 28:20)

Mary's prayers had been answered.

As time progressed the child grew and developed within her. She had begun to show her pregnancy, and she was radiant with happiness and relief.

Finally, Mary felt confident that her life had been turned around for good.

But then, another hurdle came into her path.

Scene 2: The Birth of Our Savior

Playlist: " Greatness of our God" by the Newsboys

Introduction: *Caesar Augustus announced that a census would be taken throughout the land, and all men should be registered.*

Joseph, of the house of David, was required to travel to Bethlehem, his ancestral home in order to fulfill the new law **(Luke 2:1).**

❖❖❖❖❖❖❖❖❖❖❖

Pearl: *It appeared on the surface that political reasons determined where Jesus would be born. It is important to remember that **God is in the details**, and the ultimate cause of the reason that Jesus was born in Bethlehem was God's will.*

*God is 'on the throne' and in the details, and it was God who guaranteed that the Messiah, of Davidic lineage, would be born in Bethlehem. This is in accordance with the Old Testament prophecy in **Micah 5:2,4.***

"But you, O Bethlehem Ephrathah, who are too little to be among the clans of Judah, from you shall come forth for me one who is to be ruler in Israel, whose coming forth is from of old, from ancient days."
"And He shall stand and shepherd his flock in the strength of the Lord, in the majesty of the name of the Lord his God.
And they shall dwell secure, for now he shall be great to the ends of the earth, and he shall be their peace."
(Micah 5:2,4)

♦♦♦♦♦♦♦♦♦♦♦

Pearl: *Interestingly, Mary, although also a descendant of the house of David, was not required to make the trip to Bethlehem. The decree only mandated that the **men** of the land were to travel to their ancestral home to be registered.*

However, Joseph did not want to leave her behind, as she was very far along in her pregnancy. Mary was near term, and Joseph did not want to leave her in Nazareth to give birth alone.

God is always in the details! Mary ended up traveling to Bethlehem.

♦♦♦♦♦♦♦♦♦♦♦

So the two set out on a road-trip for Bethlehem, the 'City of David,' in Judea. The long journey to Bethlehem was a difficult one for Mary.

Mary rode to Bethlehem on a donkey, and being well along in her pregnancy, the trip was definitely not a joy ride.

Mary's back ached, and it was hard to get comfortable, no matter how she tried to position herself. The pilgrimage to Bethlehem from Nazareth took several days, and each day Mary felt like she grew larger with-child.

The donkey, seeming to understand Mary's condition, was patient and cooperative. Walking carefully and rhythmically towards their destination, the donkey was well aware of her honorable burden.

Finally, the expectant couple arrived in Bethlehem, just a short time before Mary would give birth.

Luke 2:6-7
"While they were still in Bethlehem, the time came for the baby to be born, and she gave birth to her firstborn, a son. She wrapped him in cloths and placed him in a manger, because there was no inn available for them."

The inn in Bethlehem had been full, since many people had arrived to register for the census. The innkeeper had turned them away, thinking they were peasants who most likely couldn't pay for a room.

Mary and Joseph therefore found shelter in the inn's stable, keeping warm with the farm animals surrounding them.

Giving birth that very night, Mary and Joseph placed their child in the manger of barn housing the farm animals. The gentle animals of the flock gathered round the Divine event, their kind souls wanting to help keep the baby warm and safe.

After the birth of the Divine child, Mary gazed into his eyes with wonder. She and Joseph held him, and Mary nursed the baby. They then gently placed him in the manger of the barn in which they had found shelter so he could sleep peacefully.

The night was cold, but Mary and Joseph kept warm in the barn among the presence of God's animals. The livestock in the barn gravitated towards the baby seemingly in awe, wanting to stay close. The warmth of their bodies and breath emanated from them, filling Mary with peace.

◆◆◆◆◆◆◆◆◆◆◆

Pearl: *Shepherds, known for their uncouth reputation, were about to visit the baby Jesus that night. Their presence at the scene highlighted Jesus' future ministry, which was known to reach and accept all people, even social outcasts.*

*Shepherds seemed to have special significance in God's plan, as David had been a shepherd prior to being anointed King by God **(1 Samuel 16)**.*
◆◆◆◆◆◆◆◆◆◆◆

In the region of Bethlehem, out in the fields were shepherds keeping watch over their flocks at night. Some of the men had dozed off for the night, but a few stayed awake to protect the livestock from predators and thieves.

Suddenly, in the dark fields on this cold night a blinding, bright light appeared out of nowhere illuminating the entire area.

The light appeared as a cloud from heaven like burning fire, and was unlike anything the shepherds had seen before.

Terrified, the shepherds standing watch fell to the ground, shielding their eyes as they gazed toward the sky to try to determine the origin of the intense brilliance.

The men were huddled together quaking in fear, when the loud booming voice of an angel of the Lord said,

"Fear not, for behold, I bring you good news of great joy that will be for all the people.
For unto you is born this day in the city of David, a Savior, who is Christ the Lord.
And this will be a sign for you: you will find a baby wrapped in swaddling cloths and lying in a manger."
(Luke 2:9-13)

Then unexpectedly, thousands more angels appeared praising God, their voices harmoniously singing,

"Glory to God in the highest, and on earth peace among those with whom he is pleased."
(Luke 2:14)

✦✦✦✦✦✦✦✦✦✦✦

Pearl: *The angels proclaimed that Jesus, the Son of God had "taken the form of a servant, being born in the likeness of men"* **(Philippians 2:7)***. The time had come for God to send forth his Son, born of a woman, to redeem those whom God is pleased to call to Himself.*

God's love for His Creation drove Him to send His Son, who was in the position of king of the Universe, to the position of weakness for the sake of sinful mankind.

Christ descended from heaven to earth to become 'flesh', and be born to a woman as an ordinary Jewish baby.

There was nothing ordinary about Jesus however, as he was sent to earth to die.

Ultimately bound for the cross for our sacrificial atonement of sins, it was all part of God's Master plan.

✦✦✦✦✦✦✦✦✦✦✦

After the dramatic announcement of the angels, and the men had calmed their nerves, they immediately headed to see this glorious miracle of God.

Once in the town of Bethlehem, the shepherds easily found the barn, as it was aglow with Divine illumination.

The shepherds respectfully entered the serene setting to find the baby Jesus peacefully lying in the manger. Surrounding the scene were Mary, Joseph and all of the barn animals.

It was a scene just as the angels had described.

The shepherds made known to Mary and Joseph, and all who would later listen, what the angels of the Lord had told them. Together, they glorified and praised God for the miracle of the baby, Jesus.

Mary listened intently as the shepherds told of the heralding angels, treasuring the glorious moments and pondering them in her heart *(Luke 2:19).*

At the end of eight days, when he was circumcised, he was named Jesus.

This was the name given by the angel of the Lord before he was conceived *(Luke 2:21).*

When the time came for the purification according to the Law of Moses *(Lev 12:3-4),* Mary and Joseph took Jesus to Jerusalem to present him to the Lord and offer a sacrifice *(Lev 12:8).*

An elderly man named Simeon was at the temple, eagerly waiting to see the Lord's Christ, the Messiah, before he died.

Under guidance of the Holy Spirit upon seeing Jesus, Simeon took the baby into his arms with joy.

Filled with the glory of the Lord, Simeon proclaimed,

"Lord, now you are letting your servant depart in peace, according to your word; for my eyes have seen your salvation that you have prepared in the presence of all peoples, a light for revelation to the Gentiles, and for glory to your people Israel."
(Luke 2:29-32)

Simeon also forewarned of future opposition to Jesus, as well as Mary's future sorrow at Jesus' crucifixion *(Luke 2:33-36)*.

Questions to ponder:

+ How much did Mary know about the future of Jesus?
+ Was she emotionally prepared to be the mother of the Son of God?
+ Did the relevant story of how Abraham was asked to prepare his son Isaac for sacrifice to the Lord, reverberate with Mary at this time?

Grand Finale:

Playlist: "Living Hope" by Phil Wickham, "East from West" by Casting Crowns

God's picture-perfect plan of the offspring born to a woman had been fulfilled. But the rest of the prophesy of **Genesis 3:15**, still had yet to unfold. The Devil had to be defeated, in order for humanity's relationship to be restored with the Lord.

Through the ages, Jesus's ancestors, being the branches of the **Tree of Life** leading to the Messiah, the Christ, had been pruned and carefully nurtured by the ultimate Gardener, God.

Throughout thousands of years, the Tree of Life had been cultivated to ultimately culminate with the Messiah, Jesus Christ, who will conquer the Devil once and for all.

This has been the story of the human ancestors of Jesus Christ.

The ones who lead to, and contributed to the fulfilment of God's promises of a seed from a woman who will conquer evil.

This seed flourished into a seedling, and eventually into a miraculous tree.

Symbolically, we can relate this ancestral tree to Jesus, being the Tree of Life.

Throughout the ages, God shaped and pruned this growing tree as the caring Gardener. He, in His Masterplan, created it to take the perfect form of Jesus, the Messiah.

Revelation 22:1-5
"Then the angel showed me the river of the water of life, bright as crystal, flowing from the throne of God and of the Lamb through the middle of the street of the city. Also, on either side of the river, the tree of life with its twelve kinds of fruit, yielding its fruit each month. The leaves of the tree were for the healing of the nations. No longer will there be anything accursed, but the throne of God and of the Lamb will be in it, and his servants will worship him. They will see his face and his name will be on their foreheads. And night will be no more. They will need no light of lamp or sun, for the Lord God will be their light, and they will reign forever and ever."

The Tree of Life in God's created Garden of Eden, once banned to us as sinful humanity, has once again been restored through the grace of God, and his gift to us of Jesus Christ.

261

The healing of the nations has been completed due to His destruction of the Devil, sin and death.

Prophetically, the Tree of Life is available for healing of all people, or 'nations,' as has been the theme intertwined throughout Biblical history.

No longer are we prisoners of sin and subject to death, but through Jesus Christ we can enjoy an eternal relationship with God.

God has reformed and transformed our relationship with Him, through his Master Plan of His Son, Jesus Christ.

Psalm 103:1, 10-13 (A Psalm of David)

"Bless the Lord, O my Soul, and all that is within me, bless his holy name."

"He does not deal with us according to our sins, nor repay us according to our iniquities. For as high as the heavens are above the earth, so great is his steadfast love toward those who fear him;

As far as the east is from the west, so far does he remove our transgressions from us.

As a father shows compassion to his children, so the Lord shows compassion to those who fear him."

Bibliography:

1. English Standard Version Study Bible (ESV). 2008, Crossway Bibles, a publishing ministry of Good News Publishers, Wheaton, Illinois, USA
2. The Daily Bible, New International Version (NIV). 1984 by Harvest House Publishers, Harvest House Publishers, Eugene, Oregon. F. LaGard Smith (ed)
3. The Holy Bible, Authorized King James Version (KJV). 1965 by J.G. Ferguson Publishing Company and Good Counsel Publishers, Chicago, Illinois.
4. Judgement of the Nephilim, Ryan Pitterson. 2017, Days of Noe Publishing, New York, NY, USA.
5. Jesus' Family Tree; Seeing God's Faithfulness in the Genealogy of Christ. Benjamin Galan and Paul H. Wright. 2014 Bristol Works, Inc. Rose Publishing, Torrance, California.
6. *Heroes of the Bible sermon series* and personal communication by Pastor Jason Fritz, Illuminate Community Church, Scottsdale, Arizona.
7. Sermon excerpts from Ravi Zacharias. RZIM.org
8. Judaica Books of the Prophets, The Book of Joshua. A New English Translation of the Text, Rashi and a Commentary Digest. 2002, The Judaica Press, Inc. Brooklyn, NY, USA.
9. Judaica Books of the Hagiographa – The Holy Writings. The Books of Esther, Song of Songs, Ruth. A New English Translation of the Text, Rashi and a Commentary Digest. Translation of Text, Rashi, and other Commentaries by Rabbi A. J. Rosenberg. 1992, The Judaica Press, Inc. Brooklyn, NY, USA
10. Judaica Books of the Prophets, The Book of Samuel 1. A New English Translation of the Text, Rashi and a Commentary Digest. Translation of Text, Rashi, and other Commentaries by Rabbi A. J. Rosenberg. 2002, The Judaica Press, Inc. Brooklyn, NY, USA.
11. Judaica Books of the Prophets, The Book of Samuel! A New English Translation of the Text, Rashi and other Commentaries by Rabbi Moshe C. Sosevshy. Edited by Rabbi A.J. Rosenberg. 2002, The Judaica Press, Inc. Brooklyn, NY, USA.
12. Judaica Books of the Hagiographa – The Holy Writings. The Book of Chronicles 1. A New English Translation of the Text, Rashi and a Commentary Digest. Translation of Text, Rashi, and other Commentaries by Rabbi A. J. Rosenberg. 1992, The Judaica Press, Inc. Brooklyn, NY, USA
13. Judaica Books of the Hagiographa – The Holy Writings. The Book of Chronicles 2. A New English Translation of the Text, Rashi and a Commentary Digest. Translation of Text, Rashi, and other Commentaries by Rabbi A. J. Rosenberg. 1992, The Judaica Press, Inc. Brooklyn, NY, USA
14. The Midrash; Kleinman Edition, Midrash Rabbah. Wasserman Edition of Bereishis / Genesis Volume 1 Bereishis – Noach. 2017 Artscroll Mesorah Publications, Ltd.

15. The Midrash; Kleinman Edition, Midrash Rabbah. Wasserman Edition of Bereishis / Genesis Volume II Lech Lecha - Toldos. 2017 Artscroll Mesorah Publications, Ltd.
16. The Midrash; Kleinman Edition, Midrash Rabbah. Wasserman Edition of Bereishis / Genesis Volume III Vayeitzei - Vayishlach. 2017 Artscroll Mesorah Publications, Ltd.
17. Ruth, Loss, Love and Legacy. Kelly Minter. Lifeway Press, Nashville, TN. 2009.
18. Israel Bible Center: Dr. Eli Lizarkin-Eyzenber. Israelbiblecenter.com
19. Revelation: The Christian's Ultimate Victory. John MacArthur. Thomas Nelson. 2007.
20. The Book of Revelation Made Clear. Tim Lahaye and timothy E. Parker. Nelson Books, an Imprint of Thomas Nelson. 2014

Glossary Of Hebrew Terminology:

Midrash: (Hebrew: Investigation). Biblical exegesis by ancient Judaic Rabbis. Includes their commentaries on the Hebrew Bible.

Talmud: A collection of discussion on the scripture concerning Jewish civil and ceremonial law.

Halachah: The collective body of Jewish religious laws derived from the written and oral Torah. The legal part of the Talmud and supplement to the scriptural law.

Rabbinic Law: Written and oral Law of the Torah. Also known as Mishnah.

Mitzvot: Commandments of the Torah. There are 613 mitzvot in the Torah.

Torah: (Hebrew: " Mosaic Teachings" or "Mosaic Law"). The first five books of the Old Testament.

Ketuvim (Greek: Hagiographa). The Sacred writings, or Holy Writings. The third division of the Hebrew Bible. It consists of the poetic books, the Megillot, or Scrolls, and the prophets.

Megillot: The Scrolls. These are the Song of Songs/Solomon, Ruth, Lamentations, Ecclesiastes and Esther. They are part of the 11 books of Ketuvim in the Hebrew Bible, the Tanakh.

Tanakh: The Hebrew Bible. Consists of 24 books in 3 parts. The 5 books of the Torah (Pentateuch), 8 books of the Nevi'im (prophets) and 11 books of the Ketuvim (writings). Tanakh is an acronym consisting of the 3 parts.

Pentateuch: The Greek translation of the first five books of the Old Testament (Torah).

YHVH: The English transliteration for the Hebrew Tetragrammaton for the name of Israel's God. It is frequently anglicized as Yahweh, or Jehovah. In translating YHVH, both Jewish and Christian translators substituted the word LORD. Jewish belief holds that this name is too holy to be pronounced at all. LORD is a rough translation of another Hebrew name for God, Adonai.

Ha Shem: (Hebrew: The Name) The Jewish people traditionally referred to the most Holy name of God by using the Hebrew word, Ha Shem, meaning The Name. Occasionally the longer Hebrew phrase for God's Covenant name, Ha Kadosh Baruch Chu is used, meaning Holy One, Blessed Be He.

Acknowledgement

Acknowledgement: I am grateful to Richard Miller for graciously loaning me his personal collection of Judaica Books of the Prophets and the Hagiographa (A new English translation of the Hebrew Masoretic text and commentaries by Rashi and other Rabbinical scholars), and the books of the Midrash Rabbah for the purpose of study and exegesis of the Hebrew bible. These books are listed in detail in the bibliography. Information taken from these sources were invaluable, and served to deepen my understanding of Old Testament Scripture, which I humbly attempt to pass on to the reader.

About the Author

Jana Jones McDowell DVM, DAVCA, DAVECC has spent a lifetime practicing Veterinary Medicine and former Professor at a College of Veterinary Medicine.

A Christian, Dr. Jones began her research into Biblical studies a number of years ago, focusing on "context."

Her research revolves around the "context," with the study and application of the Judaica Books of the Prophets and the Hagiographa (A new English translation of the Hebrew Masoretic text and commentaries by Rashi and other Rabbinical scholars), and the books of the Midrash Rabbah. The basis of this was the exegesis of the Hebrew bible with application to the origins of Christianity.

Now retired, Dr. Jones spends time researching and applying the depth of her studies into books that provide Christians with a deeper understanding of the Word.

Dr. Jones and her husband, reside in the southwest with their horses, bengal cat named Ravi and their border collie, Sarah.

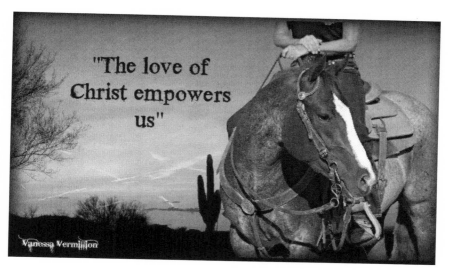

267

Other Books by the Author

(Click on the image to be taken to Amazon)

Made in the USA
Middletown, DE
19 November 2022

15511441R00161